Kremlin Wives

Kremlin Wives

Larissa Vasilieva

Translated from the Russian
by Cathy Porter

ARCADE PUBLISHING • NEW YORK

First North American paperback edition 2014

Excerpts from *Commissar: The Life and Death of Lavrenty Pavlovich Beria*
by Thaddeus Wittlin © 1972 by Thaddeus Wittlin, reprinted by permission of
Macmillan Publishing Company.

Arcade Publishing books may be purchased in bulk at special discounts for
sales promotion, corporate gifts, fund-raising, or educational purposes.
Special editions can also be created to specifications. For details, contact
the Special Sales Department, Arcade Publishing, 307 West 36th Street,
11th Floor, New York, NY 10018 or arcade@skyhorsepublishing.com.

Arcade Publishing® is a registered trademark of Skyhorse Publishing, Inc.®,
a Delaware corporation.

Visit our website at www.arcadepub.com.

10 9 8 7 6 5 4 3 2 1

Library of Congress Cataloging-in-Publication Data is available on file.

Cover design by Robert Reed
Cover photos from the author's archives : bottom, from right to left: Josef
Stalin, Semyon Budyonny, Vyacheslav Molotov, security guard, Anastas
Mikoyan, Ashken Mikoyan, Maria Budyonny, unknown; insert: Raisa
Gorbachev, Mikhail Gorbachev

Print ISBN: 978-1-62872-559-9

Printed in the United States of America

Contents

List of Illustrations   vii

Introduction   ix

Chronological Glossary   xiii

Chapter 1   Honest Nadezhda   1

Chapter 2   The Woman Question and Men's Response   33

Chapter 3   The Legend of Larissa —
               Woman of the Revolution   38

Chapter 4   The Daughter-in-law   47

Chapter 5   The Despot's Wife   56

Chapter 6   Empty Bed, Cold Heart   78

Chapter 7   The Soviet Esther   81

Chapter 8   The Three Wives of Marshal Budyonny   92

Chapter 9   In the Inquisitor's Chair   103

Chapter 10   The President's Wife   116

Chapter 11   "The Personal Has No Social Significance"   131

Chapter 12   A Pearl Set in Iron   136

Chapter 13   Bluebeard's Women   161

Chapter 14   Nina Kukharchuk's Kitchen   186

Chapter 15   Victoria's Quiet Victory   205

Chapter 16   The Mystery of Tatyana   218

Chapter 17   Anna of Three Hundred Days   220

Chapter 18   The Raisa Phenomenon   225

Select Bibliography   234

Index   243

List of Illustrations

Nadezhda Krupskaya   12
Inessa Armand   12
Nadezhda Krupskaya and Lenin   26
Nadezhda Krupskaya and Lenin   26
Nadezhda Krupskaya   26
Larissa Reisner   41
Olga Davidovna Kameneva   51
Alexander Kamenev   51
Lev Kamenev and Galina Kravchenko   51
Nadezhda Alliluyeva and Vasily Stalin   62
Josif Stalin and Nadezhda Alliluyeva   62
Olga Stefanovna Mikhailova-Budyonnaya   95
Olga Stefanovna Mikhailova-Budyonnaya   95
Maria Vasilievna Budyonnaya   95
Maria Vasilievna Budyonnaya   95
Ekaterina Ivanovna Kalinina   127
Ekaterina Ivanovna Kalinina   127
Mikhail Ivanovich and Ekaterina Ivanovna Kalinin   127
The Molotovs and the Stalins   139
Paulina Zhemchuzhina Molotov   157
Vyacheslav, Paulina Zhemchuzhina, and
   Svetlana Molotov   157
Paulina Zhemchuzhina with her grandson   157
Nina Teimurazovna Beria   166

LIST OF ILLUSTRATIONS

Tatyana Okunevskaya	166
Nikita Sergeyevich Khrushchev with his family	199
Nikita Khrushchev with Leonid Brezhnev and Anastas Mikoyan	199
Nikita Khrushchev, Anastas Mikoyan, and Kliment Voroshilov with their wives and children	201
International Women's Day, March 8	213
Leonid and Victoria Brezhnev	213
Raisa and Mikhail Gorbachev	231
Raisa Gorbachev	231
Raisa Gorbachev	231

Introduction

IF THE LIVES THE Soviet leaders led behind the Kremlin walls are still a subject of fascination and mystery, those of their wives remain a complete enigma. Throughout the seventy-five years of Soviet history little or nothing about these women was made public. Were they merely shadows of their sometimes terrifying husbands? I suspected not. In fact, I was sure they played a central role in the dramas that unfolded inside the Kremlin, and I became determined to uncover their stories. I wanted to discover who they were, how they spent their days, and what their relationships were, both to the men of power and to those around them.

A variety of sources were available to me. There were the scholarly volumes of memoirs and research published in Russia and abroad, but these works, predominately written by male authors, refer only fleetingly to the women of the Kremlin. I started, then, by reading all the available memoirs and biographies of Lenin's wife, Nadezhda Krupskaya; of Inessa Armand, an important early Bolshevik as well as Lenin's mistress; and of Alexandra Kollontai, another celebrated revolutionary. These books, however valuable, were official publications, generous on politics and dialectics, scant on the personal aspects of these women's lives. I also read a number of memoirs written by the wives of "enemies of the people," tragic, disturbing — and restrained.

There were, too, the hearsay, rumors, and legends that had been circulating over the years, which, though largely unsubstantiated, nevertheless provided useful leads.

A few of the Kremlin women who had survived their years behind the forbidding walls agreed to talk with me. Each new meeting set me the delicate task of addressing historical accuracy while not insulting the woman interviewed, and at the same time encouraging her to share her life story. Their accounts drew me on to meetings with relatives and friends of Kremlin women who had died. I have countless hours of interviews on tape. Each tells a fascinating story, and each has its predictable share of entangled half-truths. These interviews inevitably led me to other important sources: archives, manuscripts, documents, and letters.

Another point of access was through my own family connections and my life as a writer. As the daughter of the engineer who designed the now-famous World War II Soviet tank, the T-34, I was exposed at a young age to the elite circles of Soviet society. Later my name as a writer and supporter of women's rights eased my access to the people I interviewed and to the archives where I searched for insights into my subjects' lives.

All these sources were invaluable. Ultimately, however, I realized that if I were to complete the project, I would have to gain access to the KGB files in the Lubyanka headquarters. In the spring of 1991, I asked the Writers' Union to request on my behalf access to the files pertaining to the Russian wives arrested during the purges of the 1930s and 1940s. For months I heard nothing. Then, in August 1991, in the wake of the coup and three days after the statue of Felix Dzerzhinsky — founder of the Cheka, a forerunner of the KGB — had been toppled from its imposing pedestal on Lubyanka Square, my phone rang. It was an official from KGB headquarters. He informed me without ceremony that my request had been granted, but that I had to come immediately.

I reached Lubyanka Square and entered the infamous building that for so long had stuck terror into the hearts of so many. I was led upstairs to a large room overlooking the square, formerly the office of KGB chiefs Beria, Yagoda, Yezhov, and Andropov. Behind it was Dzerzhinsky's old office. I sat down in a huge armchair set before a long, T-shaped table, facing a portrait of Lenin and a bust of Dzerzhinsky. Alone in the inquisitors' office, I picked up the receiver of a telephone switchboard emblazoned with the emblem of the USSR. The line was dead. The office was completely cut off from the world. I eyed nervously the stack of files sitting there on the polished table. It seemed incredible that I was here of my own free will, knowing that when my allotted hours were up I could leave. I thought of all those who had come here and never left. My mind conjured up the image of the tortured, the sounds of doors clanking and keys grating in locks. I thought of the lives of the people whose files sat before me.

And then, feverishly, I began to read. The women of the Kremlin came alive again in my mind. Some, whom I already knew through their memoirs and letters and through interviews with friends and foes, came into clearer focus. Others, whom I knew only vaguely or not at all, cast new light on my subject. Before that first visit to the KGB files was over, I knew I had found many of the missing pieces I needed to complete my project.

I wish to acknowledge, then, the nameless KGB official who granted me access to the files. I am also deeply grateful to the playwright Ivan Vasilievich Popov, who had worked closely with Lenin in exile. In the summer of 1953, fearful of committing his unique and potentially damaging knowledge to paper, he used my memory as a notebook, and I have drawn on his information while writing this book. I particularly want to thank everyone — the Kremlin wives I met, and all the children, grandchildren, and friends who knew the women of the Kremlin and who found time in these difficult days to share precious information about themselves and their loved ones.

Chronological Glossary

Specific names and events mentioned in the text are given in italics. Subsequent mentions are not italicized.

1861 — Tsar Alexander II emancipates the serfs and introduces reforms.

1860s and 1870s — Radical men and women discuss ways of abolishing the autocracy. Some are drawn to the nonviolent ideas of *Tolstoy*. Others, the *Populists*, travel to the villages to urge peasants to rise up against their masters. Many are arrested. Women's schools and higher education courses are established, including the *Bestuzhev Courses for Women*.

1870 — First factory strikes in St. Petersburg.

1877–1878 — Two great show trials of Populist revolutionaries.

1878 — Populist revolutionaries adopt terror tactics; numerous assassinations and attempted assassinations of prominent government officials.

1881 — Revolutionary terrorists assassinate Alexander II. Six leading terrorists, including one woman, *Sofia Perovskaya*, are hanged.

1890s — Revolutionaries abandon terror tactics and turn to the ideas of *Karl Marx*, who called on workers to use their industrial power to overthrow the class system.

1895 — Marxist groups in St. Petersburg united by *Vladimir Lenin* into the *League of Struggle for the Emancipation of the Working Class*. Lenin arrested.

1896 — Large-scale textile workers' strikes in St. Petersburg. Many women workers involved.

1900 — Lenin leaves Russia for Switzerland to escape arrest.

1901 — Formation in Russia of the *Socialist Revolutionary Party*, heirs to the terrorists of the 1870s.

1904 — Outbreak of the *Russo-Japanese War*. Strikes and demonstrations throughout Russia.

1905 — Russia's first revolution. January: thousands killed by police in peaceful demonstration outside *Tsar Nicholas II's Winter Palace*. Russia's towns and villages hit by waves of strikes, riots, and demonstrations. Revolutionaries incite turmoil by conducting propaganda meetings and addressing strike gatherings. October: formation of the St. Petersburg *Soviet*, or Council of Workers' Deputies, to coordinate the strike movement. Tsar Nicholas issues manifesto promising reforms. December: mass uprising in Moscow is suppressed. Revolutionaries rounded up and sent to prison and exile. Many escape abroad.

1906 — The tsar establishes the *Duma*, a legislative body with limited representation and powers.

1906–1908 — Suppression of the revolution: strikes banned, revolutionaries arrested. *Alexandra Kollontai* urges her fellow revolutionaries to turn their attention to the needs of women, calling on factory women to join the revolutionary movement and writing a book outlining a socialist approach to women.

1911 — Lenin and his wife, *Nadezhda Krupskaya*, then based in Paris, become the focus of the future Bolshevik leadership. *Inessa Armand*, Alexandra Kollontai, and other exiled revolutionaries in Paris write articles and address meetings to spread socialist ideas and recruit men and women to the revolution.

1914 — August: start of *World War I*. St. Petersburg renamed *Petrograd*.

1915–1917 — Strikes and food riots throughout Russia. Lenin and the Bolsheviks in Switzerland urge Russian soldiers to turn their weapons against those in power at home and make the imperialist war into a revolutionary war.

1917 — March: women storm the streets of Petrograd. The riots spread, the capital is brought to a standstill. Tsar Nicholas II abdicates and a new *Provisional Government* takes power. April: Lenin and other exiled revolutionaries return to Russia and agitate in factories, military garrisons, and warships for Bolshevik power. Riots and demonstrations throughout Russia. July: revolutionary sailors attempt to storm the Winter Palace and are crushed. Bolshevik leaders go underground and in September institute the *Cheka,* the Extraordinary Commission for the Struggle against Sabotage and Counterrevolution, under the leadership of *Felix Dzerzhinsky.* October 25–26: at the Second All-Russian Congress of Soviets held at the *Smolny Institute,* the Bolsheviks declare themselves in power, and workers and sailors storm the Winter Palace and oust the Provisional Government. The Bolsheviks form a new government, the *Soviet of People's Commissars,* with Lenin as its president, *Leon Trotsky* as commissar of foreign affairs, Kollontai as commissar of social welfare, *Yakov Sverdlov* as head of the central executive committee, and *Anatoly Lunacharsky* as commissar of enlightenment. November: First Congress of Petrograd Worker Women.

1918 — March: the capital moves from Petrograd to Moscow in anticipation of a German invasion of Russia. Brest-Litovsk peace treaty signed with Germany. Armies of fourteen states, including the *White Czech Legions,* attack Bolshevik Russia as the civil war begins in earnest. Leading Bolsheviks tour the front in *agit-trains,* urging people to fight the Whites. July: Tsar Nicholas II and his family shot in Ekaterinburg. August: Lenin shot and seriously wounded by a woman terrorist in Moscow. Beginning of the *Red Terror.* Numerous *purges* of the Party and the army. November: First All-Russian Congress of Worker and Peasant Women held in Moscow.

1919 — Establishment of special women's department of the Party, the *Zhenotdel.* Eighth Party Congress creates a Political Bureau (*Politburo*), a small group within the Central Committee, and the Organizational Bureau (*Orgburo*), to check Party records and staff.

1920 — Kollontai appointed director of *Zhenotdel* after the death of Inessa Armand.

1921 — Adoption of the *New Economic Policy* (*NEP*), favoring a limited return to private enterprise.

1922 — The Cheka is replaced by the GPU, the State Political Administration, later known as *OGPU.* April: *Josif Stalin* given post of general secretary; Lenin's health begins to fail.

1923–1924 — The Party organizes discussions on ethics and the family.

1924 — Lenin dies. Petrograd is renamed *Leningrad*.

1927 — Trotsky and *Grigory Zinoviev* expelled from the Party.

1928 — More oppositionists to Stalin arrested and imprisoned.

1929 — Trotsky is exiled to Turkey, and *Nikolai Bukharin, Alexei Rykov*, and other prominent Bolsheviks are removed from positions of influence by Stalin. April: First Five-Year Plan. December: Stalin calls for accelerated collectivization of the peasantry.

1934 — OGPU comes under the administration of the People's Commissariat of Internal Affairs, the *NKVD*, under which name it is known. December: the assassination in Leningrad of government member and loyal Stalinist *Sergei Kirov* is the signal for savage new Party purges.

1936 — The first public show trials, of Grigory Zinoviev and *Lev Kamenev*. Adoption of the Stalin Constitution.

1937 — Stalin's terror starts in earnest. Execution of hundreds of Red Army leaders.

1937–1938 — The second show trial, of old Bolsheviks *Karl Radek* and *Yuri Pyatakov*.

1938 — March: the purges continue with the execution of Bukharin and fifteen others. December: *Lavrenti Beria* takes over from *Nicholai Yezhov* as head of the secret police.

1939 — August: Russia signs nonaggression pact with Germany. Two weeks later Hitler invades Poland.

1940 — Trotsky assassinated in Mexico.

1941 — June: Nazi troops invade Russia. Moscow threatened.

1943 — February: Soviet troops defeat Nazis in the battle of Stalingrad.

1945 — May: victory over Germany.

1946 — Mounting postwar terror, with campaigns against the Jews.

1953 — Anti-Semitic campaign culminates in the *Doctors' Plot*, in which Kremlin doctors are accused of poisoning Soviet leaders at the behest of international Zionism and the CIA. March: Stalin dies. June: arrest and execution of Beria. End of the Stalinist terror. *Nikita Khrushchev* emerges from the ensuing power struggle as new Party secretary.

1954 — Formation of the *KGB*, the Committee for State Security, under the Ministry of Internal Affairs.

1956 — February: the high point of post-Stalin liberalization comes with Khrushchev's "secret speech" on Stalin at the Twentieth Party Congress. Prisoners released en masse and disgraced intellectuals rehabilitated. October–November: uprisings in Poland and Hungary cause panic in the Soviet government.

1964 — October: Khrushchev is ousted from power and replaced by Alexei Kosygin and *Leonid Brezhnev*.

1966–1967 — Stalin partially rehabilitated. Dissidents arrested and forced to leave Russia.

1967 — *Yuri Andropov* is appointed head of the KGB.

1968 — Soviet invasion of Czechoslovakia.

1969 — Clashes between Soviet and Chinese border troops.

1979 — December: Soviet invasion of Afghanistan.

1980 — Summer: Olympic Games staged in Moscow.

1981 — Martial law imposed in Poland. Brezhnev's health in decline. He receives his fourth Order of Lenin.

1982 — The country suffers severe food shortages. Growing pressure on the ailing Brezhnev to resign. November: Brezhnev dies of a heart attack. Andropov becomes Party secretary. Talks with China open and relations with the U.S. become warmer. Hints that Soviet troops will be withdrawn from Afghanistan.

1983 — Andropov pursues his campaign against corruption, profiteering, and bureaucracy with raids on bars, cinemas, and shops. Arms talks with the U.S. government continue in Geneva. September: Korean Airline plane containing 269 people, including many Americans, shot down by Soviet fighter aircraft.

CHRONOLOGICAL GLOSSARY

1984 — January: Andropov launches his "limited industrial experiment," designed to give increased economic powers to factory managers. February: Andropov dies and is succeeded by *Konstantin Chernenko*.

1985 — March: Chernenko dies, to be succeeded by *Mikhail Gorbachev*, whose efforts to modernize and liberalize the country are encapsulated in the concepts of *perestroika* and *glasnost*, restructuring and openness.

Kremlin Wives

1

Honest Nadezhda

Vladimir Ilyich Ulyanov, 1870–1924 (revolutionary name — Lenin), born in Simbirsk. Joined the revolutionary movement while studying law at Kazan University in the 1880s. Imprisoned in 1895 for his part in establishing the Marxist Union of Struggle for the Emancipation of the Working Class. Married Nadezhda Krupskaya during his subsequent exile in Siberia. From 1896 to 1917 he lived mainly in exile abroad, working for revolution in Russia and returning to Petrograd in April 1917 as leader of the Bolshevik party. After October 1917 he was president of the Soviet of People's Commissars (the Sovnarkom), a post he held until his death seven years later.

IN THE SPRING OF 1918 a forty-nine-year-old woman moved into the Kremlin. Her face was plain, but her lips were full — perhaps evidence of a passionate nature, though few would have dared to suggest this of her. She had protruding, wide-spaced eyes whose heavy lids gave her face a sleepy expression. Her forehead was broad, and her straight hair was parted in the middle and drawn into a bun at the nape of her neck. A few wisps escaped onto her cheeks. Her figure was shapeless, but her bearing suggested that she had attended a good high school for girls. Her hands were elegant, but her neglected nails suggested someone more interested in action than in talk. The woman was Nadezhda Konstantinovna Krupskaya, the wife of Vladimir Lenin, leader of the Bolshevik Revolution.

The new tsaritsa, as some at first called her, had spent most of the previous fourteen years in exile, and was therefore largely unknown in Russia prior to 1917. She had known the miseries of isolation, and since communication at that time was primitive, this isolation was virtually total. Although Russia may not have been ready for Krupskaya, Krupskaya was ready for Russia — far more so than the German princesses who had occupied the Russian throne for the past two hundred years. Since childhood she had set for herself nothing less than the ambition of achieving happiness for all the Russian people. Later, when Lenin's global strategy extended beyond the Russian borders ("Workers of the world, unite!") this suited her perfectly.

Official Soviet culture was to cast an aura of sanctity around this woman's life, and the unctuous memoirs of those who knew her did little but inspire sarcasm about the "saintly" lady:

- "Krupskaya was the model of a faithful wife? With those looks, did she have a choice? Nobody but Lenin would have liked her!"
- "Lenin, faithful? Don't make me laugh."
- "What did she know about children? She never had any!"
- "After the revolution she fought for literacy but banned books because she said they were damaging to proletarian children."

Born in St. Petersburg in 1869, the only daughter of Elizaveta Vasilievna and Konstantin Ignatievich Krupsky, Nadezhda Krupskaya grew up surrounded by love. When she was three years old her progressive father was dismissed from his government post for what were ambiguously called "undesirable attitudes" and for "exceeding his authority," and the Krupskys moved to the provinces. After eight years of dislocation and hardship and petitioning the government to rescind its decision, Konstantin Ignatevich and his family were finally allowed back to St. Petersburg, where they settled in a squalid apartment in the slums.

Nadezhda, deeply affected by what had happened to her father, was quick to grasp that his problems transcended the family and had to do with the woes of Russia. She inherited his progressive ideas and was just as comfortable with the poor children in the yard as she was with the aristocratic daughters of her mother's friends.

Anxious to give their daughter a good education and to introduce her to modern thinking, the Krupskys enrolled her in Princess Obolenskaya's Gymnasium, a progressive high school created by Populist intellectuals of the 1860s and 1870s, and one of the best private girls' schools in Russia. Here Nadezhda met not only aristocrats and girls from wealthy families, but also the daughters of revolutionaries, who dreamed of dedicating their lives to the betterment of the common people. Idealistic teachers offered girls an inspiring example. Indeed, the word "revolution" was frequently heard in the Krupsky home.

By the second half of the nineteenth century, it was permissible for a woman in Russia to leave her family and seek an education. Surrounded by injustice, Krupskaya longed to do something about it, and since the tsarist state was resistant to reform, she was inevitably drawn to the revolutionary movement and to the struggles it brought. Women were permitted to be revolutionaries (and expected to act as men's faithful assistants), and a few enjoyed great authority within the movement.

Vera Zasulich (1849–1919) was active in various revolutionary circles before shooting and wounding St. Petersburg's governor-general in 1879. After many years in prison and exile, Zasulich worked with Lenin in exile abroad. Solitary and uncompromising, Zasulich remained deeply hostile to the Bolshevik Revolution and died disillusioned with life.

Vera Figner (1852–1942), a Populist turned terrorist, was sentenced to death for her part in the assassination of Tsar Alexander II in 1881. The sentence was subsequently commuted to twenty years in prison. After her release, she lived in Moscow, where for many years she observed with a certain detachment the Bolsheviks' application of her ideas.

Sofia Perovskaya (1853–1881), hanged for her part in Alexander II's assassination, was the first woman in Russia sentenced to death for a political crime.

These Russian women opened the way to a new generation of revolutionary women.

Soon after Krupsky's death in 1883, his widow and daughter were visited by Nikolai Isaakovich Utin, a well-known revolutionary, who helped fourteen-year-old Nadezhda find her first private teaching job. Nadezhda's school friend Ariadna Tyrkova, who subsequently joined the Revolution on the other side of the barricades as a member of the White Army, described her friend's life several years later:

She lived with her mother in an apartment off the inner courtyard of the Durdins' building on Znamenskaya Street. They led a quiet, dull, old-fashioned life, and their cramped three-room apartment always smelled of onions, cabbage, and pies. In the kitchen stood the cook's bed, spread with a red calico cover. In those days even a poor clerk's widow was unable to manage without domestic help; I knew nobody who did not have at least one servant.

The complacent 1870s gave way to the turbulent 1880s (beginning with Alexander II's death in 1881), and Elizaveta Vasilievna watched with a mixture of hope and apprehension as her daughter was taken under the wing of the revolutionaries. Ariadna Tyrkova again gives us a look:

> We talked constantly about the failings of society, and these discussions sprang from love of life and the urgent demands of magnanimous youth. . . . In many educated Russian families, the more sensitive of the young people were infected at a young age by the microbe of social unrest. Of all my friends the most deeply infected was Nadya Krupskaya. She had defined her views and marked out her path long before the rest of us, and far more irrevocably. She was someone who would surrender herself to a feeling or an idea totally and forever.

After graduating from Princess Obolenskaya's school with a governess diploma in 1887, Nadezhda started coaching the other girls there for their final exams. A letter of recommendation shows how effective the young teacher was: "For the past two years domestic governess N. K. Krupskaya has worked in the evenings with ten pupils. . . . The girls' success is evidence of her outstanding pedagogical abilities, her wide-ranging knowledge, and her meticulous approach to her work."

It seemed as if Nadezhda was destined to be a career teacher and a spinster. She made no attempt to make herself appealing to men. Elizaveta Vasilievna's maternal dreams of a good match for her daughter began to fade. She saw a career as a teacher as the best her daughter could hope for. "I'm like the Russian countryside — without bright colors," Nadezhda said to comfort her.

Ariadna Tyrkova recalls, "Nadya did not indulge in flirtation, amorous adventures, or sexual games. She didn't go skating, dancing, or boating, and she talked only to her school friends and the elderly women friends of her mother. I never saw any male guests at their apartment."

Indeed, plain Nadezhda pitied her married friends for enslaving themselves in marriage and throwing away their talents on a man. She had chosen not to dedicate herself to the world of home and family but to take a lonelier route. The first sign on this path was in the form of a newspaper ad placed by Leo Tolstoy. He hired educated girls to take well-known works of literature and rewrite them in a simpler language so that peasants could understand them. Nadezhda saw the ad and immediately wrote to Tolstoy volunteering her services:

> Esteemed Lev Nikolayevich! Recently I have realized more and more clearly how much toil, energy, and health I waste in my exploitation of others' labor. I have lived like this in order to acquire knowledge, in the hope that this would enable me to be useful later on. Now I see that the knowledge I have gained is of no use to anyone, since I cannot apply it to my life, even to make some small amends for my own inactivity — and I do not know what is to be done about it. . . .
>
> I know that editing books for the common people is important work that demands much knowledge and experience, and that I am only eighteen years old and know very little. . . . But I am appealing to you because I think that to do work that I love may help me to overcome my ignorance and inexperience. So if possible, Lev Nikolayevich, please send me one or two of these books, and I will do what I can with them.

Tolstoy's daughter Tatyana sent Nadezhda *The Count of Monte Cristo,* Alexander Dumas's romance of revenge, and she sat down to edit it. It was a silly task, as she herself realized the further she progressed, but since she was not one to abandon a task half-done, especially one from the great Leo Tolstoy, she persevered.

While awaiting his response to her work, she visited several groups of Tolstoyans, but her down-to-earth nature was put off by their lofty abstractions. She was attracted to younger revolutionaries, seeking some sign from them that would set her on the right path. Nadezhda did not believe in half-measures.

Ariadna Tyrkova observed, "She would pore endlessly over a phrase in a textbook, struggling to understand exactly what it meant. But once she did grasp it she would absorb it forever, just as later she would absorb the teachings of Karl Marx and Ulyanov-Lenin."

It was in the spring of 1890 that Nadezhda read Marx's *Das Kapital,* later describing it as a "drink of fresh water." And from that moment it became clear to her that her path lay neither in isolated acts of terrorism nor in Tolstoyan self-perfection. She understood that the only important thing for her was the mighty workers' movement. The year 1890 marked the transformation from the naive girl seeking her own path into the revolutionary. She would discover the force that was to guide her the rest of her life.

Hungry for further education, Nadezhda was enrolled in the prestigious Bestuzhev Courses for Women, but in the autumn of 1890 she abandoned them and concentrated all her energies on teaching.

Ariadna Tyrkova's memoirs describe how revolutionary work transformed her friend:

> She would shower me with radiant love, clasping my hands in hers and smiling in bashful tenderness. She had fine white skin, with a delicate pink flush spreading from her cheeks to her ears and chin, and although I had often pitied my Nadya her plainness, she looked quite lovely. Behind this soft and pretty face, however, I sensed another Nadya. She had begun the revolutionary work that would become her life's passion.
>
> It started with workers' evening classes outside the city gates. Her kind blue eyes would sparkle as she told me in a rote, sing-song voice of the importance of awakening the workers' class consciousness. . . . I was happy for her and realized what a joy it must be to discover some all-consuming goal.

Seeing that her revolutionary daughter paid no attention to household chores, Elizaveta Vasilievna supervised all the cleaning and cooking in the apartment. A devout woman, she was frightened by her daughter's growing atheism, and told Ariadna Tyrkova: "You're as bad as my Nadya. You'd be wiser if you went to church and prayed for grace and forgiveness!" The naturally tolerant Nadezhda did not try to convert her mother, and the two women lived peacefully together.

Now all Nadezhda needed was someone with whom she could share her revolutionary passion. Blushing, she would casually mention to Ariadna Tyrkova "a certain comrade" who meant a lot to her. Nadezhda never mentioned his name, and many years later Ariadna assumed that it had been Lenin. But four years before meeting Lenin, Nadezhda had become friends with a Marxist engineering student named Klasson and was a regular participant in his revolutionary circle. They studied *Das Kapital* together, they read and argued. Shared ideas may have led to embraces — although Nadezhda's strict moral code and preference for lofty emotions makes this unlikely. A true Marxist could conquer everything. Monks and nuns mortified the flesh by fasting and praying; she used Marx and Engels.

She recalled giving a worker Tolstoy's *War and Peace;* he handed it back to her the next day saying: "It's to be read lying on the sofa, and that is of no use to us!" Another worker named Zhukov wrote: "She was talking about India and the life of the Indians, and then she suddenly started talking about our life." Clever, open-minded, and fascinated by new ideas, the young teacher with the pink cheeks and long auburn braid was popular with her students, and after the lesson ended they would argue over who would get to walk her home at night. The man who generally succeeded was Ivan Vasilievich Babushkin. Tall, elegant, mustached, and blazing with youth and health, he took her arm and escorted her through the dark back streets of Petrograd.

All winter Nadezhda Krupskaya toiled away at her evening classes, her innumerable pamphlets, and her books. One of these was an economics book by a Marxist named Herman Krasin. She was about to put it aside, when she saw that the book's margins were filled with neatly written notes, and, struck by the reader's originality and caustic tone, she read on. None of her comrades was capable of thinking in such global terms; certainly not Klasson.

On her way to work that evening she ran into Klasson on the street. He asked if she and her friend Zina would come to his room later for a Marxist debate to be held under the guise of a Shrovetide pancake party. She didn't really want to go; she felt she had outgrown the circle. Klasson insisted. A man from the Volga would be there, he said, a strange character who had torn Krasin's views to shreds. Nadezhda remembered the notes in Krasin's exercise book and decided to go.

She recalled, "There were lots of people there. The discussion was about the future. Someone mentioned the importance of the literacy committee, and this produced a dry, sarcastic laugh from the 'man from the Volga.'"

Hearing the "man from the Volga" speak was like being struck by a bolt of lightning. She suddenly realized that revolution was not only possible but imminent. That evening she made enquiries, and though she rarely told her mother about her revolutionary activities, she told her all about Vladimir Ulyanov. He was twenty-four years old (he looked older) and came from minor nobility. His father, now dead, had been a school inspector in the Siberian town of Simbirsk. His mother, née Blank, was the daughter of a former police doctor, and his elder brother was Alexander Ulyanov, member of the terrorist People's Will party, executed in 1887 for the attempted assassination of Tsar Alexander III.

One evening toward the end of summer, the two of them happened to meet on the steps of the library and walked back through the streets of St. Petersburg to her apartment together. They talked more about revolution.

This encounter sealed her fate. The great passion in her life was and always would be the revolution; for this she lived, worked, and dreamed. And Vladimir Ulyanov-Lenin became the embodiment of her dream. She trusted him implicitly, and for his cause would go to the ends of the earth, asking nothing for herself, accepting whatever role he chose for her. Many women dedicated themselves to the revolution but chose the wrong man; Nadezhda had chosen the right one. She was a star student, after all, and star students seldom make mistakes. By 1894 Lenin's mother, Maria Alexandrovna Ulyanova, had had ample experience with revolutionaries, and from her first meeting with Nadezhda she knew that this young woman was exactly the wife she would have wished for her son. She was not pretty, but that meant he would not be distracted by jealousy. Naturally it would have been better if she had money, but her poverty gave her a certain dignity and the strength to bear life's misfortunes. Lenin and Nadezhda were unable to marry immediately, since in 1896 she was arrested and sentenced to six months in prison for her role in the St. Petersburg strike movement, and the following February he was exiled to the Siberian village of Shushenskoe.

Historians have puzzled over her strange reply when from exile Lenin wrote to her in prison and asked her to be his wife. "Your wife? Why not?" she wrote back. What is clear from this is that she would have accepted anything he proposed. As either wife or comrade, with her talent and zeal, she would make him leader of the revolution. As for Nadezhda's mother, she would accept anything just so long as Nadezhda was not relegated to the background. After Krupskaya received Lenin's letter, she petitioned to be transferred to Lenin's place of exile. Her request was granted and she set off for Siberia.

Nadezhda's mother accompanied her. This poor widow of a

would-be revolutionary had faithfully visited her daughter in prison, and now followed her to the Siberian village of Shushenskoe where she was to live with her deported son-in-law, serving them, taking care of the household, and listening to all their endless discussions about the working class and world revolution. When the two convinced atheists were forced by the authorities to be married in church, she was overjoyed. God had blessed them, whatever they might say about Him; now Lenin would have to take Nadezhda with him wherever he went.

Elizaveta Vasilievna was an educated woman, and in her youth had written poetry, but she was temperamentally unsuited to politics and had little appreciation for what preoccupied the couple. Revolution for her meant chaos, godlessness, the shattering of everything stable and familiar, and while she cooked four meals a day for these atheists and anti-Christs, she wanted nothing to do with their activities for "the people's happiness."

Kind Elizaveta Vasilievna accepted her new life with fortitude — everybody in Russia had to put up with such things now. Later of course there would be children, and she looked forward to that time. She loved her future son-in-law with all her heart, and he reciprocated. He knew that an orderly married life was possible only with her help. Throughout his life Lenin was surrounded by worshipful, subservient women: his mother, his wife, his sisters and their friends, his revolutionary comrades, his secretaries, maids, and servants. His behavior toward them was always informed by purely political motivations, and he had an extraordinary talent for directing female energy toward a greater goal.

"Ilyich and I would lie awake at night dreaming of the mighty workers' demonstrations in which we would one day take part," wrote Nadezhda about those years in Shushenskoe. It was in exile that modest Nadezhda discovered the powerful, passionate woman within. The period from 1898 to 1900 was one of the happiest of her life. There, she enjoyed love, closeness to nature, spiritual communion with the man she idolized, and the fact that she had no rivals in the whole of Shushenskoe. Of all the women there she was the youngest and prettiest. Her pink cheeks, her long thick braid, her youth, her slim figure, and her simple St. Petersburg dresses were the object of the village girls' longing stares. According to a revolutionary named Lepeshinsky, everyone was charmed by her and men fell in love with her.

One day in October 1899, the Lenins visited a handsome revolutionary named Viktor Konstantinovich Kurnatovsky. Kurnatovsky had endured poverty, prison, and exile, and now lived in a town some twenty miles away, where he worked over twelve hours a day at the local sugar factory. The rivers had frozen, snow was falling, and as Kurnatovsky led the newlyweds around the factory, the normally reticent Krupskaya astonished him with her acumen and her encyclopedic knowledge. He soon became one of their closest friends. Wrote Nadezhda, "We were newly married, and this helped us through our exile. If I don't write about it now it doesn't mean there was no poetry or youthful passion in our life, we just couldn't bear anything petit-bourgeois. Ilyich and I met as fully-formed Marxists, and this shaped all our life and work together."

Krupskaya's artless details of their life in Siberia show how central Lenin's needs were to his comrades.

> Things were cheap in Shushenskoe. Vladimir Ilyich's eight-ruble "salary" bought him a clean room, food, washing, mending. Of course dinner and supper were very plain. Every week they would slaughter a sheep for Vladimir Ilyich, and he would eat it every day until he could eat no more. They would put his week's supply of meat in the trough in which they mixed the cattle food, and the farm girl would chop it into cutlets for him. There was more than enough milk for Vladimir Ilyich and his dog, a fine Gordon setter named Zhenka, whom he taught to fetch and carry and perform all sorts of tricks.

With the arrival of Krupskaya and her mother, Lenin's life improved still further:

> We lived as a family. That summer we couldn't find anyone to help with the housework. Mother and I struggled with the Russian stove and I kept spilling dumpling soup all over the floor. In October a girl called Pasha moved in to help us. She was thirteen, scraggy and sharp-elbowed, and she took on all the housework for us. I taught her to read and write, and she adorned the walls with Mother's instructions: "Never, never spill the tea!"

The two able-bodied women handed over the household chores to a thirteen-year-old girl and didn't seem to feel any guilt about exploiting a child — something they fiercely denounced in others.

At times a new and uncharacteristically hard tone appears in Nadezhda Krupskaya's memoirs. Most of the exiles living in the area then were either former People's Will terrorists (the "old men") or younger Marxist Social Democrats. When one of the Marxists escaped without forewarning, the "old men" were angry about not having the time to clean their rooms in case of a search. "Vladimir Ilyich said, 'There's nothing worse than these exile tragedies. They're a distraction. The old men's nerves are shot. It's not surprising after hard labor and all they've endured, but we mustn't get involved. We have our work to do, we must save our energy.' "

Left to herself, Krupskaya would happily have gotten involved, but as she gradually turned into Lenin's shadow she learned to agree with him on everything. She stood behind him when he engineered the final break with the "old men": "The decision had already been taken, and we just had to carry it through as painlessly as possible. We broke with them because it was necessary, but we did so with more regret than anger. Afterward we had nothing more to do with them."

In lonely places of exile, where people lived by respect and consideration, the episode was a mortal blow for the "old men." Nadezhda understood the cruelty of the break, but she learned to deny feelings of remorse. Her beauty faded, partly due to the onset of the thyroid condition that was to torment her for the rest of her life. Her illness, far from distracting Nadezhda Krupskaya from the revolutionary path, helped her to hold to it.

In Russia, Stalin's name is connected with something huge and terrifying; Lenin's name means little to Russians now. There is the famous statue of the good, curly-headed young Lenin, one hand resting on a pedestal, the other tucked into the belt of his trousers. And there used to be portraits everywhere of the middle-aged Lenin, bald and kindly, with his small beard and narrow eyes, the father of the USSR. Lenin as a romantic figure, a lover, the image of him infatuated with Inessa Armand, is missing.

In 1889, fifteen-year-old Inessa Theodorovna Stephane and her sister Renée, orphaned daughters of a couple of itinerant French actors, traveled from Paris to the large estate of Pushkino outside Moscow, where their aunt taught music and French to a family of wealthy Russianized French textile merchants, the Armands.

Pretty, intelligent, sweet-natured, and musical, the two girls flew like exotic birds into the Armand family, whose three sons, Alexander,

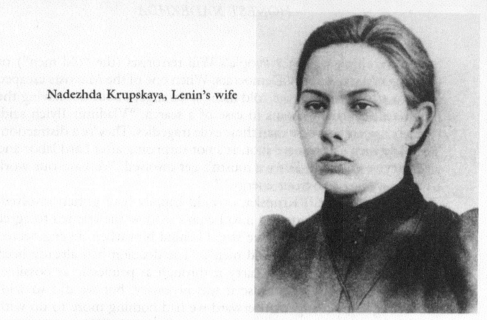

Nadezhda Krupskaya, Lenin's wife

Inessa Armand

Vladimir, and Boris, were ready to love them with all the passion of their romantic hearts. Their lowly status made the sisters unsuitable as wives, but the Armand brothers held progressive views and led their lives in a conscious attempt to undermine the merchant house of Armand.

In 1893 nineteen-year-old Inessa married Alexander, and over the next eight years they had four children: Alexander, Fyodor, Inessa, and Varvara. Like Nadezhda, Inessa was stirred by a new social consciousness and longed for activity. Inspired by Tolstoy's ideas on popular education, she set up a school for peasant children on the Armand estate. It was there that she read Lenin's *Development of Capitalism in Russia*, and this started her on the revolutionary path. Rejecting Tolstoy's image of women as "brood mares," she chose as her model the sexually and politically emancipated heroine of Nikolai Chernyshevsky's novel *What Is To Be Done?*, who sets up a women's sewing cooperative and lives in a ménage à trois with her husband and his best friend.

Alexander Armand's wife had no further to look than to his younger, more extremist brother, Vladimir, who had embraced Marxism and had always been close to Inessa. In the summer of 1903, while on holiday with Vladimir, she discovered that she was pregnant. Alexander accepted that she was in love with his brother, and she and their four children moved to Moscow to live with Vladimir. That autumn in Switzerland she gave birth to her fifth child, Andrei.

For his part Vladimir unquestioningly accepted Inessa's revolutionary views and spent the rest of his life following her to prison, exile, and abroad, while the noble-minded Alexander continued to love and support her, bailing her out of jail, taking the children whenever she was unable to do so, and doing whatever she asked of him. Some have condemned Inessa for abandoning her children for political causes that sent her to prison and exile, yet she seized every opportunity to see them, and reunions with them were always joyous. She seemed to have made the best of her life, but it took a heavy toll. In the autumn of 1908 she wrote from exile to her friends, the Askenazys: "The conflict between personal, family interests and those of society is the most serious problem facing the intelligentsia today. One or the other invariably has to be sacrificed. All of us have to face this painful choice, and whatever we decide is always equally painful."

A few days after writing this letter, Inessa escaped from exile, and after a short stop in Moscow to see her children and Alexander, she crossed over into Finland. From there she traveled to the French Riviera, where Vladimir was hospitalized for an infection. She wrote to the Askenazys, "I never suspected that he was so ill, I was only aware of a minor operation to lance the abscess. . . . Yet two weeks after I arrived he was dead. For me his death is an irreparable loss. All my personal happiness was bound up with him, and without personal happiness it is hard to live."

In this same letter, however, she also proves she is already thinking and looking ahead: "I am now in Paris, and will try to busy myself here. I want to make contact with the French Socialist Party. If I can, I shall be able to gather experience for future work."

Inessa had long been in correspondence with Lenin, and worshipped him as her teacher. It was sometime in 1909, while still deep in mourning for Vladimir, that she first met him in person. We don't know where the meeting took place. It might have been at the Russian library on rue Gobelin, or at the Bolshevik print shop on the rue d'Orléans, in a crowd of Paris Social Democrats at a cheap émigré canteen, or in Brussels, where Inessa was living.

Krupskaya wrote, "In 1910, Inessa Armand left Brussels for Paris with her small son and two daughters. She immediately became one of the most active members of our Paris group. She was an ardent Bolshevik, and our people in Paris quickly grew attached to her."

Krupskaya and her mother welcomed Inessa with affection. Both Inessa and Elizaveta Vasilievna had aristocratic tastes, both of them smoked, and they loved sitting together for hours chatting. Perhaps Elizaveta Vasilievna realized that it would be difficult for her son-in-law not to fall in love with the beautiful Inessa and was trying to protect her daughter by befriending Inessa. But Krupskaya prided herself on her ability to rise above petit-bourgeois conventions of jealousy and marital fidelity. She was a born conspirator, capable of doing anything to further the interests of the revolution, and it is hard to imagine her falling apart because of a rival who was above all else a comrade.

Krupskaya may well have had her own dramas at the time. In the ten years since she had last seen Victor Kurnatovsky, he had been sentenced to hard labor and then to death. The death sentence was commuted to permanent exile in Siberia, whence he escaped to Japan. From Japan he traveled to Australia, where he lived in great poverty as a woodcutter, and in 1910 he arrived in Paris, exhausted and barely alive.

Krupskaya wrote, "He had an exceptionally difficult life at the end. In the autumn of 1910, just after his arrival, Ilyich and I visited him in hospital. He had terrible headaches, and was in constant pain. . . . After he recovered a little he fell in with some 'compromisers,' and their views crept into his talk. After that our friendship faded."

One recalls Lenin's cruel treatment of the "old men" in Shushenskoe. He acknowledged only those who agreed with him; differences were unacceptable. It is not hard to see why as a result of suffering that Lenin could not even imagine, Kurnatovsky finally wanted to reconcile himself to life. But this did not suit Lenin, or Krupskaya, and they drifted apart.

> He rented a little room on the boulevard Montparnasse. I once visited him there and took him our newspapers. I told him about the Party school in Longjumeau, and we had a long heart-to-heart talk together. He accepted unquestioningly the Central Committee's line then. Ilyich was delighted, and visited him often at the end. In the autumn of 1912, when we were in Krakow, we learned that Kurnatovsky had died.

If like the émigré writer Mark Aldanov, one believes that during 1910 Krupskaya was tormented by jealousy of Inessa Armand, her visit to Kurnatovsky may well have eased her suffering. But given that she would commit no act that might blemish her name, or that of her husband, it seems more likely that she simply wanted to see Kurnatovsky before he died, out of respect for their former friendship.

Moreover, during the years from 1912 to 1914, Krupskaya saw even more of Inessa Armand in Poland than she had in Paris. Krupskaya was ill at the time because of her thyroid, and her condition was exacerbated from the years of prison, exile, and endless moves that took such a heavy toll on all revolutionary women's health, and were deemed the sacrifices worth making in the name of the common cause.

> Inessa arrived in Poronin in the middle of a meeting. . . . She was already displaying symptoms of tuberculosis, but she had lost none of her energy and attended to Party matters with greater passion than ever. All of us in Krakow were overjoyed to see her.
> The whole of our Krakow group was very close to Inessa that autumn. She was brimming with joy and vitality. The house seemed

warmer and more cheerful when Inessa was there. My mother was especially attached to her. . . . During her visit Inessa told me a great deal about her life and her children, and she showed me their letters. There was a delightful warmth about her stories. . . . She was an excellent musician and urged us to attend some Beethoven concerts. She herself played several works by Beethoven on the piano. Ilyich especially loved the *Pathétique,* and he constantly asked her to play it. He loved music.

The Krakow idyll of Nadezhda, Lenin, and Inessa did not last for long. Of Inessa's sudden departure from Krakow Krupskaya writes:

It was always assumed that she would remain in Krakow and write to Russia asking for her children to be sent out to join her. I even helped her look for accommodations. But life in Krakow was very secluded, rather like our life in exile, and there was no outlet there for her energy, which she had in such abundance then. She decided first to travel around and visit our overseas groups and deliver a series of reports, then to settle in Paris. Before she left we talked a great deal about women's work. Inessa insisted passionately on the widest possible propaganda among working women, and the publication in St. Petersburg of a special magazine just for them.

Is it possible that since 1909 the founder and leader of the Leninist revolution had not only a wife, but a mistress, who worked as tirelessly as the wife — writing articles for the Bolshevik press, traveling around Europe organizing conferences, and translating revolutionary articles into various languages?

Although she served the revolution just as loyally as Krupskaya, Inessa Armand did not feel obliged to see to Vladimir Ilyich's daily needs. Not only was Lenin well looked after already, but she realized that such entanglements would be awkward if not damaging, and that it was better to leave things as they were.

Yet Armand often paid a heavy price for her independence. The playwright Ivan Popov, who knew her well before the revolution, describes how in 1916 he and Inessa both believed that Russia should defend itself against Germany. She had written letters to Lenin expressing doubt about his calls for revolutionary war. After receiving Lenin's reply she advised Popov, "Leave, don't look back. You're young, you're a poet — this life isn't for you. I have nowhere to go. I'm under his spell. If I leave now all my sacrifices will be for naught."

"As regards the defense of the country, it would be extremely unpleasant for me if we disagreed. Let us try to see eye to eye," wrote Lenin to Armand.

They did eventually see eye to eye, because Inessa acquiesced to her leader. As for Popov, this was the end of the Bolshevik period of his life, although he continued to remain in contact with Inessa.

When revolution broke out in Russia on February 23, 1917, the Lenins were in Zurich. Krupskaya describes their reactions to the news from Petrograd:

> That afternoon after dinner, when Ilyich had already left for the library and I had cleared the dishes, Bronsky appeared with the words: "Haven't you heard? There's revolution in Russia!" We hurried down to the shores of the lake, where all the newspapers were hanging up under an awning. . . . It was true, revolution had broken out in Russia. All Ilyich's plans were working.

Almost immediately, Lenin, Krupskaya, and Inessa Armand traveled in the same compartment of the famous "sealed train" across Germany to Petrograd, back to the Russia that they had left so many years ago.

When Lenin was given a hero's welcome home, the two women stood a few steps behind him on the station platform. And as Lenin stood on an armored car exhorting the milling crowds on the streets to support the world socialist revolution or shouted to the crowds from the balcony of Kshesinskaya's palace, slim, elegant Inessa and bulky Krupskaya stood below, looking up adoringly while they listened to his words.

February 1917 was Krupskaya's moment of glory with Lenin, and after the speeches were over it was she who went back with him to his sisters' apartment on the Petrograd side of the city. "Ilyich and I said almost nothing that night; we did not have the words to express what we felt. . . . Ilyich gazed around the room. It was a typical Petersburg apartment, and we knew that at last we were back, and that our life in Paris, Geneva, Bern, and Zurich was behind us."

The revolution would take years to succeed, and before Krupskaya stretched an uncertain future that might even have included prison. Prison had not frightened her before, but as she approached forty it was becoming a harrowing prospect. These worries were more pressing for Lenin, however, and for the first time in many years they were forced to separate.

The fall of the tsar brought revolutionaries by the hundreds running to Russia from all over Europe, eager to get a piece of the power now handed over to the masses. The European powers facilitated their return in the hope that internal power struggles would weaken the monster of Revolution and keep Russia preoccupied.

Released from her role as Lenin's secretary, Krupskaya threw herself into the turmoil of Petrograd life and the part of the revolutionary process that she had reserved for herself: the ethics of the new society and the education of women and children in the spirit of Marxism. Determined that the Marxist transformation bear fruit, she compiled a number of detailed amendments to the Bolshevik program on popular education and published an appeal to the All-Russian Congress of Teachers. She wrote an article about Lenin, explaining in accessible language who he was and what he stood for. She was elected to the Duma (Parliament) by Petrograd's Vyborg District. She employed her teaching gifts to recruit men and women workers to Bolshevik literacy commissions. And she became secretary of the Bolshevik Central Committee in order to monitor what was happening in the Party while its leader was in hiding.

The list of Krupskaya's activities is endless. Her life's work was the revolution, and the revolution was giving her life. Just a month earlier she had been a sick, prematurely aged woman; now she was almost beautiful again. She and Lenin managed only a few brief meetings. She kept him informed of what was happening. The more heavily he relied on her, the more she blossomed.

Krupskaya's activities in Petrograd were mirrored by those of Inessa Armand in Moscow, where with her usual passion she was putting Lenin's ideas into practice. She also gave speeches, organized groups of women workers and soviets of workers' deputies, and was elected to the Moscow city Duma. Her article "Why Does the Bourgeoisie Slander the Bolsheviks?" explained, as Krupskaya had, who Lenin was. She started a magazine entitled *Worker Woman's Life*, and in the little village of Pushkino, which years earlier had welcomed her into its embrace, her labor work undid the achievements of generations of Armands.

On the morning of October 24, 1917, Nadezhda Krupskaya was

in Petrograd's Vyborg District when she was handed a note from Lenin to the Bolshevik Central Committee: "To delay the uprising is death!" She hesitated, then hurried off to join him at the Smolny Palace, where Lenin had emerged from underground. From then on she and Lenin were inseparable. People flocked to him, and he walked through the crowds followed by his wife — servant, housekeeper, workhorse of the revolution.

There were persistent rumors that Lenin wanted to live with Inessa and that the Politburo had disapproved. Some say Krupskaya offered to move out so that Inessa could move in. Others say that she ordered Inessa to leave for the provinces. Most evidence, however, seems to indicate that the two women remained on friendly terms and worked well together.

In March 1918 the Bolshevik government moved from Petrograd to Moscow, and until the mid-1950s, after the death of Stalin, the upper echelons of the Soviet state occupied the fortified center of Moscow's Kremlin.

The Kremlin lies at the heart of the four concentric roads within which Moscow is situated. The fourth road was built just over twenty years ago to ease Moscow's traffic problems. The third, the Garden Ring Road, dividing central Moscow from the suburbs, was once lined by apple trees, but these were destroyed in the 1930s. The second separates the residential and business sections. Official Moscow with its various institutions lies on the boundary of the first ring and in the middle is the Kremlin itself; the Bolsheviks replaced the tsars' golden eagles with red stars above the high redbrick walls and pointed battlements.

Within the Kremlin grounds lie the imperial palace, the ancient theater building (rebuilt under Khrushchev as the Palace of Congresses), three ancient Orthodox cathedrals, and the belfry of Ivan the Great, which for years was Moscow's tallest structure. There were also numerous auxiliary buildings, living quarters for the servants.

Until the mid-1930s the Kremlin was a lively place: cars of every possible foreign make whisked by, officials hurried about, mothers strolled with children, visiting dignitaries went sightseeing.

Into the residences formerly occupied by the royal court, the Bolshevik leaders moved with their wives, servants, and dependents, a huge noisy throng of people. To reach them one went through a heavy door and along a vaulted, brightly lit corridor covered by a red carpet with a green patterned border. At the end of the corridor hung a large mirror, making it seem even longer. As the leader of the new state, Lenin was given an apartment right next to his office in the Soviet of People's Commissars. The Lenins' apartment was modestly furnished, as befitted the leader of the proletariat. Krupskaya thought this appropriate, although when her husband delighted in the proximity of their new quarters to his office she shook her head and said, "It's convenient all right — no sleep, no rest, no holidays, just work!"

Living in the Kremlin meant being in direct contact with Lenin, and later Stalin, and involved a high degree of trust and intimacy, particularly while the war with the Whites still raged. As Soviet society became calmer, some officials left the Kremlin and with the new government's approval moved into town.

Common interests and experiences meant that underground revolutionaries tended to marry within their own circle, and most Kremlin couples were well matched. The new tsaritsas, as they were called, soon adjusted to their new roles. First it was prison, now the Kremlin. They had earned it. Most Kremlin wives, like Krupskaya, did not slave over a stove or wash the dishes. More serious occupations awaited them, and they threw themselves into literacy programs; caring for the old, sick, and hungry; adopting orphans; and setting up nurseries and day-care centers for working mothers. Although state nurseries quickly caught on and special ones were available for the children of the elite, many wives preferred to have their children looked after at home, and some overcame their scruples and hired nannies, cooks, maids, and governesses who had worked for the bourgeoisie.

New governments always relish disclosing the abuses of their predecessors, before engaging in their own. Former political prisoners, exiles, and émigrés — most no longer young — were drawn to the Kremlin and from its heights surveyed unimaginable riches: works of art, fabulous jewels, princely estates. Their conduct was shaped by a life on the run: paranoia, cunning, betrayal, self-serving lies, rigid hierarchies. From their values emerged a Party run on the principles of "democratic centralism," which the new commissars used to transform the Kremlin into a prison. But they were too intoxicated by victory to realize this.

The new commissars had a puritanical mission. They had risked their lives to expose the evils of the old regime: the workers and former serfs had risen off their knees and ensured a bright future for all mankind. This, with minor variations, was the Bolsheviks' basic theme, and the future belonged to them. How it was to take shape involved interminable arguments. The Leninist slogan "Loot the looters!" could be interpreted however one wished, and from the first days of the Revolution raged a relentless internal power struggle behind the Kremlin walls.

Nadezhda Krupskaya played a major part in this struggle. By assuming total responsibility for the people's education she was establishing herself as far more than a mere female adjunct to Lenin. It was on her initiative that religious education was banned from every school in the land.

Memories of her childhood may have justified Nadezhda's hostility to religion:

> Why did I need religion as a child? I suppose it must have been loneliness. I read and saw a lot, but could never give form to my thoughts and feelings so as to make them comprehensible to others. This was especially tormenting to me as an adolescent. I always had a lot of women friends, but we met on a completely different plane. That was why I needed God. I felt it was His job to understand what was happening in the soul of every human being. I would sit happily for hours on my own, looking at the icon lamp and thinking thoughts that could not be put into words, and knowing that there was someone close by who understood me. The elimination of the vestiges of religion was later hindered by people's ignorance of natural social phenomena. That is why Marxism cured me so radically of any form of religion.

The message is contradictory and not entirely convincing, but it is at least clear that Nadezhda Krupskaya sought to replace her religion with Marxism. Yet her dogmatism is unattractive, and her views are especially unappealing when we remember that they are directed at children. "Anti-religious education should start young, even before school, since children interest themselves in such questions very early these days."

Krupskaya's own childlessness could not but affect her work with them, and the fact that she did not really know or understand them may account for a certain lifelessness in the educational programs she forced into being. Nonetheless, these programs were a great deal more humane than most education circulars drawn up by men. Nadezhda was very often gentle and generous with the many people who solicited her help.

One of these, a woman named Nina Kuritsyna, recently wrote to me:

> In 1937 my sister Lena was suffering from rheumatism and a heart condition and needed hospital treatment. Mother was in despair. She lived in a little village in Siberia with her six younger children. I was a student at Rybinsk, and I made up my mind to write to Krupskaya. Her reply arrived just over a week later, and the following day I was called to the Rybinsk medical center, where I was handed a free travel pass, valid for the whole summer, to give to my sister so that she could attend a sanatorium, and an extra allowance to Mother for the children. . . . My sister is alive today, thank God, and I never forgave myself for not thanking Nadezhda Konstantinovna for what she did for us.

Whatever her individual acts of kindness, had Nadezhda Krupskaya wielded supreme power, her cultural inquisition would have been far more effective than Stalin's, for she was better educated than he was.

However gentle she might have been, Nadezhda Krupskaya believed the execution of the tsar and his family in the summer of 1918 was unquestionably correct and necessary. She also believed that "librarians and teachers should be selected with great care, since the most important thing is not talent or spiritual qualities, but a class approach to people and books."

A standard feature of Soviet policy from the start was the banning of books. Nadezhda's part was instrumental. The émigré writer Roman Gul wrote, "After the Revolution Lenin handed over the task of Russia's enlightenment to his wife. This spiritually and intellectually limited Party dogmatist issued three circulars in rapid succession, each remarkable for their unambiguous declaration that the bloodletting had started."

Generations of Russians were shielded from their country's finest art and literature. The poetry of Sergei Esenin was criticized for its "religious-patriarchal basis and street psychology." The works of Dostoyevsky were outlawed for their "extreme conservative views and pathological images." Blok, Bulgakov, Platonov, Akhmatova, Gumilyov, Voloshin, Tsvetaeva, and later Pasternak were all denounced as well. In November 1923 Gorky wrote to the poet Vladislav Khodasevich, "I can now inform you of the mind-numbing news that Plato, Kant,

Schopenhauer, Solovyov, Taine, Ruskin, Nietzsche, Leskov, and Leo Tolstoy have now all been banned, thanks to Nadezhda Krupskaya."

Having toiled throughout her life to promote literacy in Russia, Nadezhda was now destroying all that she had created. Having grown up in a world of forbidden books, underground leaflets, and illegal strikes, she probably saw nothing criminal or contradictory about her actions; the banning of books lies deep in Russia's history and long preceded the Bolsheviks.

Krupskaya would have been shocked to be called an inquisitor because of her efforts to purge future generations of decadent literature. She dreamed of creating a new comrade for the new society — pristine, pure, freed of the shackles of history, unencumbered by traditional gender roles.

Fierce defender of everything Bolshevik, Krupskaya's own persona was masculine by the old standards, and her educational circulars treated boys and girls as virtually indistinguishable. Other Kremlin wives had only to follow her example.

In the years that followed the revolution, euphoria was replaced by grim survival and a seemingly endless rollcall of disasters: civil war, nationwide famine, counterrevolution, Fanya Kaplan's shooting of Lenin, Sverdlov's sudden death, and in September 1920, the death of Inessa Armand.

That summer Inessa had exhausted herself working to organize the International Women's Conference in Moscow. "Inessa could barely stand straight," wrote Krupskaya. "Even her energy was not up to the colossal task she had set herself." When the conference was over, many of Armand's friends urged her to leave Moscow for a rest. Lenin wrote to her: "If you won't visit a sanatorium, why not go south to the Caucasus? Sergo* will organize rest, sun, and interesting work for you there. Will you think about it? I warmly press your hand."

She took Lenin's advice and left for the Caucasus, where she fell ill with cholera, and on September 23 died alone. Her body was brought back by train to Moscow for burial one damp autumn evening. Elizaveta Drabkina, member of a detachment of Bolsheviks defending the government against terrorist attack, recalled seeing a grief-stricken Lenin, propped up by Krupskaya, following two bony black horses

* *Sergo Ordzhonikidze was a leading Bolshevik.*

pulling a zinc coffin through the streets of Moscow. The next day Armand's ashes were interred next to the Kremlin wall on Red Square. Among the flowers was a wreath of white lilies bearing the inscription: "To Comrade Inessa, from V. I. Lenin." Bolshevik protocol did not strictly entitle Inessa Armand to burial in such a location, but it was Lenin's way of thanking her — or assuaging his own feelings of guilt.

To this day, members of the Armand family fiercely deny any idea of a love affair between Lenin and Inessa. Yet some people, including her friend Ivan Popov, insist that she had a sixth child who died, and that the baby's father was Lenin. They say that the baby's grave can be found in Switzerland.

Another leading Bolshevik feminist of the time, Alexandra Kollontai, openly speculated that Inessa Armand's death may have hastened Lenin's demise. He had arrived at the end of his work, and her death was the final blow. Lenin had created the machine that destroyed the old system, but this machine needed new people and these new people were already breathing down his neck, impatient to do what he himself was no longer capable of doing. Lenin's energy was waning, and his aristocratic intellectual temperament could not tolerate the savagery he had unleashed.

As plots and enmities within the Party multiplied, a most improbable group of people united to claim proprietorship over Russia. By the time of Lenin's last illness the civil war had wound down, but within the Kremlin walls the battles were raging. Lenin's illness frightened Krupskaya, and for the first time she worried about what would happen if he were to die. Refrains of "The Moor has done his work, the Moor must go" could be heard, and discussions about Lenin's successor were already underway. Some of this talk reached Krupskaya, but she ignored it, convinced that no one but Lenin could see the true path.

Whatever the rumors about Inessa Armand, Krupskaya and Lenin were a deeply united couple. She had given herself to him. They shared a profound belief in the power and primacy of the the working class. After twenty years of marriage, their passion might well have lessened, yet none could doubt the power of their attachment. She was his alter ego.

When Lenin fell ill, Krupskaya took her place by his sick bed. The best doctors prescribed complete rest. Ignorant of medical matters, but duly respectful, the Central Committee entrusted the supervision of the doctors' regime to its general secretary, Comrade Stalin. More precisely, Stalin himself assumed this responsibility with the Central Committee's backing, and it served his purposes well.

Lenin's secretary had already secretly brought Stalin the "Testament" that the sick leader had dictated to her, and in which he warned the Party leadership: "Stalin is too rude, and this defect, though quite tolerable in our midst and in dealings among us Communists, is intolerable in a general secretary. I therefore propose that comrades consider some way of removing Stalin from this post and appointing someone else."

The week after Stalin was made responsible for the leader's health, Lenin asked to be allowed to dictate his diary. Stalin, Kamenev, and Bukharin held a meeting with the doctors at which it was agreed that he be allowed to dictate for five to ten minutes each day. Meetings were prohibited, and friends and servants were forbidden to talk politics with him. They were told that this would agitate him.

His doctors had not insisted that he be totally isolated. It was his anxious comrades who decided this was absolutely vital. Krupskaya realized that only work would keep Lenin alive, and on December 21 she wrote under his dictation a message to Trotsky about the foreign trade monopoly. In a telephone call to Krupskaya shortly afterward, Stalin shouted at her in the foulest language for conniving with his archenemy. He threatened to report Krupskaya to the Party's Central Control Commission for disobeying the doctors' orders.

After more than twenty years of marriage a wife knows her husband better than any doctor. Yet the Party could always prove that it knew best, and the Party was above everything. Although Krupskaya's nerves were already at breaking point, she defended herself with her usual dignity, writing to the Control Commission to propose that it should investigate this purely personal conflict.

> I am not exactly new to the Party. In thirty years I have not heard a single rude word from any of my comrades. The interests of Ilyich and the Party are no less dear to me than they are to Stalin. At present I need all the self-control I can muster. I know better than any doctor, and certainly better than Stalin, what can and cannot be discussed with Lenin, since I know what agitates him.

Krupskaya with Lenin in the early days of victory

The widowed Krupskaya

Krupskaya and Lenin in Gorky,
shortly before Lenin's death

This quarrel with Stalin took place as Lenin entered the last phase of his illness, in December 1922. Lenin learned of it only on March 5, 1923, and immediately dictated to his secretary a letter to Stalin in which he said:

> You were rude enough to swear at my wife over the telephone. Although she agreed to forget what you said, both Kamenev and Zinoviev heard about it. I do not easily forget slights against me, and I need not tell you that I take personally any slight against my wife. I therefore demand that you take back everything you said and that you apologize to her. Otherwise you may consider all relations between us at an end.

After dictating this letter Lenin was observed by his secretaries and by his attending physician, Doctor Kozhevnikov, to be in an extremely agitated state. The next morning, after his secretary had read the letter back to him, he asked her to deliver it in person to Stalin and to wait for his reply. Soon after she left his condition deteriorated, his temperature rose, he lost the power of speech, and the left side of his body became paralyzed.

Lenin never returned to active life again. Some, including Trotsky, claimed that Stalin had killed Lenin with a slow-acting poison. According to others, Stalin informed the Central Committee that when Lenin became ill he had asked for poison to put an end to his suffering. Stalin's treatment of Nadezhda Konstantinovna may have been the only poison, but it had the required malevolent effect.

Lenin's letter to Stalin defending Nadezhda was surely one of the most honorable things he ever did. It cost him his life. He lived less than a year after writing the letter. Krupskaya never left his side. She knew now that his departure would open a new page of history, and that the power so hastily gathered into his hand would soon be clutched in another, more terrifying fist.

Did she wonder if it had all been for nothing? Almost certainly not. She believed in the victory of his ideas, even as they were being hijacked before her eyes by Stalin. She was made of iron. During Lenin's long illness she came to terms with his death, and at his funeral in February 1924 she did not shed a single tear. At his grave she addressed the mourners thus:

> These past few days, as I stood over Vladimir Ilyich's coffin, I have been thinking about his life, and this is what I want to say to you.

His heart beat with a passionate love for the workers, the oppressed. Comrades, he never said this himself, and I would probably not have done so at a less solemn moment. But now that our beloved, precious Vladimir Ilyich is dead, I have one great request to make of you: do not let your grief for Ilyich be diverted into superficial reverence for his personality. Do not build monuments to him, or palaces in his name, or hold grand celebrations in his memory. He attached little importance to such things when he was alive, and found them distasteful. Remember that much still has to be settled in our country.

These are more than the words of a grieving wife, they are the words of a revolutionary fighter looking ahead. Krupskaya knew that now she needed to find whatever support she could.

Immediately after Lenin's death she wrote to the writer Maxim Gorky:

Yesterday we buried V. I. He remained to the last as he had always been, a man of enormous will, in full possession of his senses, laughing and joking and tenderly concerned for others. On Sunday evening he had a visit from Professor Auerbach, the oculist, and after he had left Lenin called him back wanting to make sure he was getting enough to eat. When he read in the newspaper that you were ill, he grew very upset and kept saying, "Is it true? Is it true?"

According to Krupskaya, Lenin was active to the last. But another source, the artist Yuri Annenkov, maintains that Lenin had by then entered an infantile state. He writes in his memoirs:

Wanting me to do a last sketch of Lenin, Lev Borisovich Kamenev invited me in December 1923 to visit the little town of Gorky, where Lenin's illness had forced him to take refuge with his wife. I can see as clearly as if it were yesterday the spacious yellow house where they were staying. We were met by Krupskaya, who said there could be no question of my doing a portrait, and indeed the man wrapped in a blanket reclining on a chaise-longue, looking past us with the vacant smile of one who has passed into a second childhood, could not possibly serve as a portrait of Lenin, only as an illustration of his terrible illness.

One can understand why Krupskaya would not wish even her old friend Gorky to see the leader of the revolution in this condition, determined as she was for him to remain in popular memory as good, noble, and powerful. Yet on that same day she wrote another, rarely mentioned letter to Leon Trotsky in the Caucasus. Just before Lenin died Trotsky had gone south to the resort of Sukhumi for a holiday. Stalin had sent him a telegram there advising him not to return for the funeral. Trotsky did not wish to attend Lenin's funeral, and he took Stalin's advice even though later he blamed his absence at the funeral on Stalin.

In his memoirs, Trotsky described how while in the Caucasus he had reflected on Lenin's life and death, and about Krupskaya,

> who had been his friend for so many years, had seen the world through his eyes, and was now burying him and faced intolerable loneliness. I wanted to send her some words of sympathy and affection, but I could not bring myself to. All words seemed frivolous compared to the weight of events, and I feared they would sound clichéd. I was therefore shaken by feelings of gratitude to receive a few days later a letter from Nadezhda Konstantinovna.

Krupskaya's letter, to which Trotsky refers, read:

> Dear Lev Davidovich,
>
> I want you to know that as Vladimir Ilyich was looking through your book a month before his death, he stopped at the passage where you discuss Marx and Engels and asked me to read it aloud to him. He listened closely, then looked at it again himself.
>
> I also want to tell you that V. I.'s feelings for you, beginning when you first visited us in London after your escape from Siberia, remained with him all his life.
>
> I wish you health and strength, Lev Davidovich, and I embrace you warmly.

If one is to believe Krupskaya, Lenin remained intellectually active up to his last month and Trotsky was on his mind just before his death.

Insensitive as ever to anyone but himself, Trotsky writes in his memoirs: "Krupskaya confirmed that despite a long antipathy, Lenin retained the warmth he had felt for me in London, but now perhaps on a loftier historical plane. All the folios of the falsificators would not outweigh before the judgment of history that little note of Krupskaya's, written just a few days after Lenin's death."

Krupskaya's note looks to the future, while briefly evoking the dead man's affection for Trotsky, and seems more intended to extend the hand of comradeship, solidarity, and possible political alliance.

Krupskaya knew she must act. Aware that the choice between

Stalin and Trotsky was a choice between two evils, she chose Trotsky, despite the fact that she must have known that he would not win. Trotsky's monstrous vanity aside, perhaps she felt that the two of them might have confronted Stalin and together waged an effective struggle within the Party. But as Trotsky slipped away and Krupskaya was left without allies, she stifled her personal grief once again in the interests of the higher cause. She had not given her life to the Bolshevik Party for a peasant like Stalin to blunder in and destroy it.

At the Thirteenth Party Congress in May 1924, the first after Lenin's death, Krupskaya delivered a supplementary paper on work in the countryside:

> There is a conveyor belt between the vanguard of the Communist Party and the working class, and this conveyor belt is now securely in place. Vladimir Ilyich spoke of this system of conveyor belts from the proletarian vanguard to the working class itself, and from the working class to the middle and poor peasantry. The first of these conveyor belts exists already. The establishment of the second conveyor belt, from the working class to the peasantry, has still to be developed.

Her speech was greeted with loud applause. Observing the ecstatic welcome which met Lenin's widow at factory and Party meetings, Stalin may well have realized that the people needed this old woman as a replacement for the former tsaritsa, whose murder in Ekaterinburg was still fresh in everyone's memory.

It was widely known that he had insulted Krupskaya, that no one had dared to intervene, and that he had accused her of driving Lenin to an early grave with her inept nursing. It was also known that he had accused her of insulting her beloved husband's memory by not visiting his embalmed body at the Mausoleum. Distressed by Stalin's insistence on this ritualistic veneration of Lenin's remains, Krupskaya had begged that Lenin's body instead be buried. She lived just a step away from where he lay in waxy suspension, and the endless lines to view the body were a symbol of all the other lines in her country.

The actress Galina Sergeyevna Kravchenko, daughter-in-law of Commissar Lev Borisovich Kamenev, recalls:

> In 1930 or 1931 Krupskaya came to Lev Borisovich in tears and begged him to protect her from Stalin's rudeness. Lev Borisovich tried to comfort her, but I don't know if he was able to do anything for her. She looked puffy and unwell, but she remained nevertheless a

splendid, gentle woman. I soothed her and she put her head on my shoulder, sobbing, "It's so hard, Galechka, so hard!"

By the time of the Fourteenth Party Congress in December 1925, Krupskaya was voicing her fears about her brainchild:

> The authority of the Party has arguably been weakened. . . . Our Party was formed many years ago in the struggle against the Mensheviks and Socialist Revolutionaries, and we learned to shower our opponents with curses. Such language is obviously quite unacceptable for Party members to use when debating with each other.

She then invoked Lenin, who, were he alive, would have warned the Party machine against an excessive enthusiasm for capitalism. There was great applause from the audience, and she was awarded extra time.

More storms of applause greeted her at the Fifteenth Party Congress in 1927, when she voiced her fears about the cultural revolution and problems of reeducating society according to Bolshevik guidelines. At the Sixteenth Congress in 1930 she greeted the collectivization program as "a genuine agrarian revolution — a perestroika of the peasant economy on socialist foundations." She castigated Trotsky, now cast out of the USSR, for "having misunderstood the peasant question." She suggested that the full weight of the Party be used to promote the course of collectivization, and she urged each Party member to employ "unceasing Leninist vigilance, lest in struggling with every new twist and turn they forget their priorities and lose sight of the main purpose of the struggle."

Krupskaya didn't let up. Like all the other speakers at the Seventeenth Party Congress in January 1934, she missed no opportunity to mention Stalin's name. Yet while playing by Stalinist rules of the game, she cleverly avoided unctuousness, and even managed to retain some of her dignity in speaking of him: "At our last congress Comrade Stalin brought up the question of general education. This question is naturally of the utmost importance and something the Party has discussed from the start. . . . But we knew that only when the conditions were right could we fulfill this enormous task."

In other words, Comrade Stalin, Lenin and I were discussing such things when you were still attending seminary.

Stalin was sensitive to even the smallest barb, and according to the caustic Karl Radek, he replied: "If she doesn't shut her mouth the Party will appoint old Elena Stasova [an old Bolshevik comrade of

Lenin] as Lenin's widow in her place!" On the evening of February 26, 1939, Nadezhda Krupskaya invited her friends to celebrate her seventieth birthday. Stalin did not attend the party but he sent a cake. Later that evening Krupskaya was stricken with severe food poisoning and rushed to hospital. She died the following morning. At her funeral, it was Stalin who carried the urn with her ashes.

Nadezhda Konstantinovna Krupskaya outlived Lenin by fifteen years, and it must have been painful for her to witness the agony of Bolshevism as it was transformed into Stalinism. Her colleagues at the Commissariat of Education spoke in loving terms of her. She was respected for her kindness as well as her uncompromising toughness. Despite being tormented by her thyroid condition, she worked, issued exhortations, published articles, and endlessly wrote and rewrote her memoirs. Those memoirs make it clear that Krupskaya was deeply involved early on in constructing the Bolshevik system. And after Lenin's death, she valiantly continued to implement his ideas, though most of her efforts were in vain.

Despite the many qualities of her eleven volumes, they were never absorbed into mainstream Communist thought and today survive only for scholarly and historical purposes. In Moscow, where the uncrowned Queen of the Revolution lived for almost twenty years, the legacy of Bolshevism was played out by its children and grandchildren, who finally destroyed it.

2

The Woman Question
and Men's Response

SOME SAY THE FIGHTING on the night of October 25, 1917, between revolutionary soldiers and sailors and White Guard units, was bloody. Others maintain that the Bolsheviks' coup d'état was a rapid and bloodless revolution in which the cannons that the battleship *Aurora* fired at the tsar's palace were blanks. What is rarely mentioned is that the revolutionaries fought a small detachment of palace guards and the Petrograd Battalion of Women. In other words, the Bolsheviks' victory that night was over women.

One of the Bolsheviks' greatest successes was an almost immediate eradication of illiteracy in Russia. Having taught Russia to read and write and tackled some of its more pressing political and economic problems, the Party machine turned to the role of women, the family, and marriage. Militants such as Inessa Armand and Alexandra Kollontai devoted much attention to women's rights in the years before and after the revolution. These women were not Kremlin wives but Kremlin comrades. They were also the first Soviet women to endorse the ideas of "free love" in the Soviet Union.

Intelligent, beautiful, and as delicate-looking as porcelain, Alexandra Kollontai put women's sexuality at the center of the Communist agenda. The new collective living could inspire higher forms of love and compassion, she wrote in her essay, "Make Way For Winged Eros." "It is irrelevant to the tasks of the working class whether love takes the form of a lengthy settled union or a passing liaison."

People were disturbed and agitated by Kollontai's ideas, and in an article entitled "Marriage and Family Law," Krupskaya riposted:

"Monogamy is the most normal form of marriage, and corresponds most closely to human nature."

No "woman question" exists strictly as such, since every question concerning women concerns men, too. Krupskaya and Kollontai, traditionalist and progressive, stood on opposite sides of the issue of monogamy, but to limit either to that position would be to trivialize their complex and often contradictory lives.

The Kremlin, the seat of Soviet power, was also a vast communal apartment complex. Ever fearful of counterrevolution, the leaders wanted to live as close as possible to the pulse of government. They lived where they ruled. Run by iron rules, the Kremlin had its own army of cleaners, typists, secretaries, and guards. Leaders and support staff lived together in comfortable proximity and shared domestic duties, and Kremlin wives were expected to be discreet and modest, like Krupskaya. A few women enjoyed the right to be different in their manners and dress, however, and Alexandra Kollontai was one.

In 1920 Kollontai, forty-eight, was the acknowledged leader of the Bolshevik women's movement. Although Kollontai and Krupskaya were poles apart on the monogamy issue, there were no real political differences between the two women. In many ways they were in agreement about how socialism would reshape and improve family life. Krupskaya, like Kollontai, was against bourgeois forms of the family, and although she opposed Kollontai's theories of free love she magnanimously reconciled herself to Alexandra Mikhailovna Kollontai's flamboyance. Prudish Krupskaya, who had never in her life allowed herself to be tempted by another man, could not have approved of Kollontai's open relationship with a sailor sixteen years younger than her and Soviet military leader, Pavel Dybenko, but she kept her feelings to herself, knowing full well how important and useful Kollontai's education and international connections were to the young Soviet republic.

Kollontai's writings about free love were perhaps partly a justification of her affair with Dybenko. But the theory had a huge impact upon Soviet society as a whole throughout the 1920s and 1930s, and was a subject of continuous vocal discussion. In the Kremlin especially, marriage came to be regarded as a bourgeois throwback, and some Kremlin leaders, such as Lev Kamenev and Grigory Zinoviev, supported second families outside the Kremlin walls.

As the vanguard of the new Soviet family life, Kollontai's role was challenged by events in her own life. By refusing to build a conventional home with Dybenko she made it increasingly hard for them to sustain intimacy, and in 1923, tormented by his continual affairs, she broke off the relationship. After Dybenko tried to kill himself, the Party sent her as ambassador to Norway. When Dybenko followed her there she sent him away, writing to Stalin: "Please do not link the names of Kollontai and Dybenko in the future." Stalin, who liked to meddle in other people's romantic dramas, asked Dybenko on his return to Moscow if he had broken off with Kollontai. When the sailor replied that indeed he had, Stalin said, "You're a fool then!" Dybenko was arrested fifteen years later, and Kollontai did not lift a finger to save him; she was aware that it might have cost her her life to do so, despite her role as ambassador for Stalin.

By 1924 Inessa Armand had died, Kollontai had stopped promoting free love, and Krupskaya had no more rivals on women's issues. Perhaps to avoid her own contradictions, Krupskaya let the Party machine resolve questions involving the sexes. She wrote:

> The non-Party masses see the Party as pioneering new forms of the family and of family life.
> The family will for a long time be a major factor in our life. We are still a long way from the ideal.
> We must deal mercilessly with Communist husbands discovered under the influence of their wives to have departed from Communist ethics.

Other leading Party ideologists' followed Krupskaya's example, believing that the Party should have the last say in dictating the conduct of family life. Here is a sampling of their statements:

> The Party has the right to inspect the family life of each one of us and enforce its line there. . . . Members of our Party do not give enough thought to individual propaganda, especially inside their own families. (Lyadov-Mandelstam)
> The Party has dealt with many disorders, and will also deal with disorders in Communists' family lives. (V. Solts)
> We have the right to demand of Party members that Communism take the spiritual lead in family matters. The Communist who cannot conduct his domestic life properly and introduce the guiding principles of Communism into the family is worth very little. (Commissar of Enlightenment Anatoly Lunacharsky)

Communism, they believed, should first liberate and then transform the new Soviet woman, so that she could take her rightful place in the struggle for the new order:

> Communism and the true liberation of women will start only with the start of a mass struggle, led by the proletariat in power, against the petty domestic economy: in other words restructuring it on the lines of the larger socialist economy. (B. Yaroslavsky)
>
> The woman of the future is being forged in our socialist plants and factories. Here we can see the slow but promising growth of a new type of woman, whose beauty has nothing in common with the eternal female beauty exalted by poets of the past. Aspects of this new type of woman are being reproduced by our new poets and writers, but since it is still in the dynamic of growth it is not yet fully amenable to artistic embodiment. (V. Solts)
>
> Women's weakness, once sung by poets as well as the "eternal feminine," must be judged by us an inevitable consequence of women's slavery as a result of historical conditions that will only be removed under communism. (Yaroslavsky)

By 1924, the family structure would become a leading focus of power struggles and restructuring — twin phantoms of male power — and the notion of the family unit be challenged at its root. Lyadov-Mandelstam concluded:

> What is needed is a radical change in the way we bring up our children. If the schools and children's homes of bourgeois society could artificially produce a bourgeois citizen, then this is where we must strike our first blow. . . . Can a collective person be produced in an individual family? To this we must say a categorical no. A child with the collective mentality can be reared only in a collective environment. Even the best parents ruin their children by bringing them up at home.

The result of all these discussions was a Politburo decree on the "woman question," the first in the Party's history, which embodied all these arguments and remained officially in force until 1989.

The Bolsheviks' policy of promoting women's equal rights — and in particular their right to do heavy work — encouraged women to enter the lower, local levels of power. An article that appeared in *Pravda* on November 7, 1932, noted that "increasing numbers of women" were active in the rural and urban soviets. It notes that in small villages their number had increased from 151,298 in 1927 to 316,697 in 1931.

For the first time in Russian history, women began making their presence felt. Women were relentlessly bombarded with government leaflets exhorting them to shed their previous traditional roles in the family structure. Many rose high in the Soviet hierarchy.

Inside the Kremlin, the wives of the Soviet leaders lived a life of privilege. However, if Molotov, Voroshilov, and Kaganovich were known to share ideas and political decisions with their respective spouses, it was always in the strict intimacy of their households. No Kremlin wife's opinion was ever officially welcomed. Those who challenged that fact — such as Molotov's wife, Zhemchuzhina, as we shall see — were promptly arrested.

3

The Legend of Larissa — Woman of the Revolution

WHEN BOLSHEVIKS from the battleship *Aurora* stormed Petrograd's Winter Palace on the night of October 25, 1917, people claim to have seen on board a tall, statuesque woman of unearthly beauty, with pale features and auburn braids wound around her head. It was she, they said, who gave the order to open fire on the palace. History records that the only woman known to be on the *Aurora* that night was the anti-Bolshevik Countess Panina, who led one of three delegations sent by the Petrograd Duma to the Winter Palace, the Smolny Institute, and the *Aurora*, which were all turned back. Yet in the years that followed the legend persisted, and in Soviet literature, film, and theater the image of the leather-jacketed, gun-toting woman revolutionary — standing on the bridge of a warship at the height of the battle, urging the sailors on and outdoing even the bravest of them in courage — became standard.

That image is based on the life of Bolshevik commissar Larissa Reisner, whose exploits during the Civil War were first depicted in the play *An Optimistic Tragedy*, by Vsevolod Vishnevsky, a Bolshevik sailor on board the same ship as Reisner during the battles on the Volga.

Larissa Mikhailovna Reisner was not a Kremlin wife, but the men she associated with were men of the Kremlin. She was born into a cultured, Bolshevik-sympathizing St. Petersburg family in 1895, shortly after Nadezhda Krupskaya had already joined the Leninist struggle for the liberation of the working class. Poet, revolutionary, and journalist, Reisner lived hard in her short lifetime — she died in 1926 — through World War I, two revolutions, and a civil war. She flashed white-hot across the sky of the revolution like a comet, and her trace was a symbol of the new women's glory. Known as the "Woman of the Revolution," Reisner wanted to create a new type to match the Woman of the French Revolution. She used her own life as the example. In her way, she succeeded: she was immortalized in the prose, drama, and poetry of her time.

Every piece that appeared after her death mentions her beauty. The poet Vsevolod Rozhdestvensky recalled his fellow students gasping when she entered the St. Petersburg University auditorium in 1911 as one of its first women students. "Tall and elegant in a modest gray suit of English cut, her thick, dark hair wound around her head like a crown, there was something haughty and un-Russian in her regular, almost chiseled features and her sharp playful eyes."

According to Vadim Andreyev, son of the poet Leonid Andreyev, who lived with the Reisners as a boy, "Walking along the street, she seemed to bear her beauty like a torch. Even the coarsest objects gained a new tenderness from her presence. Men would stand rooted to the spot as we passed, and few who knew her failed to fall desperately in love with her."

The writer Yuri Libedinsky described her as a "classical goddess or Nordic Valkyrie:" "I felt that to talk to her would bring extraordinary happiness." The British journalist Andrew Rothstein recalled entering her compartment during a train journey to Latvia, and being enchanted by "her beauty, the charm of her language, and her passionate commitment to communism." Even Osip Mandelstam's wife, Nadezhda, who was extremely skeptical about Larissa, was struck by her "Germanic beauty."

Larissa's poetry resembles her — cool and beautiful. As a schoolgirl she immersed herself in poetry, and in 1915 she helped her father start publishing a literary journal named *Rudin*. She tenderly and perhaps passionately loved Alexander Blok, known as the King of Poets, and gave him a collection of *Rudin's* issues. Perhaps she hoped that proximity to his poetry might miraculously transform her into a great poet. But Blok, who regarded women poets with barely disguised indifference, never acknowledged her poetry.

Before the Revolution, she became close to Blok's rival Nikolai Gumilyov. Gumilyov's wife, the poet Anna Akhmatova, was said to have been jealous of their relationship and made angry scenes. But Gumilyov seems to have had little positive to say about Larissa's talent.

In one of his letters to her he wrote, "You have beautiful honest eyes, but you are blind. Strong young legs, but no wings. A powerful and elegant intellect, but with a strange emptiness at the center. You are a princess turned into a statue."

Perhaps to soften the blow, he went on: "But no matter! I know that somewhere in Madagascar all will change, and that on a warm evening of buzzing beetles and blazing stars, in a thicket of red rosewood trees near a bubbling spring, you will tell me wonderful things that I have glimpsed only in my finest moments. Good-bye, Leri, I shall write to you."

Gumilyov's words are an accurate assessment of Reisner's poetic abilities. She had strong feelings, but however much she longed to be a poet, she simply lacked the talent.

Reisner may have seemed cool and proud, but she had a huge energy for life and expression, and the Revolution gave her an opportunity to display it. She worshiped Lenin. As she put it: "I am not a timid soul, but when I am near Ilyich I forget myself and become as shy as a little girl." Since all the female places in Lenin's circle were occupied, she stayed on the fringes.

Shortly before October 1917 she did revolutionary propaganda work with sailors at the Kronstadt naval base. There she met Fyodor Raskolnikov, a sailor of peasant origin and the leader of the Kronstadt Bolsheviks, with whom she fell in love. Immediately after the revolution she worked under Anatoly Lunacharsky, Commissar of Enlightenment, to help preserve the imperial artifacts in the Winter Palace from the marauding masses. In the summer of 1918, as the Civil War reached its height, she resigned her position with Lunacharsky and set off as Raskolnikov's wife to fight with the Baltic sailors of the Volga flotilla.

That summer Larissa Reisner sailed the length of the Volga, the Kama, and the Belaya rivers helping the Red Army defend towns and villages from the White Guards and the White Czech legions. Many of the abandoned estates lining these rivers contained furniture, food, and clothes, and she would often appear on board dressed in a variety of ladies' costumes and girlish summer dresses. During the battle for Kazan she twice infiltrated the Whites' lines, dressed first as an aristocrat, then as a peasant, and started a rearguard action.

The example of Larissa's courage may have determined the course of many of the battles during the Bolsheviks' victorious Volga

Larissa Reisner

campaign, and her pen and her personality turned her part into legend. A sailor named Kartashov recalled ecstatically how she appeared on their battleship and ordered them to scout out the White flotilla. The commander objected that it would be too dangerous, but she insisted, boarded a cruiser, and sped off toward the Whites' ships: "She stood smiling at the helm, happy to be going into danger, then disappeared from view, and only from the shooting of 37-millimeter guns could we establish the cruiser's whereabouts. We opened defensive fire, there were some artillery shots, and a few minutes later she maneuvered the cruiser back safe and unharmed."

This flamboyance guided her pen in her numerous essays from the Civil War fronts and later from Afghanistan. Everything had prepared her for this role: her parents' revolutionary sympathies, her own dedication to the Bolsheviks, her literary ambitions, and the naval victories of Commander Fyodor Raskolnikov furthered the cause. Raskolnikov was a powerful figure, a monument to revolutionary courage and enthusiasm who softened only before Larissa. His prospects were dazzling. Her beauty and courage were legendary. As a team they made it seem as if everything was possible.

It may be hard for us now to imagine how the lice-ridden peasant sailors, exhausted by interminable war, could appreciate Larissa's rather stilted speeches to them. Her extraordinary ideas and style seemed hopelessly out of place in the midst of poverty and destruction. "Why not please the eye if you can?" she wrote, arguing that it was her glorious femininity that gave the sailors courage, reminding them that they had women waiting for them back home. Yet rather than representing the girl back home, she presented men with the challenge of the new woman: wide-ranging intellect, courage, and tenderness.

About a month after the shooting of the imperial family in July 1918, Larissa sailed down the Volga from Sviyazhsk to Nizhny Novgorod on the former royal yacht, the *Mezhen*. According to a fellow sailor named Berlin, "Larissa Mikhailovna was in high spirits. She quickly made herself at home in the quarters of the former tsaritsa, and upon learning from the crew that the tsaritsa had scratched her name on the window of her cabin, she mischievously crossed it out and scratched her own next to it with a diamond."

We might forgive Larissa Mikhailovna her extravagance when we remember what she accomplished despite a background of hunger, family breakup, and economic havoc. She never refused herself anything, whether risking death in battle or living like a queen while others starved. Yet she was honest, unlike those who said nothing or feigned poverty. "We're creating a new state," she wrote. "People need us. It would be hypocritical to deny ourselves the things people always acquire when they come to power."

Nadezhda Mandelstam wrote, "Larissa did not merely love poetry, she believed in it. In the first years of the Revolution, among the conquerors numbered many lovers of poetry. I don't know how they managed to reconcile poetry with their Hottentot morality — it's good to kill, it's bad to be killed."

Others managed it quite successfully, in fact; Stalin for one. Poets sometimes prove accomplished murderers, and their words can have a keen edge. It is not surprising that the bullet and the word were in perpetual opposition.

Larissa Reisner contracted tropical malaria at the front. The illness took a heavy toll on her health, but her courage never flagged. After leaving the front lines, she went on to conquer St. Petersburg's poetry circles. According to her friend and fellow poet Lev Nikulin, the city's inhabitants would see Larissa and Blok riding around the city's islands on horses requisitioned from the front, indulging in long conversations about poetry and revolution. People mumbled that "society strolls" were out of tune with a time when the population was suffering such privation.

Vsevolod Rozhdestvensky was also struck by the unabashed luxury of Larissa's life. When he, Osip Mandelstam, and their fellow poet Mikhail Kuzmin went to visit her at the Petrograd Admiralty building, where she lived, he noted:

> The duty sailor led us down the dark, echoing corridors to her apartment. Outside the door our arrival was announced so ceremoniously that we were overcome with shyness. Larissa was waiting for us in a small room draped in exotic fabrics. Bronze and brass buddhas, Kalmyk idols, and Oriental majolica dishes glimmered in the corners. The floor was covered with a white felt Caspian nomad tent. On a low wide sofa lay stacks of English books and a thick classical Greek dictionary. A ship's signal flag was adorned with a revolver and an old cadet's cloak. On an old Oriental table gleamed innumerable cut-glass perfume bottles and highly polished bronze boxes and bowls, most likely acquired from the same Kalmyk settlements. Larissa was draped in a heavy gown embroidered with gold thread, and were it not for

the thick chestnut braid around her head, she could have been mistaken for some Buddhist idol.

Rozhdestvensky's description of the famous commissar's quarters proves that the iron revolutionary was also a woman of refined taste and spiritual aspirations.

In March 1921, Raskolnikov was appointed to head Soviet Russia's first diplomatic mission in Afghanistan. Larissa traveled with him to Kabul, where she quickly became the center of attention at the diplomatic mission. Here she wrote a series of sketches published in 1923 as *Afghanistan*. She no longer had any illusions about herself as a poet. On November 24, 1921, Larissa wrote to Anna Akhmatova from the mountains of Afghanistan, where she was sheltered from all that was happening in Russia — including Gumilyov's execution, which had taken place three months earlier.

> Dear, respected Anna Andreyevna, the newspapers have traveled nine thousand *versts* to tell us of the death of Blok, and for some reason it is only with you that I feel able to express how sad and absurd this seems. Only you, because it is as though the column standing beside you has fallen, a column just as fine, white, and exquisitely molded as you. Now that your equal, only, spiritual brother is no longer here, your greatness is even more apparent. My dear, most tender poet, are you writing poetry? There is nothing greater than this. For one line of yours people should be pardoned an entire, evil year.

Despite her influence with the new government, Larissa made no effort to save Gumilyov — who had been arrested for planning the Kronstadt rebellion — from the firing squad. In her memoirs, Nadezhda Mandelstam recalls that, when she and her husband visited Larissa, she told them that her mother had allegedly persuaded Lenin to send the Cheka a telegram canceling the execution. The telegram must have been delayed, and the execution was carried out. This story had great currency for many years. Yet Nadezhda Mandelstam had also visited Larissa's mother while Larissa was away, and found her deeply distressed that her daughter had done nothing to prevent Gumilyov's arrest.

After two years in Kabul, Larissa Reisner suddenly left Raskolnikov and returned to Moscow. Raskolnikov took her departure badly. He wrote, "I know there are many men far cleverer than me, but you will never find anyone who is so boundlessly devoted to you and loves you so passionately after seven years of marriage. . . . Remember, I not only love you, I respect you infinitely."

Larissa Reisner was a tangle of contradictions. She could turn simple immorality into an exploit. Osip Mandelstam recalled that Larissa once threw a party solely to enable Cheka agents to arrest the guests. Yet she would also take a basket of food to Anna Akhmatova when she was ill, and what is striking is not that she was able to procure food — for everything was available to her — but her deep reverence for poetry.

Finally reconciled to the fact that she herself was no poet, Larissa turned to prose, and worked hard to become a journalist. Her writing displayed a new rigor, a release from excessive prettiness. Behind this transformation stood the extraordinary figure of Karl Radek-Sobelsohn.

Witty and cynical, Radek was one of a small group of Bolshevik leaders who continued to be active after Lenin's death. Although not at all handsome, he won Larissa's heart. In 1923 she traveled with Radek to Germany as a journalist, and wrote about the aborted Hamburg uprising in a book called *Hamburg on the Barricades*. When she got back to Moscow, she was hailed as a successful journalist and became a special correspondent for *Izvestia*. She also published a book of essays, *Coal, Iron and Living People,* about her travels around Russia and her adoption of a little boy.

In the name of the Revolution Larissa had fought, danced, written poetry, and dazzled. It took all her strength, and at the age of thirty, Larissa suddenly collapsed with typhoid fever. She refused to accept that she was dying until nearly the end. In the last minutes of her life she briefly regained consciousness and said: "Now I understand the danger I am in."

The poet Varlaam Shalamov, who had worshiped Larissa Reisner from afar, described her funeral:

> A beautiful young woman, heroine of the Civil War and the hope of literature, has died of typhoid fever at the age of thirty. No one can believe it. We think we are dreaming. But Reisner is dead. . . . Her coffin lay at the House of the Press on Nikitsky Boulevard. The courtyard was filled with people — soldiers, diplomats, writers. The coffin was borne out, and we saw her burnished chestnut hair coiled like rings around her head. Following the coffin walked Karl Radek, supported on each side by his friends.

Radek's grief began an eleven-year fall from grace: his support of Trotsky, his betrayal of Trotsky, his panegyrics to Stalin, his terror of prison, his false testimony against countless comrades, his willingness to do anything to save his skin.

It may have been just as well that Larissa died before Radek and Raskolnikov, as they were destroyed by the machine to which they had devoted all the energy of their passionate natures. One can only wonder what her fate would have been had she been alive in 1937, given her connection with the men who became "enemies of the people."

Boris Pasternak mourns her loss in his poem "Memories of Larissa Reisner":

> In depths of legend, heroine, you walk,
> Along that path your steps will not fade.
> Tower like a mighty peak above my thoughts;
> For they are at home in your great shade.

It is not only Larissa Reisner's loss Pasternak is mourning, but the loss of a particularly female mystique, without which it was hard to survive the cruel realities of life in the Soviet Union. The irony is that while Larissa tried to become a poet, she became better known years later as its muse, when Pasternak gave her name to the heroine of his greatest novel, *Doctor Zhivago*. Larissa Reisner and Lara are different in many ways, but Larissa's name was for Pasternak an abiding symbol of inspiration, faith, hope, and love.

An inspiration to men whose job it was to fight, Larissa Reisner represents a type often encountered in Russian history: a figure larger than life, acting on the huge stage of history itself. She could play the spy infiltrating enemy lines, the commissar urging her soldiers into battle, the poet summoning words to her cause, the journalist tackling the toughest truths. She ignored the elements, scoffed at gunfire, drank from fetid pools, swung herself into the saddle beside cavalry commanders, fully confident that the costumes in her wardrobe were endless and that she would find another part to play.

4

The Daughter-in-law

Lev Borisovich Rosenfeld, 1883–1936 (revolutionary name — Kamenev), born in Moscow, the son of Russianized Baltic Germans. Raised by radical parents, he studied law at Moscow University, where he joined the revolutionary movement and spent the ensuing years traveling around Russia as a propagandist and strike organizer. In 1913 he followed the Lenins into exile in Poland. Returning with them to Petrograd after February 1917, he became editor of Pravda. *After October 1917, he became chair of the Moscow Soviet. The end of Kamenev's career began in 1927 with a long course of political capitulation to Stalin. In 1928, he and Zinoviev denounced the Trotskyites. Four years later they were expelled from the Party. Readmitted in 1934, he was accused in January 1935 of being morally responsible for the assassination of Kirov and sentenced to five years in Siberia. The following July, at a trial where his brother was the main prosecution witness, Kamenev received an additional five-year sentence, and in August 1936 he and Zinoviev were the stars of the first Moscow show trial, the Trial of the Sixteen, which sentenced these "mad dogs" to death for having formed a terrorist group allied to the Gestapo. In a last attempt to save his wife and children, Kamenev begged his sons to "spend their lives defending the great Stalin."*

LEGEND HAS FORGED an odd link between Larissa Reisner and the murdered royal family. When the poet Vladislav Khodasevich visited the Kamenevs in the Kremlin in 1919, Kamenev's wife, Olga

Davidovna, the sister of Trotsky, spoke tenderly to him of their fourteen-year-old son, Lyutik, who had joined the Volga flotilla and sailed on the royal yacht with Raskolnikov and Reisner. She told Khodasevich that Raskolnikov had dressed the boy in a sailor suit, with jacket, cap, shoes, and striped jersey, and the little boy had stood guard outside the door armed with a revolver. The image disturbed Khodasevich. Were these the clothes of the murdered tsarevich Alexei?

Olga Davidovna continued unabashed:

> When Lyutik was little he was questioned by the tsarist police, but they got nothing out of him. He's only fourteen but he's already organized the Kremlin boys into a military league of young Communists.* Lyutik sits in on all our meetings, and when everyone's gone he says, "Mama, don't trust Comrade so-and-so, he's a bourgeois and a traitor to the working class." He was right about two old and trusted Communists, and now we ask his opinion about everything!

Galina Sergeyevna Kravchenko was born in 1904 in Kazan. She was beautiful and would become a star of the silent screen. Her parents, although not wealthy, took their pretty young daughter on a world tour.

On their return to Russia the family moved to Moscow, where she entered a girls' school on Lubyanka Square (before the KGB had its headquarters there). A talented dancer, she left school to attend ballet classes that became part of the Bolshoi Theater. Her teachers predicted a brilliant career for her as a ballerina.

Tall, blond, graceful, and vivacious, Galina had already danced in several ballets and operas when she happened to meet the film director Vsevolod Pudovkin, who persuaded her to switch from ballet to film. A beautiful ballerina, talented acrobat, gifted aerialist, swimmer, and equestrian, Galina Kravchenko was the model Soviet girl. She could also shoot, drive a motorcycle, and box. "Boxing is like dancing," she said. "It's about lightning reactions, thinking first and moving fast."

One day in 1929 the film director Volodya Schneider, just back from China with his wife, telephoned the beautiful twenty-six-year-old star. "Get dressed and come over!" he said. "An interesting man is coming — you'll fall in love with him!"

---

* *Lyutik Kamenev's boy soldiers later became the Komsomol.*

I resisted and deliberately put on a plain cotton frock. But the man Volodya introduced me to looked very handsome and elegant in his summer uniform. When it was time to leave he offered to see me home. As we were walking, a tram came along Theater Square. I jumped on, waved, and said that I didn't like being taken home. I never forgot the sight of his surprised eyes gazing after me. He began phoning me, and his voice was soft and bewitching. He told me he rode a motorcycle. I had a passion for motorcycling, too. At that time people were allowed to train on the Leningrad Highway after midnight. My new friend started taking me there on his Harley-Davidson. He told me I was the first girl he had allowed to drive it.

Galina Kravchenko's new admirer was a pilot, a graduate of the Zhukovsky Military Air Force Academy. His name was Alexander Lvovich, but everyone called him Lyutik, and he was the son of Olga Davidovna and Lev Kamenev.

Galina and Lyutik married in June 1929, and for almost seven years she lived with the Kamenevs in their six-room apartment on Manezh Square, opposite the Kremlin.

Lev Borisovich's head was always in the clouds. He was an optimist, and all he ever thought about was books, art, and music. He never discussed politics at home. He owned nothing, everything belonged to the state. When he went to Italy to negotiate with Mussolini the Italians gave him a magnificent car, but he handed it straight over to the Central Committee the moment he got back.

Olga Davidovna worked as head of the Society for Cultural Relations with Foreign Countries, and then as head of the Department for Film Promotion. She was always out working. She had been shot in the leg and head many years before. She was clever, and people said she had been pretty in her youth, but now she was moody and difficult. She could be cruel, too. Lyutik would come home exhausted and take his boots off, and a few minutes later she would phone ordering him to pick her up. She had her own government car, she just wanted to show him off to her friends at work. Trotsky, Olga Davidovna's brother, had been deported in 1927, two years before I arrived. Olga Davidovna never mentioned him. Trotsky's wife, Natasha Sedova, had left the country with him, but Seryozha, Trotsky's younger son, had refused to follow. Seryozha used to visit us. He was a delightful, modest young man, with two children. He was later shot, and his children were deported. I don't know how they ended up.

Olga Davidovna knew exactly what was happening and antici-
pated everything. I was shocked by her pessimism. "Enjoy yourself
while you're young, Galenka," she used to say. "Things are going to
be bad for us." When I asked her what she meant, she would say,
"You'll see, terrible grief awaits us."

The Kamenevs had a younger son, Yura, who was still at school.
He was a wonderful boy, noble, sweet-natured and poetic. There was
also the cook and Lyutik's old nanny, Mrs. Terentevna. She was very
strict. She hadn't liked any of Lyutik's previous girlfriends but she
loved me right away. We would come back late from the theater or
friends to find a light supper waiting for us on the table, with three
kinds of vodka.

Lev Borisovich was in love with a woman named Glebova. She
had two sons, one by her first husband, the other by Lev Borisovich —
there was the same sixteen-year gap between her two as between Lyutik
and Yura. Lev Borisovich's other family had almost nothing to do
with us, although we all knew about them.

Lenin's sister, Anna Ilyinichna, lived in the apartment above us.
She was a horrible woman — always sending her maid down to tell
us to make less noise. We used to have lots of young people and artists
around. Once we had a New Year's party with a hundred and fourteen
guests, including the film director Sergei Eisenstein. Lev Borisovich
worshiped Eisenstein. We showed all the latest Soviet and foreign films,
then took turns shooting at the ceiling with an air-gun. . . . That an-
noyed Anna Ilyinichna.

Galina took responsibility for picking up the family's food. The
Kamenevs gave her five hundred rubles a month each for the meals,
and every day she would drive Lev Borisovich's car to collect lunch
and dinner from the special Kremlin stores, located across the river
in the House on the Embankment. There were two sections, one for
high government officials, the other for Party workers. Although only
Lev Borisovich and Olga Davidovna had special privileges, the food
allotted to them was more than enough for nine people, and invariably
every meal came with half a kilo of butter and half a kilo of the finest
black caviar. There were unlimited supplies of "dry rations" — that is,
uncooked foods, prime cuts of meat, superb fish, delicatessen, gro-
ceries, cakes, sweets, and spirits. On Shrovetide, hot pancakes in covered dishes would be rushed back to the apartment.

Clothes were more of a problem. In 1932 Lev Borisovich asked me
to buy him some socks when I was in town. I came back empty-

Kamenev's wife and Trotsky's sister,
Olga Davidovna

Alexander Kamenev, "Lyutik"

Lev Kamenev with his daughter-in-law, Galina Kravchenko

handed. He was amazed when I told him there wasn't a single pair of socks to be had in Moscow. I had my clothes made for me by the special Commissariat of Internal Affairs dressmaker on Kuznetsky Most. I sometimes met Stalin's wife there during the early 1930s — we used to sit together waiting for our fitting. I can't say we knew each other well. I found her gray and uninteresting, and I didn't like her taste in clothes — all her things were so drab.

In the autumn of 1931, when Galina Sergeyevna was seven months pregnant, Lyutik drove her around the Crimea in a Ford he had received from the United States. They joined five other couples at the Politburo guest house at Mukholatka, all of whom were also the children of Politburo members, but Lyutik and Galya occupied Stalin's suite, consisting of bedroom, office, and sitting room. "Mukholatka was so luxurious — I could never stay anywhere else after that. At first we were bothered by the presence of guards, but soon we didn't even notice them. It was like a fairy tale."

In December 1934, Galina and the film director Mark Donskoy were returning by train from shooting a film in the Crimea, when they learned of the murder of Kirov.* Lyutik, white as a sheet, met her at the station. On December 16 they came for Lev Borisovich, and shortly afterward Glebova was arrested and Lyutik lost his job. On the night of March 5, 1935, three months after Lev Borisovich was deported to Siberia, Lyutik was arrested.

> Four soldiers, including one colonel, ransacked the apartment. They went through the cupboard containing my films and the colonel pulled out reel after reel, one containing a unique shot of Lev Borisovich with Lenin. They pulled out every single film, unwound them all and looked at them in the light, then threw them on the floor, so the floor was piled with coils of unwound film and it took me a month to put them back again.
>
> On March 20 they came for Olga Davidovna and she kissed Yura good-bye. She was sentenced to three years' exile in Gorky. Vitalik and I were evicted from our government apartment, and Yura, Seryozha, Vitalik, and I all moved into the headquarters of the Central Committee at 27 Gorky Street, which before the revolution had been a a second-class hotel.

* *Politburo member Sergei Kirov was assassinated in Leningrad on December 1, 1934. His death served as the pretext for Stalin's subsequent campaign of terror.*

In 1938 Yura decided to join his mother in Gorky. I tried to persuade him not to, but he insisted. He never returned. He was arrested in Gorky with his mother and shot.

Lyutik went to prison twice, the first time in the Butyrki. When we visited him there Vitalik said, "Papa lives in a ditch!" He looked terrible. He said, "For God's sake write to Josif Vissarionovich and get me out of here!"

I wrote a letter to Stalin and posted it, and twenty-four hours later I telephoned his secretary, Poskrebyshev, a repulsive individual. His response was encouraging: "Josif Vissarionovich has read your letter, and agrees to your request."

Next thing I received a call from the prison telling me that my husband was leaving for Alma Ata at seven that evening, and to bring a leather coat, some money, and a suitcase to the Kazan Station.

I ran all the way, handed in the things at a special office, and demanded a receipt. "I know you're all crooks!" I said. I was young and fearless then. At the ticket office they told me the train was leaving at five past seven. I dashed along the carriages frantically looking for the barred windows. Right by the engine I saw the crimson service caps, and suddenly there was Lyutik, freshly shaved and looking his usual cheerful self. He saw me, and put up three fingers to indicate three years. We said a long good-bye.

Behind me stood a man in a crimson cap. When the train had left he said: "Go quick. I let you say good-bye — now scram or I'll be in trouble!" I thanked him.

This time, Lyutik didn't come back. We loved each other very much. We were never apart. It makes me mad when the papers say he stood on the highway waiting for Stalin or Vishnevsky's car to pass so he could shoot them. We were always together. Even when he was studying at the Military Academy I used to pick him up in the car.

Galina Sergeyevna eventually married again, and had a daughter. In the summer of 1951, when the baby was away in Georgia for the summer, nineteen-year-old Vitalik was arrested before her eyes. As she came home in the small hours after spending the evening with a friend, she saw Vitalik, who had been unable to sleep and had come out to walk her back.

They came for him a few minutes later. There were three of them. They spent the whole night rummaging through our things looking for contacts. They were unbelievable boors. They found two letters from Lev Borisovich to me, one written at the Kremlin hospital on the day Vitalik was born, and enclosing a little revolver from Alexandra Mikhailovna Kollontai. It was a real St. Bartholomew's Night — that was the night when they took all the teenage children of the "enemies of the people."

They took my whole family, apart from my little daughter. All our government acquaintances and actor friends avoided us, of course, I don't blame them. In those days people looked out for themselves. Not everyone. The writer Anna Antonovskaya, the director Abram Romm, and his actress wife, Olga Zhizneva, went on seeing me. But my career went into decline. They removed me from the picture *Happy Flight* when it was almost finished, and replaced me with another actress. At a film festival in February 1935 I wasn't even nominated for an award. Everyone was looking at me as Abel Enukidze read out the list of prizewinners at the Bolshoi Theater, but he looked away. He was a sweet man but he played around with little girls and dancers. Stalin warned him about this, and about his political ambitions.

They persecuted my second husband too. Before we lived together several men would follow him up the street when he came to visit me, and they would look up at my window until he left. They didn't leave me in peace either, of course. They started harassing me again in 1938, when I was summoned to be interrogated. I was already married then, with another family, but a man started telephoning me to say that if I didn't help him he would have me deported or sent to prison. Someone suggested that I write to a certain General Korutsky in the NKVD, and Korutsky agreed to see me and said the man had not been authorized to telephone me and wouldn't be bothering me again.

I survived to make more films. But the truth is that I was devastated. I could have done so much more creatively. I remember them all: charming Lev Borisovich, unhappy Olga Davidovna, beautiful Yurochka, and my unforgettable Lyutik. And I think, did they really exist or did I dream it?

Documents relating to all the murdered members of Galina Sergeyevna's family cover an entire table. Papers show that they were killed, and that it was in vain.

Lev Borisovich Kamenev. Died: 8.25.1936. Age: 53. Cause of death: word deleted. Place of death: Moscow.

Olga Davidovna Kameneva. Died: 9.11.1941. Age: 58. Cause of death: two words deleted. Place of death: word deleted.

Yuri Lvovich Kamenev. Died: 1.30.1938. Age: 17. Cause of death: word deleted. Place of death (between these words someone has inserted "registered"): Moscow.

Alexander Lvovich Kamenev. Died: 07.15.1939. Age: 33. Cause of death: word deleted. Place of death: word deleted.

She has two more bitter communiqués. The first, dated November 11, 1955, reads:

Regarding the case of Vitaly Alexandrovich Kravchenko, born 1931, sentenced by Special Session of the USSR Ministry of State Security on August 18, 1951, it has hereby been decreed on November 5, 1955, by the Juridical Collegium for Criminal Affairs of the Soviet Supreme Court, that the case is annulled due to absence of *corpus delicti*. (Signature illegible.)

The second is a death certificate:

Vitaly Alexandrovich Kravchenko. Died: 8.3.1966. Age: 34. Cause of death: poisoning. Place of death: Moscow.

5

The Despot's Wife

Josif Vissarionovich Dzhugashvili, 1879–1953 (revolutionary name — Stalin), born near Tbilisi in Georgia, the son of a shoemaker. Expelled from Tiflis Seminary as a revolutionary and worked for the Bolshevik underground and in exile until February 1917, when he returned to Petrograd and was elected to the Party Central Committee. After October 1917 he was made commissar for nationalities and spent most of the Civil War at the front. In 1922 he became secretary of the Party Central Committee. Having concentrated power in his hands after Lenin's death in 1924, he embarked on his campaigns of forced industrialization and collectivization, which resulted in the purges and terror of the 1930s and 1940s. World War II elevated Stalin to the status of a myth but also isolated him, and the backlash followed quickly upon his death.

As THE SOVIET GOVERNMENT prepared to move from Petrograd to Moscow at the beginning of 1918, each of its leaders had his life's companion by his side. Lenin had Krupskaya, Trotsky had Natalya, Kamenev had Olga Davidovna — the only wifeless one was Josif Stalin.

Behind Stalin lay years of exile in Siberia and Northern Russia, a life without home creature comforts or a woman's touch. He might have retained the faint memory of his first wife, Ekaterina Svanidze, who died of tuberculosis in 1909, leaving him with their young son, Yakov. In his memoirs, Trotsky describes Ekaterina Svanidze as a "young uneducated Georgian girl," yet we know that this "uneducated girl" was educated at home by governesses until the age of fourteen and that her brother studied at Berlin University; Bolshevik psychology determined that anyone from the country must necessarily be poor and uneducated.

By the spring of 1918 it had become urgent for the widowed Stalin to find himself a new wife. Since he had nowhere to live in Petrograd because of a housing shortage, his revolutionary friend Sergei Alliluyev had offered him a room, but he could not continue indefinitely to stay at friends' homes and be fed by their kind-hearted wives. There were those who hinted that if Stalin was unable to find a wife it was because no woman could endure his savage temper.

His mother urged him to go back to his village in Georgia, pick himself a strong pretty girl, and take her back to the Kremlin with him. He agreed that it would be good to find a woman with whom he could speak his own language at home, but that was out of the question. He had no time to go to Georgia, and what would his comrades say? For all their talk about the masses, professional revolutionaries were an elitist group. A simple Georgian peasant girl would be no wife for the future leader of the People's Government, surrounded by powerful, intellectual, aristocratic women such as Nadezhda Krupskaya and Trotsky's wife, Natalya Sedova; with a Georgian peasant for a wife, Stalin would be at the mercy of Trotsky's sharp tongue.

Where else was he to find the right woman for his new station in life? In the next room, doing her homework, was the Alliluyevs' elder daughter, Nadezhda. A sweet little girl, slender and graceful, she was in many ways the image of Stalin's ideal woman.

Nadezhda was also little more than a child. Years earlier Stalin had saved her life in Baku. She had fallen in the water when playing on the dock, and he had pulled her out just in time. She was pretty, clever, young, the daughter of a true Bolshevik, unspoiled and untouched. She had not endured putrid tsarist prisons like Kamenev's wife or been degraded by exile like Voroshilov's Ekaterina Davidovna, who was said to have taken a fellow Bolshevik as a lover before her marriage. Alliluyev's wife was highly promiscuous, and in fact had just run off with yet another man. As a result, Nadezhda had to do all the cooking; Stalin found it incomprehensible how his friend Alliluyev could put up with his wife's affairs.

Stalin had met the Alliluyevs in December 1900, the year before

Nadezhda's birth, when they lived in the Georgian capital of Tiflis, as it was called then. Shortly after Stalin's arrival, the talented Victor Kurnatovsky returned from exile in Siberia, where he had made such an impression on the young Nadezhda Krupskaya. Kurnatovsky united all the Bolsheviks in Tiflis and told Stalin about the Lenins. He changed Stalin's life.

Alliluyev's wife first chased Stalin, then Kurnatovsky, and Nadezhda had arrived in September 1901, nine months later. Stalin worried at first that she would turn out to be as promiscuous as her mother, but this wasn't the case. As the goddaughter of the prominent Georgian Bolshevik Abel Enukidze, she would not be out of place in Kremlin circles. She was young, but she would soon grow up. Stalin sensed his time was coming: the right woman by his side would be key to his success. Nadezhda was a blank page on which he could write whatever he liked. She would be his princess!

Meanwhile, in the next room, Nadezhda was writing to a Bolshevik woman named Anna Ivanovna Radchenko, who had taken a motherly interest in the girl. She had written Radchenko a number of times in the past:

> Last summer I was so lazy I didn't prepare for or take any exams. I went to take them this morning. I think I've passed everything except Russian composition.
> May 1916.

> It'll soon be the holidays and we'll probably spend Christmas here in Petrograd. It takes too long to go anywhere and it's too difficult and expensive.
> December 1916.

> I can't wait for summer. I'd like to come and stay with you and get a job. I think I'm old enough now, I'm nearly sixteen.
> January 1917.

On February 26, 1917, the eve of revolution, she wrote:

> We've been out of school for four days because of the chaos in Petrograd, so I have some free time. Things are very, very tense here, and I long to know what's happening in Moscow.

And the following day:

We're all fed up because for four days Petrograd has had no public transportion. But now at last we can celebrate — February 27! Papa's so excited. He's been by the phone all day. Abel Enukidze arrived today at the Nikolaev station in the middle of the celebrations, and he was amazed.

Nadezhda spent the summer of 1917 at the Radchenkos' dacha outside Moscow, and for a few days the Alliluyevs entertained the Lenins at their apartment, where Stalin met the couple for the second time. (He had first met them in Krakow. Lenin exceeded all Kurnatovsky's stories, but Stalin disliked Krupskaya; he had no liking for homely activist women.)

On her return to Petrograd, Nadezhda resumed her correspondence with Anna Radchenko:

We can still get food here. Eggs, milk, bread, and meat are available but expensive. We can just scrape by, although we're in low spirits, like everyone else. Sometimes you feel like crying, it's so depressing. You can't go out anywhere. There are rumors that the Bolsheviks are planning something for October 20, but I don't expect there's anything to it.
October 19, 1917.

I'm fine, but depressed as usual. The school isn't managing too well. The electricity is turned off twice a week, so we only go in four days. I wanted to buy Ivan Ivanovich more cigarettes, but there was such a long line I gave up. You have to get up at dawn and even then they only give you a few.
Good-bye for now, I have to do my wretched Bible Studies.
December 11, 1917.

Happy New Year! Things have completely changed here at home. Mama's not living with us any more, because we are grown up now and want to do and think as we please and not dance to our parents' tune. We've become real anarchists — it drives her mad! That's not the main reason, though. The fact is she has no life of her own here with us, and she's still a healthy young woman. So now I've had to take over all the housework. I've grown up a lot this past year and I've become quite adult. I'm glad. The trouble is that I've become rude and irritable, but I'll probably grow out of it.
February 1918.

I'm glad you finally got the cigarettes I sent you. I'm sick of all this housework, but I think Mama will soon be back to take over again. She's lonely without her noisy brood, and of course we'll be delighted.

There's terrible hunger in Petrograd. We get just an eighth of a pound of bread each day, and some days there's none at all. I even cursed the Bolsheviks. But they've promised to increase our rations after February 18. We'll see!

I've lost twenty pounds, I had to take in all my skirts and underclothes as they were falling off me. I've lost so much weight people are saying I must be in love!
February 1918.

Her being in love is not totally improbable, since within days of this letter to Anna Radchenko Nadezhda dropped out of school, apparently without regret, and traveled to Moscow with Stalin as his personal assistant at the Commissariat of Nationalities.

Although they were not officially married, we may assume that from the first days of Nadezhda's life in Moscow her relations with Stalin changed from those of a child toward the kindly uncle who had saved her from the water. In the euphoria of the revolution, Stalin's friends were ecstatic. They all adored their dear little Nadezhda, who had grown up before their eyes. Now they were all one happy Bolshevik family! Not everyone regarded their relationship so warmly. Nadezhda was just sixteen, he was thirty-nine. According to the 1918 Family Code, which Stalin later endorsed, she was underage, making their relationship illegal and him guilty of corrupting a minor. But already in 1918 Stalin evidently did not apply the same criteria to his own behavior as he did to others'.

On his arrival in the new capital, Stalin was allocated a study and living quarters in the Kremlin, but since he had no offices for his Commissariat he decided to appropriate some, and had Nadezhda type out a notice reading, "These rooms taken by the People's Commissariat of Nationalities." Stalin's colleague Semyon Pestkovsky described how he and Stalin were preparing to post this notice at a certain guest house that Stalin had selected when they found someone had beaten them to it. Another notice on the door read, "These rooms taken by the Supreme Council of the Commissariat of State." Stalin immediately tore it down and pinned up Nadezhda's. But he had not yet hit his stride, and the battle for the rooms was still won by those who arrived first.

In the last years of her life, Nadezhda's younger sister Anna denied that Stalin and Nadezhda had lived as man and wife in Moscow, and insisted that in June 1918, when she accompanied him to the Tsaritsyn front along with four hundred Red Guards, it was as a comrade. Nadezhda's father, Sergei Yakovlevich, was on the same train, and shared a sleeping compartment with several others. The train moved slowly and was delayed at several stations. According to Anna, one night Alliluyev heard his daughter screaming and rushed into her compartment to find her sobbing that Stalin had raped her. Enraged, Alliluyev threatened to shoot him, but Stalin threw himself at his feet and begged for his daughter's hand.

Nadezhda, the innocent schoolgirl, spent her honeymoon in Tsaritsyn, a strategically crucial steppe town steeped in blood and heat, and located at the confluence of the Volga and Don rivers. Knowing that if it fell it would open the Whites' path to Moscow, Stalin requested that the Council of People's Commissars grant him extraordinary powers to oversee the delivery of food supplies, a request that was granted.

Voroshilov later called Tsaritsyn the "Red Verdun." The town was an armed camp. Streets and crossroads were crowded with Red soldiers and the jails overflowed with prisoners. Outside town the front extended over thirty-five miles, and the rivers were patrolled by two cruisers, a destroyer, and a steamship armed with artillery and machine guns. Assisted by Chervyakov, a member of the Executive Committee, Stalin purged the Red Army command by arresting almost the entire general staff and sailing them down the Volga on a barge that accidentally sank.

Tsaritsyn was the turning point of Stalin's career. Among brothers and sisters, Reds and Whites, who took up arms and fought to the death, his name was pronounced only in hushed whispers. While Nadezhda had absorbed Bolshevism with her mother's milk, nothing had prepared her for the cruel realities of that summer. Was this scorching revolutionary love in the midst of bullets and death to set the pattern for their life together?

On her return to Moscow from this frontline honeymoon, Nadezhda found work on Lenin's staff, and she and Stalin finally registered their marriage. It seems curious that they did not register their marriage before. According to Nadezhda's sister, it was because she hesitated marrying this man whom she did not love. Yet her daughter,

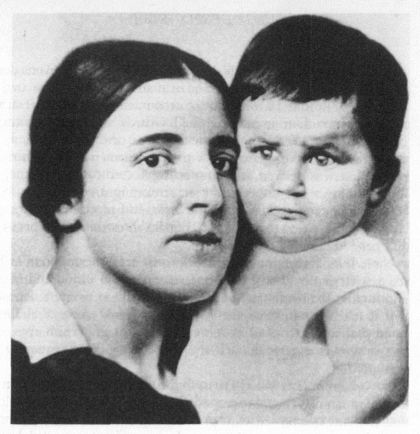

Nadezhda Alliluyeva with her son, Vasily

Josif Stalin and his wife, Nadezhda Alliluyeva

Svetlana, asserts the contrary in her book *Only One Year:* "Olga Al-liluyeva, Stalin's future mother-in-law, was well disposed to him but disapproved of Mama's marriage, doing her best to talk her out of it and calling her a 'silly fool.' She could never accept this alliance; she knew Mama was deeply unhappy, and later thought that her suicide was a result of 'all this foolishness.' "

It may well be that the Bolsheviks were simply indifferent about registering their marriages in the first decades of the revolution. Ideas of free love, although never the norm, had a deep influence on the Soviet people, and official marriage was denounced as a petit-bourgeois vestige. It was different when children came along of course, because they needed both parents' names on the birth certificate.

Five months after the marriage was registered, Nadezhda gave birth to a son, Vasily, and two years later to Svetlana. Following the Kremlin fashion then for adopting orphaned children, two other children lived with them: Yakov, Stalin's son by his first marriage, and the son of Stalin's late friend, Artyom. Nadezhda preferred older children and found these children easier to relate to than her own two. With Vasily and Svetlana she was strict. Stalin, for all his harshness, could be excessively lenient when it came to children.

As a member of Lenin's secretarial staff, Nadezhda proved to be an efficient, tireless worker, and despite her youth Lenin entrusted her with the most secret documents. Stalin was delighted at the prospect of being kept in touch with the latest developments; the only problem was that his young wife refused to share them with him. At first he applauded her loyalty, but there were times when he desperately needed to know what was happening and her stubbornness infuriated him.

An entry by Nadezhda in the duty secretaries' diary reads:

> Vladimir Ilyich is unwell and his sister Maria Ilyinichna asked that he not be disturbed. If he needs to know something we are to consult the appropriate person. No one is to be admitted, and no messages are to be taken. Two parcels have come from Stalin and Zinoviev, but we mustn't say a word about them without special permission.

Stalin was disappointed. He did everything for her. Her wish was law. She was living a lifestyle her parents could not have dreamed of. She had no worries about food, and although she still wore her old dresses out of nostalgia for her youth, Stalin's wife wanted for nothing. Against his principles, he hired cooks and nannies for her. She could order anything she wanted to eat and it would be brought to her. She could get tickets for any play or film. True, he was generally too busy to accompany her and this upset her, but that could not be helped.

The fact was, she felt closer to Lenin and Krupskaya, with their prerevolutionary culture and education, than she did to her rough, uncouth husband. Whenever she had problems at work — she herself admitted that her spelling and timekeeping were poor — Lenin would stand up for her. He knew she had recently had a baby and was finding it hard to cope. As for her spelling, he also knew that she had left school early, and was convinced that it would improve.

Nadezhda's new independence flattered her proud, self-reliant nature, and it seemed as though Stalin might finally have met his match. The peculiarities of his nature, later revealed to the world at large, were now turned in upon his wife and children. Trotsky's wife, Natalya Sedova, recorded her indignation at his cruelty to Yakov, his son by his first marriage:

> A little boy of about twelve with a dark, gentle little face and startling black eyes with a gold glint in them. People say that his delicate, almost miniature frame resembles that of his mother. His manners are very gentle. He told our son Seryozha, with whom he has made friends, that his father punishes him cruelly and beats him for smoking. Stalin had once thrown him out of the apartment because he smelt tobacco on his breath, and he had spent the night in the corridor with the doorman. "But he won't make me give up tobacco by thrashing me!" he said.

Trotsky received a rather different account of Stalin's attitude toward tobacco from Nikolai Bukharin, who had just returned in a state of great indignation from visiting Stalin:

> "Do you know what he does? He draws on his pipe, fills his mouth with smoke, then picks his year-old baby out of the cot and blows it in his face! The baby chokes and cries and Koba doubles up with laughter, shouting, 'Never mind, it's good for him, it'll make him strong!' "
> "But that's barbarous!" I said.
> "You don't know Koba — he's like that."

Koba was Stalin's Georgian nickname. And the baby was Vasily.

These strange domestic scenes, as strange as life itself then, achieved ever more fantastic forms over the years.

Nadezhda was at the center of the Stalin-Trotsky conflict after the Bolshevik victory at Tsaritsyn, and during the subsequent conflict among Lenin, Stalin, and Krupskaya, Nadezhda behaved impeccably. She also obviously knew things about her husband that no one else knew. When he had been drinking he loved to tell her that total power would soon be his. She had witnessed all of Lenin's comrades change after the revolution; the hostility they had once directed against the tsarist regime they directed against one another, and Stalin was the worst.

She was one of the first to hear of Lenin's "Testament," in which he described her husband as rude, uncouth and often unjust. She was forced to admit that he was right: Stalin was rude and often unjust to her, too. But she never told anyone and behaved in a perfectly correct Bolshevik fashion. Stalin found her secretive. She was bored and depressed by Kremlin life. It was like a prison. Everyone around her was in their forties and fifties, distrustful and obsessed with power. She was young, and at that time wanted only to study and enjoy herself.

In *Letters to a Friend*, Nadezhda's daughter Svetlana writes:

> This child labored under the crushing burden of her love for a man twenty-two years her senior, a hardened revolutionary just back from exile, a man whom even his comrades found difficult to get along with. She cast her lot with him like a tiny sailboat drawn to a giant ocean-going steamer. This is the way I see them, ploughing the turbulent ocean side by side. How long could the sailboat keep up with the liner? Could it weather the heavy seas?

A librarian at the Institute of Marxism-Leninism described her visit to Stalin's apartment after his death:

> A row of rooms, their windows covered in dark maroon blinds. Sofas, tables, and chairs with their covers on, and protruding everywhere the disconnected cables of Stalin's vast internal signaling system; the guards could hear every rustle he made, and knew when he passed from room to room.
>
> The apartment was divided into two halves, Stalin's and his daughter Svetlana's. She had three rooms, a few table napkins, some toys, an embroidered cushion. His quarters were like a burial vault — a huge dining room, library, office, and bedroom. Everything bore the mark of officialdom. The atmosphere was the same at his dacha.

Stalin's secretary, Yuri Bazhanov, who later emigrated, recalled the four rooms and the plain furniture, the sentry standing permanently outside the door of their apartment, and Stalin's army cap and greatcoat hanging in the lobby, At first, meals were brought to the house from the dining room of the Soviet of People's Commissars, but because of Stalin's fears of being poisoned he employed cooks to prepare his food at home.

Nadezhda clearly did not want to be a housewife and mother, and the children ran wild. Stalin hated this; he could not bear independent women. As Nadezhda's nerves became increasingly strained, she was prone to hysterical attacks. Stalin had it on good authority that Nadezhda's mother suffered from schizophrenia: she had been treated at the Kremlin's special clinic, and he had been told the diagnosis. "You're a schizophrenic!" he would shout when they quarreled. "And you're a paranoiac!" Nadezhda would shout back. "You have enemies everywhere!"

Stalin's mother had been right: a Georgian girl would have suited him far better. More and more, he found himself missing his first wife, Ekaterina Svanidze. "This creature softened my stony heart," he had said at her funeral. "With her death my last warm feelings for people have died." Cruel people are often sentimental; Stalin was sentimental in his relationship with his daughter Svetlana, and this sentimentality would clash again and again with Nadezhda's fiery temperament.

After Lenin's death in 1924, Nadezhda went to work for the magazine *Revolution and Culture*. Although her education did not go beyond secondary school, plus the secretarial experiences she had picked up in Lenin's office, she acquired new editorial skills remarkably quickly. She seemed to accept anything if it meant avoiding being in the Kremlin with her children or at her husband's dinner table.

For the children there was a nanny and a housekeeper, and Cheka guards were always on hand. The evenings were more difficult. Stalin's Georgian nature reveled in the unlimited new opportunities for heavy drinking. Nadezhda did not drink and loathed drunken dinners. Since it was virtually impossible for her to resist, she learned to live with his ways for eight years. During these difficult eight years, however, she also learned to fight back.

They slept separately now, she in the bedroom, he in his study or in a little room next to the dining room where the red government telephone was located. This telephone had become an essential accessory for the head of the government and the Party. Stalin made calls whenever he liked. Only his most trusted associates were allowed to call him, and only in exceptional circumstances. Stalin's former secretary Bazhanov wrote:

> With his family Stalin was a despot. For days on end he would maintain a haughty silence, ignoring the questions of his wife and son. If he were out of sorts, as he frequently was, he would sit through dinner in silence, expecting everyone else to be silent too. After breakfast he would sit by the window with his pipe.
>
> The Kremlin's internal telephone would ring.
>
> "Koba, it's Molotov!" Nadezhda Alliluyeva would say.
>
> "Tell him I'm asleep!" Stalin would shout.
>
> You could tell a lot about Alliluyeva from the way she took her husband's calls. Living in an atmosphere of lies, she too was forced to lie, even though Molotov was clearly not phoning to pass the time of day. It shocked Nadezhda deeply; a servant of the revolution capable of lying could not possibly be an object of respect.

She disagreed with him more and more. Disagreements about how the children should be brought up turned into fights, and in the end neither brought them up properly. They were both failures as parents. The nannies, servants, guards — an essential feature of the Kremlin mechanism — did not help to create a cozy family environment. Finally, in 1926, Nadezhda ran off with her two small children to Leningrad, hoping to make a new life for herself. Outraged and humiliated, Stalin ordered her back. She complied; but the quarrels continued, and again she dreamed of moving out permanently with the children to live with her sister and brother-in-law in the Ukraine.

When Lenin died she knew that Stalin would win. She had seen blood at Tsaritsyn and wanted no more of it. Stalin's brilliantly orchestrated popularity campaign dramatically increased his influence in the Party. His portraits were carried through the streets during revolutionary holidays, and everyone loved, feared, and respected him. Why could she not stand by him? Why could she not give her husband some support at home as he set about tackling his many enemies? She could not understand why he had accused Trotsky, Kamenev, Zinoviev, and Bukharin of being his enemies since they all were Bolsheviks, Leninists, and Party members fighting for the same cause.

To her, everything outside the Kremlin seemed interesting, even the hardest labor.

She left her job at *Revolution and Culture* and went to work at the Industrial Academy, where she studied synthetic fibers. She wanted to remain anonymous and tried not to let anyone at the Academy know who she was, leaving her car at the corner and asking her guards not to follow too closely as she walked to the building. This desire for anonymity sprang either from her innate shyness or from shame.

The autumn of 1927 was dark and heavy. Nadezhda was often ill and depressed. Kremlin life was not conducive to joy. As Stalin entered the final phase of his struggle with Trotsky, and many oppositionists dear to her heart were expelled from the Party, she was overwhelmed with the feeling that she understood nothing — but perhaps she understood everything.

Seizing rare moments of family peace to try to reason with Stalin, she would inevitably be told that these were not women's matters and sent away to plan the evening's menu instead. She had reached her limit. Often his insults to her over dinner were worse than a slap in the face. She would flush and jump up silently from the table. Terrible fights would follow.

In November 1927 the distinguished diplomat Adolf Ioffe killed himself. People knew that he had been ill, but they also knew that he was a Trotskyite, who together with Trotsky had signed the Brest-Litovsk peace treaty with Germany.

Nadezhda had loved and respected Ioffe, and she and Trotsky were among the large crowd of mourners at the Novo-Devyiche cemetery. Stalin's wife stood at the front of the crowd listening in silence as Trotsky and Kamenev spoke at Ioffe's grave, young people sang Civil War songs that invoked Trotsky's name, and Zinoviev abandoned funeral decorum to curse her husband's criminal betrayal of the Party. When the ceremony was over, she and her guards walked back to her car. A young man from Trotsky's entourage yelled out to a battalion of Red soldiers who stood keeping order at the gates: "Red soldiers! Hurrah to Comrade Trotsky, leader of the Red Army!" There was no response. Trotsky bowed his head and walked on.

During the first trials of the 1930s, several of Nadezhda Alliluyeva's former teachers were arrested in the "Trial of the Industrial Party," which soon spread to all branches of Soviet industry. Psychologically torn, she began emotionally and intellectually to side with her husband's enemies.

One could never imagine Krupskaya in such a situation. For her,

Lenin was right even when he was wrong, and he was never wrong. She idealized him; alone in the darkness of night she probably admitted a great deal to herself, and she would sometimes speak of his over-emotional, exalted "rages" that only she knew about. But she was never seen disagreeing with him in public; she always made sure that any disagreements between them were kept private, protecting him from his own mistakes and explaining to herself and others the necessity of the Leninist terror.

Nadezhda Alliluyeva was different, and younger than Krupskaya by more than thirty years. When Stalin insulted Krupskaya, Nadezhda probably sympathized with her, but she cannot have found Krupskaya easy to understand, and Krupskaya's militant atheism repelled her as she herself turned more and more to God. Religion brought peace to her turbulent soul, and she started attending church.

Galina Kravchenko recalled:

> Nadezhda Alliluyeva looked old for her age. She could have been almost forty. If a young wife marries an old husband they both end up looking the same age.
>
> She was deeply religious, and went to church. Everyone knew about it. She could obviously do things forbidden to other Party members; she had been in the Party since 1918. But you could see she was strange — even a bit mad.

However, Nikita Khrushchev, who worked with Nadezhda on the Moscow Party committee before entering the corridors of power, wrote: "I had a deep respect for Nadezhda Alliluyeva. She was so different from Stalin. I especially liked her modesty."

On November 7, 1932, during the parade marking the fifteenth anniversary of the Revolution, the entire government, headed by Comrade Stalin, lined the tribune of the Mausoleum. Beneath them on the lower tribune stood government officials and foreign guests. Ekaterina Lebedeva, wife of Alexei Lebedev, deputy chief of the Central Committee's military section, stood beside her husband with the usual lump in her throat as she watched the vast workers' demonstration passing beneath her on Red Square. Suddenly many in the crowd began to murmur: "There's Stalin's wife!"

Her gaze moved along the columns of demonstrators until she saw Nadezhda Alliluyeva marching under the banner of the Industrial

Academy. "She was tall, and her coat was flung open despite the cold. She smiled and laughed and said something to her companions, then she looked up to the Mausoleum and waved, and her white, marble face was beautiful, her wave was regal, she was radiant."

As the crowds cheered and applauded Comrade Stalin, his wife crossed Red Square. Then, leaving her companions, she turned into the Spassky Gates and emerged with her guards at the lower tribune, where she took her place beside Nikita Khrushchev. It was bitterly cold, and she shivered as she pulled her coat around her. Peering up at Stalin on the Mausoleum, she told Khrushchev she was worried he would catch cold; he was so stubborn, she had begged him to dress more warmly, but he had not listened.

The following evening the Kremlin elite celebrated the holiday at a reception in the Voroshilovs' apartment. Nadezhda Alliluyeva left early, and Stalin followed several hours later. The next morning the housekeeper found Nadezhda Alliluyeva lying beside the bed in a pool of blood. Next to her was a little revolver her brother Pavel had brought back from abroad as a present. The terrified housekeeper called the nurse, and the two women lifted the cold body onto the bed. Afraid to wake Stalin, who was still sleeping a few yards away beside the red telephone, they phoned Abel Enukidze and Molotov's wife, Paulina Zhemchuzhina. When they arrived, Stalin was woken, and he emerged into the dining-room to hear them crying: "Josif, Josif, Nadezhda's dead!"

This was how witnesses described the events of that morning to members of the Stalin household and later to his daughter, Svetlana. The passing years have inevitably tangled the thread of events surrounding Nadezhda Alliluyeva's tragic end into a knot of contradictions, and her death has been the subject of countless rumors, legends, and myths.

The half-truths started at once. On November 10, the Party Central Committee announced in *Pravda:* "On the night of November 9, active and dedicated Party member Nadezhda Sergeyevna Alliluyeva died."

This was followed by an article under the banner headlines:

TO THE DEAR MEMORY OF NADEZHDA SERGEYEVNA ALLILUYEVA, FRIEND AND COMRADE.
We have lost a dear, beloved comrade with a beautiful soul. A young

Bolshevik, filled with strength and boundlessly dedicated to the Party and the Revolution, is no more. Growing up in the family of a revolutionary worker, she was someone whose life was joined to the Revolution, at the Civil War front and during the growth of socialist construction. Unceasingly modest and vigilant, Nadezhda Sergeyevna selflessly served the cause of the Party, demanding much of herself and in her last years working tirelessly to become one of the most active student comrades at the Industrial Academy. The memory of Nadezhda Sergeyevna, dedicated Bolshevik, wife, close friend and faithful helper to Comrade Stalin, will remain forever dear to us. *Ekaterina Voroshilova, Paulina Zhemchuzhina, Zinaida Ordzhonikidze, Dora Khazan, Maria Kaganovich, Tatyana Postysheva, Ashkhen Mikoyan, K. Voroshilov, V. Molotov, S. Ordzhonikidze, V. Kuibyshev, M. Kalinin, L. Kaganovich, P. Postyshev, A. Andreyev, S. Kirov, A. Mikoyan, A. Enukidze.*

These clichéd official condolences present the head of state's wife as a sexless creature dedicated only to Party and revolutionary work.

Murder, suicide. The rumors swelled throughout the land.

Most official reports of the ceremony imply that Stalin attended the funeral. In fact he did not.

In the days that followed, articles in *Pravda* gradually regained their senses. One, written by the head of the Industrial Academy, hints at the cause of death: ". . . poor health did not impede the Bolshevik diligence she brought to her studies." This suggests that she was ill but continued to overexert herself, and died from it — yet if this were the case, one would expect to see the medical causes of death.

On November 11 *Pravda* wrote: "A dedicated young fighter in the great Bolshevik army has died mid-campaign, mid-journey, mid-studies."

The author of the article then turns abruptly from praising the deceased to commiserating with her "suffering survivor," and addresses condolences directly to Comrade Stalin: "His close friends and comrades understand the enormous weight of Stalin's loss, and the obligations that this places upon us in our relations with him."

The stream of obituaries culminated on November 16 with a message printed in bold type from Nadezhda Konstantinovna Krupskaya: "Dear Josif Vissarionych, I have been thinking of you recently and wish to offer you my hand. It is hard to lose the person one is closest to. I remember some conversations I had with you in Ilyich's office during his illness. They gave me strength at the time. Again I press your hand. Nadezhda Krupskaya."

One gets the sense that Krupskaya's words were carefully measured. She doubtless had her own views about Nadezhda Alliluyeva's death, but with no other opportunities to express them she used this condolence message to suggest her true attitude to Stalin. She had learned to deal with everything, including her husband's murderer, and she was quietly letting Stalin know that nothing was forgotten.

"It is hard to lose the person one is closest to" — reminds him of Lenin. The "conversations in Ilyich's office" — given her relations with Stalin shortly before Lenin's death — refers to his insulting telephone calls.

Her use of the uncapitalized "you," for instance, rather than the formal "You," is obviously deliberate, as is her sloppy misspelling of Stalin's name as "Vissarionych," rather than "Vissarionovich." Either the editors dared not correct her mistakes or she forbade any changes, but the solecisms were eloquent. Nadezhda Konstantinovna Krupskaya perhaps felt that she alone had the right to this kind of patronizing familiarity. Her attitude toward Stalin in his hardest hour summed up her contempt for him.

Izvestia had less to say about Nadezhda Alliluyeva's death and funeral, but one issue of the paper even carried a poem dedicated to her memory by Demyan Bedny, known as the "court poet of the Kremlin":

> Death takes its bloody toll
> Sparing the old and the lame
> And striking down those in their prime.

Bedny could hardly have failed to know of the two main conjectures — murder and suicide — of Nadezhda Alliluyeva's death, but his verses were written for the masses, and all they had to know was that she had been struck down in her prime.

When I requested material on Nadezhda Alliluyeva's death for this book, I was told that her KGB file was missing, and that Stalin had given orders that there be no inquest.

Over the years, history has distilled all the rumors into scenarios:

1. Stalin murdered her in a jealous rage because she was having an affair with his son, and her stepson, Yakov. On discovering them

together he dealt with her on the spot, promising to deal with Yakov later. This might explain why Stalin made no attempt to get his son released from a German prison camp during the war.

2. Stalin murdered her because he considered Nadezhda his political opponent; she was horrified by his policies, especially the brutalities of collectivization, and he could not tolerate it.

3. Stalin learned that she was supporting enemies of the people by joining the opposition "Group of 92," and not wishing to get his own hands dirty, he ordered her killed.

4. She had joined an anti-Stalin opposition group, and her accomplices had her removed for fear she would betray them.

5. Stalin ordered the secret police to kill her because he was sick of her jealous scenes; they no longer lived together as man and wife, and she prevented him from drinking and sleeping with ballerinas.

6. Stalin shot her because she defended Krupskaya.

An even more inventive theory was that Stalin walked into his room late that night and saw someone standing behind the heavy maroon curtains. He shot at the curtains and killed Nadezhda, who had been staring out of the window into the darkness.

The main scenario is still that Nadezhda Alliluyeva took her own life because she could no longer bear living with Stalin. Or bear the possibility — whatever her mother's assurances — that he might be her father as well as her husband.

Nikita Khrushchev wrote, "The circumstances of her death were mysterious, but it was undoubtedly caused by something Stalin did. There were even rumors that he had shot her. . . . Another version, which strikes me as fairly plausible, is that Nadezhda shot herself because of some insult to her female dignity."

Nadezhda's daughter, Svetlana, who was sixteen at the time and had more insight than anyone else into her mother's death, later wrote:

> Her self-control, her tremendous inner tension and discipline, her pent-up dissatisfaction and discontent, built up more and more pressure within until finally she was like a tightly coiled spring. And when the spring uncoiled at last it did so with ferocious force.
>
> That is what happened. What caused the spring to give, the immediate occasion was trivial in itself, so trivial one might have said it happened for no reason at all. It was a minor quarrel at a banquet in honor of the Fifteenth Anniversary of the Revolution. He said to

her: "Hey you, drink!" And she screamed: "I'm not 'Hey' to you! Don't talk to me that way!" jumping up in front of everyone and running from the table.

Other details of what happened that night are provided by Vyacheslav Molotov, Politburo member and Stalin's closest ally, speaking in the last years of his life to the poet Felix Chuev. Molotov supported his leader in everything, and one can hear his implicit condemnation of Alliluyeva. But he was at the table with them that evening and was a witness:

> There was jealousy of course, but it was probably unfounded. Stalin used to visit a hairdresser to be shaved, and Nadezhda hated it. She was so young. After the November 7 parade a big crowd of us gathered in Voroshilov's apartment and Stalin was rolling lumps of bread into balls and throwing them at Egorov's wife. Nadezhda was a bit crazy in those days, and she couldn't bear it. She left the party with my wife, Paulina Semyonovna, and they walked around the Kremlin together. It was late at night, and she complained to my wife about the hairdresser, and the way Stalin had been flirting that evening. It didn't mean anything, he was just a bit drunk, but she took it very hard. She was terribly jealous of him — it was the gypsy blood in her. Paulina Semyonovna told her it was wrong of her to abandon him at such a difficult time.

Maria Vasilyevna, Marshal Budyonny's widow, was equally critical of Alliluyeva, describing how Budyonny had commiserated with Stalin after her death: "My husband told me Nadezhda was a bit crazy. She was always nagging and humiliating Stalin in front of other people. 'I don't know how he puts up with it!' Semyon Mikhailovich used to say. 'What normal mother would orphan her children?' "

Those more sympathetic to Nadezhda Alliluyeva emphasize her profound disillusionment with the politics that had at first so attracted her, and the terrible effect this had upon her. According to Galina Kravchenko, "The evening before her death she shouted, 'I hate you all! Look at this table, and the people are starving!' "

Trotsky, in his Mexican hiding place, had his own interpretation of the tragedy:

> With collectivization at its height and mass shootings and starvation rampant in the villages, Nadezhda Alliluyeva apparently came under pressure from her father to persuade Stalin to change his rural policies.

Her mother, too, who was from the countryside, was constantly telling her of the horrors being inflicted on the peasants. When Nadezhda Alliluyeva spoke to Stalin about it he forbade her to see her mother or to receive her in the Kremlin. But Nadezhda Alliluyeva would meet her in town, and this strengthened her resolve.

During a party at Voroshilov's apartment, she dared criticize Stalin. He showered her with obscenities in front of all the guests, and when she got home she killed herself.

Anna Larina, wife of Politburo member Nikolai Bukharin, recalls in her memoirs, *The Unforgotten:*

In November 1932 I came home from the Institute and found N. I.* there. He had just been at the funeral of Nadezhda Sergeyevna Alliluyeva. He looked pale and agitated. N. I. and Nadezhda Sergeyevna had had a warm regard for each other; she had secretly shared his views on the collectivization program and had taken the opportunity to tell him so. Nadezhda Sergeyevna was a good, modest person of enchanting appearance and fragile spiritual strength. She suffered terribly from Stalin's coarse, despotic character.

N. I. recalled arriving once at Stalin's dacha at Zubalovo while he was out. As he and Nadezhda Sergeyevna walked chatting around the grounds, Stalin returned, and creeping up on them, he stared into N. I.'s face and said: "I'll shoot you!" N. I. took it as a joke, but Nadezhda Sergeyevna turned pale and shuddered.

N. I. had sat next to her at the Kremlin banquet marking the fifteenth anniversary of the October Revolution, and he told me how Stalin got drunk and threw orange peels and cigarette butts in her face. Unable to bear his rudeness, she jumped up from the table and disappeared for the rest of the evening. Next morning they found her dead.

N. I. was one of the mourners standing beside the coffin, and Stalin chose this moment to come up and assure him that he had gone straight from the banquet to his dacha, and that they had telephoned him there to tell him the news. This directly contradicts the account of Nadezhda's daughter, Svetlana, and gives the distinct impression that Stalin was trying to divert suspicion from himself.

I don't know if it was murder or suicide, but N. I. certainly didn't exclude murder. According to him, the first person after the nurse to see Nadezhda Sergeyevna dead was Enukidze, whom the nurse phoned

* *Her husband, Nikolai Ivanovich Bukharin.*

for fear of telling Stalin first. Perhaps this was why Enukidze was removed before any of the other Politburo members.

    N. I. said that before the lid of the coffin was closed Stalin asked them to wait, then he lifted up her head and kissed it. "What are his kisses worth?" N. I. said. "He's destroyed her!"

Apart from Nadezhda's father, Sergei Yakovlevich, who died of natural causes, all the Alliluyevs suffered a terrible end. Nadezhda's mother, Olga Evgenyevna, was afflicted by a serious mental disorder, and her sister, Anna, was driven out of her mind by years of solitary confinement in Stalin's prisons. But the most haunting of the stories about Alliluyeva was told to me in the mid-1950s by an elderly Bolshevik woman who had once attended lectures at the Red Professors Institute in the early 1930s and had known a girl who was friendly with Nadezhda Alliluyeva.

Nadezhda was close to a nervous breakdown, said her friend. Weeping and emotional, Nadezhda would complain bitterly about Stalin's roughness and indifference. They were estranged; virtually an alcoholic, he would go on drunken binges all night, then sleep until midday. She hated drinking and was unable to do so because of the delicate psychic condition she had inherited from her mother. Stalin would force her to drink in company, and it would enrage her. When drunk and alone with her, he was intolerable, and when he made obscene remarks about women she often came close to killing him; she was not jealous and did not let his drunken male ravings insult her dignity, but it exasperated her that when everyone shouted "Great Stalin!" only she knew how "great" he really was. He even interfered with her relationship with the children. She felt helpless. Her best years were disappearing like sand.

About a week before the anniversary, Nadezhda Alliluyeva told a girlfriend that something terrible was about to happen, and said that she was cursed from birth. When pressed to explain, Nadezhda confessed to her friend that Stalin had recently told her that she was in fact his daughter. "You're either mine or you're Kurnatovsky's!" he had yelled to her during a quarrel. He immediately retracted the statement and claimed that it was just a joke.

Her mother had had plenty of lovers in her youth, and when Nadezhda pinned her down she admitted that throughout December 1900 and January 1901 she had indeed been sleeping with both Stalin and her husband and could not be sure who her father was, but since she resembled her legal father she had always assumed it must be he. Yet Nadezhda Alliluyeva grew increasingly convinced that she must be Stalin's daughter, and thus the sister of her own children. In the last days of her life she regarded herself as damned. And so she killed herself. Afterward her girl friend was never seen again.

The contents of the suicide note Nadezhda Alliluyeva left Josif Vissarionovich, if there was one, were known only to him. Yet Stalin wept openly for Alliluyeva, and those who saw him were struck by the depth of his grief. He blamed himself for not giving her enough of his attention, he blamed the bad influence of others, and he blamed her for punishing him. He never remarried.

New generations may bring new insights to bear on this terrible event. Plays and films may yet be written about this mysterious couple — the child and the despot. But history will doubtless never know the full truth about Stalin and Alliluyeva.

6

Empty Bed, Cold Heart

ALIVE, NADEZHDA ALLILUYEVA hindered Stalin from fulfilling his historic mission. He could tolerate no obstacles on his path, especially female. Prison was the best she could have expected, to keep her from speaking out against him.

Stalin was alone again, and remained so until his death over twenty years later. Marxist visions of social equality for women were long abandoned and had come to mean simply that women had the same opportunity to do manual labor as a man and also to support him in his politics; there could be no thought of women expressing their concerns, whether emotional, social, or political.

By 1941, the Kremlin's Augean stables were thoroughly cleaned by Stalin's secret police. With the outbreak of World War II, fear of Stalin was overshadowed by fear of Hitler. As the Kremlin families were evacuated to Kuibyshev, they gained a welcome distance from Stalin, who remained alone in Moscow with his commanders.

Alone in a cold bed.

A ballerina at the Bolshoi Theater recalls wartime Moscow:

> Moscow in 1941 was empty. We had ration cards but nothing to buy with them. There were lines outside the shops all night. The frosts came early that year. Those of us still left in the capital wrapped ourselves up as best we could. Many apartments stood empty, you could just go in and take what you wanted. Nobody did, though.
>
> Moscow was empty, but in December 1941 the Bolshoi opened a new season at its annex. Stalin often attended. In the beginning we were frantic, but we soon got used to it. There was a strange, exalted atmosphere in the theater. There were always a lot of foreigners — diplomats, pilots, tank drivers. Everyone was having love affairs, and many of the ballerinas had affairs with foreigners. If one of us came

in wearing patent-leather shoes or a foreign frock it was obvious she had caught a foreigner.

Even as a ballet student in the 1930s, I knew the Bolshoi was protected by the highest of the high in the Kremlin. The ballet school was under the protection of Abel Enukidze, who used to send sweets and biscuits to the school, and organized magnificent Christmas parties with presents. I was only little then, but I heard the rumors about him and some of the older girls.

Stalin loved the opera. There were rumors that he had affairs with Natalya Shpiller and Vera Davydova, both well-known singers from the Bolshoi.

Recently Vera Davydova spoke on Russian television of Stalin's attentions to her, and of his offer of marriage. The proposal frightened her since she was happily married, and she had to explain to him that her devotion to him as her leader was incompatible with everyday love.

Throughout the 1930s and 1940s, the widowed Stalin, surrounded by the Kremlin families, all with their domestic hearths, must have felt lonely as he went home to an empty place. Brief liaisons offered such a man no satisfaction; he knew their cost. Attempts at something more serious, in his twisted and paranoid mind, would be no better: he knew in advance how they would end.

As time went on, Stalin continued his arrests throughout the Party. He took special pleasure in dealing with the wives of his enemies — Olga Kameneva, for instance, sister of Trotsky, who on his orders received a bullet through the head in the yard of Orlov Central Prison, along with the prerevolutionary terrorist Maria Spiridonova. Generally, however, prison appeared a more fitting punishment.

My own mother witnessed the terror. Shortly after my birth in 1936, Mother fell ill, but managed with great difficulty to be permitted to recuperate in the Crimea. There she was amazed to see fabulously elegant women in expensive gowns or in bathing suits. These were all wives of commissars, marshals, and Party secretaries. They lived an unreal and brief existence, socializing in groups according to their husbands' rank, and talking mainly about clothes or their husbands' work.

Mother fell ill again in 1937, and this time she had no trouble acquiring a ticket to the Crimea. But arrests were at their height, and she wondered if leaving was wise. Her mother read her fortune and reassured her that nothing would happen, so she left for the Crimea.

This time she found the beaches empty. All the fashionable women from last season were now in jail.

Old Bolsheviks returning from the camps told how both Nadezhda Krupskaya and Maria Ilyinichna, Lenin's wife and sister, visited Stalin at the height of the terror and pleaded with him for the lives of their old comrades. "Whom are you defending? You're defending murderers!" he shouted at them. The two women were led weeping from the room.

There were Kremlin women who, although free, lived in constant fear of being arrested. Women such as Ekaterina Voroshilova, Maria Kaganovich, and Paulina Zhemchuzhina clad themselves in the armor of blue Party suits, orthodox words, and Party piety — but never knew from one day to the next what would happen to them. As a result of their unceasing anxiety, they grew guarded, close-minded, and repressed. No one around Stalin escaped this fear. All lived in the shadow of imprisonment, and this made them morally weak and absolutely submissive. Stalin's personal secretary, Poskrebyshev, who served him with doglike devotion, uncomplainingly sacrificed his Jewish wife on the altar of his boss's happiness. Old Bolshevik Yuri Pyatakov confessed orally and in writing, at large and from prison, to crimes he had never committed and eagerly offered to shoot his allies. He went as far as to offer to shoot his wife, an impulse evidently familiar to many Kremlin men in those days.

The suffering that Stalin inflicted on his close associates must have helped to ease his own. Like potentates and dictators throughout history, Stalin could not anticipate the end of his reign, nor the thousand eloquent reports and testimonies from those who survived to tell the horror stories of his Siberian prison camps.

7

The Soviet Esther

Kliment Efremovich Voroshilov (1881–1969), born of poor working parents in a village near Ekaterinburg. He started working in a factory at the age of fifteen and taught himself to read. Arrested in 1905 as a strike organizer, he spent the next twelve years working for the Revolution in exile and the underground. In February 1917, Voroshilov was elected to the Petrograd Soviet, and spent the Civil War fighting at Tsaritsyn, in the Ukraine, and in the Caucasus. Appointed marshal in 1935, Voroshilov was one of Stalin's closest allies and supported all Stalin's subsequent purges of the army. Between 1953 and 1960 he was president of the Presidium of the Supreme Soviet. Removed by Khrushchev, he was denounced in 1961 as an accomplice of Stalin, but was rehabilitated in 1963.

IN THE EARLY PART of the twentieth century, large numbers of Jewish girls left their remote villages to heed the call of the Revolution and settle in the cities. Many of these girls captured the hearts of simple Russian lads with their exotic looks, and several of the Party's leaders, including Molotov, Kirov, Dzerzhinsky, Lunacharsky, and Kamenev, were married to Jewish women. The most striking example of a mixed marriage was the Voroshilovs, Kliment Efremovich and his wife, Ekaterina Davidovna.

One day in December 1944, when I was ten years old, I was picked up by the man I knew as uncle Petya, who had worked on a secret tank-building project with my father in the Urals. Uncle Petya took me with him to the Kremlin. We entered an imposing building, went up to a brightly lit corridor on the first floor, and were met by a large, unsmiling, dark-haired old woman wearing a beautiful floor-length white satin dressing gown that was clearly captured from the Germans. The woman silently led me to the kitchen and sat me down at a table, where she poured me some cocoa and spread some butter and sausage on a slice of white bread. To this day I can still remember how it tasted.

A boy by the name of Klim appeared and took me to another apartment, where a large Christmas tree stood in the corner of the sitting room. A stepladder was brought in, and I had just climbed up to decorate the top when a group of men appeared at the door. The man in front was familiar: short, with a black mustache and khaki army tunic, exactly like the photographs I had seen displayed every-where, except that his hair was gray, not black, and stuck up on his head like a hedgehog. From my ladder I could see a small round bald patch. He looked up at the tree, then at me, frozen on my ladder, and said with a slight accent: "She'll get a bump when she falls!" My heart pounded as Stalin and his friends passed into the next room. We were quickly led out of the apartment.

Later, my mother told me that the apartment I had been in was Marshal Voroshilov's. I also learned that the woman in the dressing gown was Voroshilov's wife, Ekaterina Davidovna, that uncle Petya was their adopted son, and that Klim was their grandson.

My memory of that pale face is contradicted by the author Roman Gul, whose book *The Red Marshals* describes his meeting with Ekaterina Davidovna during the height of the battle for Tsaritsyn in 1918:

> On the second floor of the abandoned mansion of a mustard-factory owner lived Kliment Voroshilov and his wife. Ekaterina Davidovna appeared in the darkened bedroom beautifully dressed in a fine karakul cape. . . . She dashed around town in a military car, and many Cheka members took a dim view of the concern the commander's wife lav-ished on her appearance at such a time.

Gul's Ekaterina Davidovna was bathed in the euphoria of revo-lutionary victory, the freedom of war, the reflections of Voroshilov's glory. How did this elegant, vital woman become a sullen "Party auntie" of the 1930s and 1940s?

Wanting to discover more about Ekaterina Davidovna's origins and her life in the Kremlin, I visited Nadezhda Ivanovna Voroshilova, my uncle Petya's widow and mother of Klim.

Today, Nadezhda Ivanovna lives in a spacious apartment on Granovsky Street, to which the Voroshilovs moved during the Khrushchev period. The spirit of those times is preserved in the huge Kremlin-style dining table, the vast prerevolutionary sideboard, the photographs of Voroshilov, Petya, Nadezhda Ivanovna, and their sons, and the large ceremonial portraits by the then-fashionable "court" artist Alexander Gerasimov. From Nadezhda Ivanovna's memories of her mother-in-law, I learned the things in Ekaterina Davidovna's past that she felt obliged to hide from the prying eyes of Soviet officials.

She was born Golda Gorbman, one of four children in a poor Jewish family living in the remote village of Mardarovka, in the Ukraine. After learning to read and write a little in her teens, Golda left Mardarovka for the Black Sea city of Odessa, where she trained as a seamstress and enrolled in an adult school. One of her teachers there, a dedicated revolutionary named Serafima Gopner, drew her into the Socialist Revolutionary Party. She was arrested in 1906 and exiled to Arkhangelsk, in the Russian Arctic.

Most of the exiles living in this kingdom of darkness were men, for whom every exiled woman was like a ray of light. Many revolutionary relationships started in exile, and the dark-eyed little Socialist soon embarked on a love affair with the dashing Georgian Bolshevik Abel Enukidze. Enukidze was something of a star in Arkhangelsk, but for Abel, Golda was clearly little more than a passing fancy. The affair did not last, and Golda was soon to be seen in the company of Klim Voroshilov, a former riveter from Lugansk and a popular Bolshevik organizer who quickly converted her to Bolshevism. From the outset they made an excellent match. Nadezhda Ivanovna told me:

> She used extraordinary tact in dealing with Kliment Efremovich. Some years after her death, he told me she had been completely honest with him from the start, so there would be no cause for reproaches or recriminations, and that she had told Klim everything that had happened between her and Enukidze. She put him on a pedestal, and he became the sole purpose of her life. She subordinated herself completely to his work and life, and never criticized him or had a moment's doubt about anything he did. This continued for the rest of her life. They seemed to be in total harmony.

Ekaterina Davidovna was released from exile before Klim, but she soon returned to be with him. As with Krupskaya and Lenin, civilians and exiles were allowed to cohabit only if they were married in church, so she converted to the Orthodox faith and changed her name from Golda to Ekaterina, which deeply distressed her parents. The rabbi denounced her before a large congregation in the Mardarovka synagogue. When Voroshilov's term of exile came to an end, they both left for his home town of Lugansk, and since he had a Wolf's Ticket,* she supported them both by working as a seamstress.

In April 1917 the Voroshilovs were among the crowd of Bolsheviks who gathered to welcome Lenin to Petrograd. There she met her former teacher, Serafima Gopner, who recommended her for membership in the Bolshevik Party.

She spent the entire Civil War at Kliment Efremovich's side. In the summer of 1918 she joined him at the Tsaritsyn front, where she worked with the First Cavalry and helped to set up a women's cooperative, taking care of orphaned children and arranging for them to be adopted. One day Marshal Budyonny brought a curly-haired four-year-old boy to her, and the the child won her heart. Since she could not have children (because of complications arising from her love affair with Enukidze), she and Kliment Efremovich agreed to adopt the child, and they named him Petya. Petya later told his wife that Ekaterina Davidovna had been an excellent mother. He remembers her using her old dress patterns to make his clothes. As Nadezhda Ivanovna told me:

> Although it was common knowledge that Petya wasn't their son, neither Ekaterina Davidovna nor Kliment Efremovich ever mentioned it. Petya loved them as much as if they were his true parents, and Kliment Efremovich would shout at him just like a real father. In the 1920s everything was very democratic in the Kremlin, everyone lived as equals, and out at the dachas they each took turns cooking. Once, Petya was sent off by the cook to fetch bread and refused to go — Kliment Efremovich was furious, chasing him around the bushes and trying to pull his ears.

From 1919 onward Ekaterina Davidovna and Petya left Tsaritsyn and followed Kliment Efremovich around the country on his various

---

* A Wolf's Ticket was issued to political prisoners or strikers, and it banned them from finding future employment.

military missions. In 1922 Ekaterina worked for Budyonny's First Cavalry in Ekaterinburg, where the Budyonnys and the Voroshilovs shared a house. Z. Yu. Arbatov, who worked in various Soviet institutions in the town, remembers visiting them there on several occasions. Arbatov was no admirer of the new regime, and his memoirs of the period, contained in the Archive of the Russian Revolution, have the ring of truth about them:

> The department of social assistance in Ekaterinburg had been taken over by a man named Shalyakhin, who immediately declared that money was being paid out to a mass of petit-bourgeois counter-revolutionary pensioners living at the state's expense, and that this money should be spent on increasing the allowances paid to Red Army invalids or widows. Having stopped their payments, Shalyakhin raised the matter at an executive committee meeting, and "jokingly" proposed various ways to quietly eliminate these old people, such as building a large crematorium to which all the pensioners could be sent.
>
> For over three months Shalyakhin battled with the pensioners. This went on until the arrival of Voroshilov's wife. Replacing Shalyakhin as head of the department, she demanded the restitution of all the decrees of Soviet power, and restored the pensioners' benefits, retroactive to when they were stopped.

Her good intentions had terrible results, as Arbatov went on to explain:

> The pensioners stripped the department like locusts; in two days all the cash in the till and three months' savings in the State Bank were gone. Shalyakhin proceeded to declare war on Ekaterina Voroshilova, attacking her to the Executive Committee, the Party, and everyone else. His propaganda had an effect in part because her smart appearance, her expensive karakul coat, and her elegant silk shawl hardly fitted the proletarian image. Only officers from the General Staff were invited to their home, and her supporters were bourgeois, not proletarian; she often said herself that the Party committee disliked her because of her bourgeois appearance and non-proletarian tastes.
>
> Voroshilov had worked for the Party since 1906, and by 1917 he had a solid record as a proletarian activist. Self-taught, he had acquired a selective knowledge of revolutionary history. His development was encouraged by his intellectual wife, and he quickly memorized whole pages from Marx and Engels. . . .

Although a former exile, she was always "dear Ekaterina Davidovna," not "comrade," and she flirtatiously welcomed the attentions of Budyonny's handsome young cavalry commanders, many of them having previously belonged to the finest tsarist cavalry regiments. When one saw her on the street with her entourage of officers, provocatively flashing a wide gold bracelet-watch, their laughter, talk, and elegant manners would remind one more of the tsar's army than of the worker-peasant Red Army.

In their apartment in a splendid old mansion, dressmakers and needlewomen worked day and night for the wives of Voroshilov and Budyonny. The Voroshilovs and Budyonnys would take car trips out of town together, or steamer trips down the River Dniepr. At dinner there was always wine, fresh fruit, and cut flowers. I was invited there to dinner on the day Ekaterina Davidovna took over at the department. She suffered terribly from Comrade Budyonny's loud and frequent belches, and toward the end of the meal, when he started sticking his fingers in his mouth to rescue some pieces of food lodged in his strong male teeth, she flung down her napkin and left the table.

But according to Nadezhda Ivanovna, things were not quite like that.

Ekaterina Davidovna was not an educated woman. She could appear so in the company of her officers, but her lowbrow tastes were always in evidence. She was intelligent — kind, too, in her own way — but not an intellectual. I don't recognize her in Arbatov's memoirs. And Kliment Efremovich used to be wildly jealous — he would have killed her if she had flirted openly!

Ekaterina returned to Moscow at the end of the Civil War, and she and Petya lived first in the Metropol Hotel, then in the Kremlin, where she remained until her death forty years later. She continued to study, graduating from the Higher Party School, working on the newspaper *Poverty*, then returning to work for the Higher Party School.

Since Petya didn't seem to satisfy fully Ekaterina's maternal longings, the Voroshilovs took in her niece, Truda, and Voroshilov's nephew, Kolya, as well as the two children of army commander Mikhail Frunze, who had died during an operation. Frunze's death was shrouded in mystery. There were rumors that doctors had "knifed" him on orders from above, and these rumors were inflamed by the publication of Boris Pilnyak's story "Murder of a Commander," which was a transparent account of the episode. Since Voroshilov's friendship with Frunze was well known, it was natural for the Central Committee to appoint the Voroshilovs as guardians of Frunze's orphaned children, and Ekaterina Davidovna's love for them dispelled all rumors surrounding Frunze's death.

In 1928, Ekaterina Davidovna fell ill and went abroad for a major operation. She put on weight. By now she had been appointed political director of the Higher Party School and was one of the most important women in the Kremlin. A fiercely loyal member of the Party, stern and uncompromising, she made allowances for nobody, least of all herself, and those who knew her, including Petya's wife, her new daughter-in-law, found her taciturn and difficult.

Nadezhda Ivanovna and Petya were school friends who first became close during a holiday in 1932 and married three years later. She found Ekaterina Davidovna highly repressed on sexual matters.

Ekaterina Davidovna and I met three years before Petya and I married. When our son Klim was born she examined the dates obsessively to the day, trying to prove that I had been a virgin when we married. I was wary of her coldness. It was three years before she fully accepted me as Petya's wife.

By the time I moved in with them, she had closed herself off. Maybe it was because of what was happening around her in the Kremlin, and she had decided to keep her mouth shut. However, the Voroshilovs nurtured our marriage, and we filled their life with all the bustle and anxieties of an extended family clan, with our elder son Klim becoming especially close to Kliment Efremovich, and the younger one, Volodya, to Ekaterina Davidovna herself. Yet she was unable to express this love. She never embraced and never showed her emotions, despite the fact that she was a person of enormously strong emotions. She simply held it all in. Her soul was dissatisfied. She was merely repressed: always neat, lived by the clock, went to bed early. We young people grew used to it, and Kliment Efremovich would spend the evenings with us.

Things were much easier with Kliment Efremovich. It must have been hard for her to be married to a man with such power, and having to tolerate his impulsiveness and sociability. His bright, expansive nature was popular with other women too, but she didn't notice or didn't want to. He did nothing in the house without her. They never argued.

She had no rings and despised jewelry. She ordered me not to wear earrings at my wedding. She always wore a severe, mannish suit, like a uniform. This said, her clothes were always well-cut, for she was a fine dressmaker.

The Ekaterina Davidovna whom Nadezhda describes had successfully assimilated the manners and habits of the aristocratic ladies, whose dresses she had worn in her youth. After the revolution, her contacts with former tsarist cavalry officers inspired her in several areas. She became a new type of "Soviet lady" benefactress, adopting orphans and helping poor pensioners in hard times. As age and circumstances turned the "Lady Bountiful" into the "Party auntie," she learned to conceal her generous impulses behind an armor of ideological correctness.

When Nadezhda Ivanovna's parents were arrested in 1937 as enemies of the people, she was both outraged and terrified that this would be a threat to her husband's career.

> Ekaterina Davidovna never said anything, but I knew what she was thinking. Once, when we were alone, she informed me that my mother was a petit bourgeois. "That's not a criminal offense," I protested. She said nothing. She had obviously been trying to understand why my mother was in prison, and this was the only way she could make sense of it. When my only sister, Vera, moved in with us, I could see Ekaterina Davidovna resented the fact that I had not asked her first. When my husband went to talk to his parents about it, she said nothing, but Kliment Efremovich said: "Don't talk nonsense — I've already informed the Politburo about our relatives being 'enemies of the people!' " Then Vera fell in love with Frunze's son Timur. This was the last straw for Ekaterina Davidovna. "One misalliance is enough for this family," she said, evidently referring to Petya and me, and Vera was ordered to break off her relationship with Timur. But they went on loving each other.
>
> I behaved as though nothing had happened. I never asked Kliment Efremovich about my parents and he never once said anything about their being "enemies of the people." Just before the war he managed to get Mother released on health grounds, and she moved in with us.
>
> Shortly before the birth of our second son, Petya went off to work in the Urals. I dropped my studies, started going out to the theater, even had an affair. Ekaterina Davidovna was outraged.
>
> Unlike most Kremlin wives, she tried not to take advantage of her husband's privileges. She thought women should work, and it gave her great satisfaction to achieve something without him. It offended her to see me sitting at home doing nothing. She would leave

for work early, and to avoid her I would pretend to be asleep in my room and have breakfast with Kliment Efremovich, who worked late into the night. Ekaterina Davidovna nagged him about me, but he would say, "You've fallen on hard times, Nadya, my girl." He once read me the fable of the grasshopper and the ant, but that was his only reproach to me.

Stalin didn't like Voroshilov and was always criticizing him. Once in 1946 they were boating on a lake together and Stalin said: "You know what you are, Klim — you're a British spy!" Kliment Efremovich turned red at this and slapped Stalin in the face, nearly capsizing the boat.

Ekaterina Davidovna told me once in a whisper, looking over her shoulder as she spoke, that she thought Stalin was envious of Voroshilov's popularity. On Kliment Efremovich's sixtieth birthday Stalin made a speech about the model Party worker, and we were all in ecstasy — until we realized he hadn't said a word about Voroshilov.

At dinner Stalin would always check that everyone's glasses were full. He would pour the wine himself and make sure we drank to the bottom, so it was impossible not to get drunk. I remember Molotov being carried out once. Stalin's manners were very coarse, and Kliment Efremovich followed suit, like everyone else in Stalin's entourage. Ekaterina Davidovna lived in a state of perpetual fear. When Frunze's children moved in with us, she was afraid that as the daughter of arrested parents I would corrupt them by making critical speeches.

Despite Ekaterina Davidovna's visible efforts to espouse Party orthodoxy and her authority in Kremlin circles, she never managed to please Stalin. He was only too aware that as a friend of his wife's, Ekaterina must have known more than he would have wished about that fateful November night in 1932. But since her behavior was impeccable, the only way Stalin could torture Ekaterina Davidovna was to refuse her any awards or medals. Since every other working Kremlin wife received an award of some kind or other, the slight became all the more apparent, and according to Nadezhda Ivanovna the hurt went very deep:

Ekaterina Davidovna's fears intensified in 1937, and remained with her for the rest of her life. After 1937, families in the Kremlin kept to themselves. Those who hadn't been arrested barricaded themselves inside their families, people stopped socializing in the evenings, and everyone grew fat, dull, and old. It was as though the Kremlin had been hit by a hurricane.

We all lived in terror. We knew that anything we said or did could land us in prison. In those years Voroshilov wasn't always invited to Politburo meetings. This was a bad sign; we were afraid they might come to take him away at any moment. And when he did attend none of us could sleep. The Politburo met after midnight, and we would stay up all night not knowing if he would return. Ekaterina Davidovna suffered in silence, never betraying her anxieties.

During the last years of her life, Ekaterina Davidovna became deputy director of the Lenin Museum. Stern, severe, and undemonstrative as ever, she regarded everything that had happened as correct — even the anti-Semitic purges of the 1940s, the arrest of Molotov's wife, and the murder of the Jewish theater director Mikhoels. Yet after the shooting of the Jews at Babi Yar in 1941, Nadezhda Ivanovna noticed a change in her mother-in-law:

She seemed to become more human. Her sister and her sister's daughter had perished in that terrible pit, and it opened her eyes to something. When the state of Israel was declared I heard her say: "Now we've got a homeland, too!" This from an orthodox Communist internationalist, anathematized in the synagogue for betraying her faith!

She softened in old age. When she fell ill I took her to the hospital and visited her there, and she thanked me in emotional tones quite unlike what I had known before. She was embarrassed at having caused me trouble.

She was always convinced that she would outlive Kliment Efremovich, and very early on she started collecting material for his museum. Having broken with her own family, she wanted everything about him to be worthy of his name. In fact, he outlived her by ten years.

Just before she died she said: "Nadya, you and Petya don't have a dacha. That's bad, you should have one." She knew that Molotov's wife, Paulina Zhemchuzhina, had everything and she had nothing, and that it was dangerous for people in our position not to have their own dacha.

I shall never forget her final parting with Kliment Efremovich. She was dying of cancer. She had told us about it, but not him. It was a stormy day in April 1959, and she was being cared for at their dacha by a team of doctors and nurses, while in the next room he was being cared for by another medical team as he lay delirious with flu. She was determined not to die before he recovered.

She grew steadily worse and started to hemorrhage, but still she begged the doctors not to tell him. Finally they decided she must go to the hospital. They broke the news to him as gently as they could, and only then did he realize how serious the situation was.

We all knew this would be their last meeting. He sat on the edge of her bed, and they sat hand in hand together like Philemon and Baucis. Then we heard her say: "Do you remember how we used to sing together in Petersburg, Klimushka?"

She sang and he joined in, and the tears streamed down our cheeks as we heard their two quavering voices sing: "Gazing at the rays of the purple sunset."

She died just a few days before their golden wedding anniversary, thinking, as always, only of him.

Immediately after Kliment Efremovich's death ten years later, KGB agents came to the Voroshilovs' apartment, examined all their documents, and removed a large quantity of them. These included the memoirs which Ekaterina Davidovna had been working on for several years. They doubtless have been destroyed. One can only surmise, however, that her memoirs, like those of Nadezhda Krupskaya, were written from the guarded perspective of a woman watched constantly, ready at any moment for them to come and take her away.

8

The Three Wives
of Marshal Budyonny

Semyon Mikhailovich Budyonny (1883–1973), born to a poor peasant family on the Don River. After the Civil War he was appointed assistant commander-in-chief of the Red Army; in 1937, commander of troops in the Moscow military district; and from 1939 to 1940 deputy defense commissar. During the war he was a member of the general headquarters of the Supreme Command.

POSTERITY HAS DEALT HARSHLY with those members of Stalin's government who died in their beds, and this is especially so in the case of Semyon Mikhailovich Budyonny. For most of the twentieth century Budyonny was worshipped as a hero. Every Soviet schoolboy longed to be like the "Soviet MacKenzie," with his horse and his saber. A new breed of horse was named after him, and endless songs testified to his horsemanship and courage in battle. He spoke the language of the ordinary people, and if he grew soft from age and adulation, nobody seemed to notice.

In his youth Semyon Mikhailovich had dreamed of being a horse breeder. Instead, he became the finest horseman in the tsarist cavalry and a graduate of the Petersburg Equestrian Academy. Enlisting at the age of twenty in 1903, he was promoted to cavalry sergeant-major, did battle with the Khunguz in the war against Japan, fought on the Austrian, German, and Cossack fronts during World War I, participated in the illustrious Baratov campaign in Persia, and was decorated with no fewer than four St. George Crosses.

In 1917, just as he was about to be promoted to officer, Budyonny suddenly went over to the Bolsheviks, joking later that he preferred to be a marshal in the Red Army than an officer in the White. During the Civil War, Budyonny's First Red Cavalry seized numerous towns from the Whites, including Rostov and the Cossack capital of Novocherkassk, and it was out of these battles that his legendary status grew.

For women attracted to physical strength in a man, Budyonny was eye-catching: stocky and well-built, he had broad peasant features, quick brown eyes, and luxuriant whiskers. Yet the woman chosen by this hero as his life's companion was neither a beauty nor an intellectual but an illiterate Cossack peasant girl named Nadezhda Ivanovna, who came from the village next to his. After marrying her in church he set off with the army and did not see her again until seven years later, in October 1917, when his cavalry regiment disbanded and he returned home to raise a Red detachment there.

Now in her thirties and knowing how to read and write, Nadezhda Ivanovna went off with her husband to fight by his side and organize food and medical supplies for the regiment's hospital unit. Budyonny had found the ideal mate, although Nadezhda apparently found it hard to accept her husband's new status. Later, as they shared a house with the Voroshilovs in Ekaterinoslov, she would often shout at him for denying her permission to invite her Cossack friends home.

In 1923, the Civil War over, the Budyonnys moved to Moscow. The following year Nadezhda Ivanovna shot herself.

Her death spawned a thousand rumors. Some said that Budyonny shot his wife because he was tired of her or because he had found out on his return to Moscow that his wife was having an affair with a student. Others that she committed suicide because he found another woman, or because she had given birth to a dead baby when he was away fighting for the tsar and buried it in the kitchen garden. Accident? Suicide? Murder?

Years later, Semyon Mikhailovich told his adult daughter (by a later marriage) that he and Nadezhda Ivanovna had grown apart and no longer had any family life together. One evening while Nadezhda Ivanovna was at the theater with some friends, he said, he came home from work to find a crowd of men gathered in the courtyard outside his apartment on Granovsky Street, blocking his way. It was dark, and since the secret police did not protect VIPs as diligently then as they do now, he removed the safety from his pistol as he walked through the crowd. Entering his apartment, he sat down on the bed and started to take off his boots. At this moment Nadezhda walked in with her friends, saw the pistol lying on the table, and laughingly pointed it at her head. Through the open door, he called out to her that the pistol was loaded. She laughed. "It's all right, I know how to —" A shot rang out, she fell to the ground, and all the witnesses in the room froze.

Whatever the truth, by the end of that year, Budyonny was re-married to an attractive woman he had met while on holiday in the Caucasus. Her name was Olga Stefanovna Mikhailova. Together with her gypsy good looks and dark, lilac-tinged eyes, Olga had a lovely contralto voice and dreamed of being a singer. Semyon Mikhailovich, himself an accomplished accordionist, loved and encouraged her musical aspirations, and after they married she entered the Moscow Conservatory, joining the Bolshoi Theater in 1930 and singing the parts of Vanya in *Ivan Susanin* and Lelya in *The Snow Maiden.*

Olga Mikhailova and Budyonny were together for thirteen years but never succeeded in managing to make a life together. Budyonny wanted children, but Olga Mikhailova didn't want to spoil her figure or to take time off from her stage work. The role of brood mare did not appeal to her any more than it had to Inessa Armand. But while Armand never quite knew what she expected from her grand revolutionary dreams, Olga was a woman of the 1920s, the daughter of a poor Kursk railway worker, and she knew quite clearly that she wanted: to dazzle audiences with her singing.

Having encouraged them, Budyonny had no choice but to honor his wife's talents, even if her career failed to coincide with his old-fashioned dreams of family warmth and children's voices. While her nephew and niece came to stay with them occasionally, their presence could not fill the childless house.

In the summer of 1937, as the madness, spy mania, and suspicion reached their height, Olga Mikhailova was arrested. Accounts of her arrest differ. Local gossip had it that the beautiful singer was a Polish spy, and that her husband had abandoned her. A version I heard as a child was that she was having an affair with a foreigner, and that Budyonny took her to prison in person in order to save the NKVD the trouble. (I imagined him, like Kazbich in Lermontov's *Hero of Our Time,* throwing his poor wife across the saddle of his bay stallion and

Olga Stefanovna in jail

Olga Stefanovna Mikhailova-
Budyonnaya, second wife
of Marshal Budyonny

Maria Vasilievna, Budyonny's third wife

Third wife of Marshal Budyonny

galloping over to the Lubyanka.) It turns out she was arrested either on the street or at the apartment of the singer Alexeyev, with whom she was probably having an affair, and spent the next nineteen years in a succession of jails and camps.

Shortly after Olga Mikhailova's imprisonment, the marriage was annulled. It was said that Budyonny's third wife was the young girl who had come to the house to help her aunt (Olga's mother), Maria Vasilievna. He had chosen her because she was near at hand, and when he went to her mother the old woman fell at his feet crying, "Make us happy, sir!"

It was also said that, after her marriage, she owned fifty fur coats, and when she hung them out to air at their dacha it was quite a sight. Everyone agrees, however, that Maria Vasilievna was a sweet, modest girl who ran the large Budyonny household splendidly. Thirty-three years younger than Budyonny, she lived happily with him for the rest of his life and bore him three children.

Ekaterina Sergeyevna remembers her thus:

> She was a good-natured woman with a lovely laugh. She was always rushing around after her three children.
>
> In the late 1940s it was an unbreakable tradition for the men to see in the New Year with Stalin, while the wives and children spent the evening at the Budyonnys' dacha. At two A.M. Stalin would release the men and they would arrive at the Budyonnys' to be met with delicious home cooking, cakes, presents, and a Grandfather Frost for the children. It was wonderful!

Today Maria Vasilievna lives in a large Moscow apartment situated in a rambling nineteenth-century building adorned with plaques bearing the names of Marshals Budyonny, Zhukov, Voroshilov, and others. She is a small, youthful-looking woman of seventy-five with a kind face and calm, bright eyes. I went to visit her and we sat in her kitchen at a huge oilcloth-covered table. On the wall behind her hung a huge family portrait done in the best tradition of socialist realism — everyone looks stout-hearted and proud. Semyon Mikhailovich is solemn and brave with his famous whiskers. Maria Vasilievna, in a glamorous dark dress with the fashionable stand-up collar and decolletage known in the early 1950s as the "Mary Stuart style," appears to be virtually the same age as her husband, not because the artist has aged her, but because he took several years off Semyon Mikhailovich. The couple sit surrounded by faceless children, clearly of no interest to the artist, whose focus is the bold Cossack warrior and the little girl from Kursk destined to be his life's companion.

Budyonny's widow is understandably distressed by the contemptuous reactions to him today. Insisting that most of what is written about Budyonny is lies, Maria Vasilievna told me candidly about her life.

In 1936, I left Kursk to study at the Dental Institute in Moscow. An aunt of mine lived in Moscow, and her daughter, my cousin Olga, was married to the famous Marshal Budyonny. I hardly ever saw Olga, she was always busy. Semyon Mikhailovich almost never saw her, either. I always felt nervous at the idea of meeting him when I went to visit their house.

Once I rang the bell and he opened the door. He asked me who I wanted to see, and I barely managed to pronounce my aunt's name.

I sometimes used to help my aunt with the cooking and housework, and after Budyonny's wife went to prison in 1937, I would often cook him dinner, and he would always thank me and smile.

One day my aunt asked me if there was anyone special in my life. There wasn't. She must have told Budyonny. The next day at dinner he asked me, "How do you feel about me?"

Not suspecting anything, I said, "You're my favorite hero!"

"How would you like to marry me then?"

I was flabbergasted. Finally I whispered: "I'm afraid!"

He laughed. "Go to your parents and ask their advice. Then give me your answer."

He left the room and I ran to my aunt, who said, "Marry him! He's a good man, I can vouch for that. He's got to marry someone, so it might as well be you. Even if Olga gets out of prison they'll never be together again. How could Budyonny be married to an ex-prisoner? Go on, marry him!"

I went to Kursk to talk to my parents. When Mother opened the door she assumed I'd been expelled from the institute. When I told her I was getting married she sat down on a chair and asked me who it was.

"Semyon Mikhailovich Budyonny!" I said.

"Have you got yourself into trouble?" Mother demanded.

I said nothing, just handed her a letter from Auntie explaining that Olga was in prison and Semyon Mikhailovich had indeed asked me to marry him.

I talked with my parents for a long time. When I started to leave for Moscow, Mother embraced me and wept: "They'll lock you away behind the Kremlin walls, and we'll never see you again!"

When I got back I went straight to Budyonny's place and cooked him his dinner. He greeted me but didn't mention his proposal. I felt awful. After he finished his soup he asked: "So, what's it to be?"

"It's yes!" I said, my ears burning.

"I was afraid to ask," he said, blushing, too. "I thought you'd say no!" Then he went off to work.

My aunt had fixed me up in the corner of a room belonging to the cleaning woman, but when he came home later that evening he said: "Don't go, stay with me. You're mistress of the house now!"

He was so confused he didn't know what to call me, and I kept calling him "Semyon Mikhailovich." That made him angry. "I'm your husband now — Semyon Mikhailovich sits on a horse!"

We were happy together right from the start. We never quarreled. Our son Seryozha was born on August 13, 1938, and our daughter Ninochka on September 6, 1939. Misha, our second son, was born in 1944. Semyon Mikhailovich was happy. He hadn't had children by his first two marriages, and he'd always assumed it was his fault.

After the first two children arrived I left the institute. It made me very sad. Semyon Mikhailovich was sad, too, but we didn't want to hand our babies over to nannies. "You look after the children, and I'll pay your wages," he said. I never worked outside again. I learned English, beekeeping, vegetable growing, how to use a sewing machine, and the usual domestic skills.

My aunt stayed with us for a while, then moved to Leningrad to be with her sister. Semyon Mikhailovich helped her find an apartment. It was hard for her to see us so happy together when her own daughter was in prison and she herself the reason for this happiness.

Semyon Mikhailovich and I grew very close. He thought the world of his children. Their favorite game was to climb into bed with him for a cuddle and to make him tell them stories.

He was obsessively afraid that something would happen to me. "I bring bad luck," he said. "One wife shot herself, another was arrested — you must be terrified!" We even moved out to another apartment so he wouldn't be haunted by memories.

He always tried to keep me away from Kremlin society, but I remember the first time he took me out was to a government reception marking the anniversary of the Revolution. He introduced me to all the other guests. I was shy because I was so much younger than anyone else. When he went up to the podium I sat with Ashkhen Mikoyan, who took me under her wing; she was a good wife and mother. As for the other wives, I didn't have much to do with them; they were all strong women and much older than me. I was just a child, and I couldn't stop thinking that I'd built my happiness on someone else's suffering, and that if Olga hadn't been arrested we wouldn't have had our three children. I found that aspect of my life terribly hard to bear.

The first time my parents visited us they traveled to Moscow in a special government train. My father later told me he'd found it very difficult and felt intimidated by Budyonny, but he walked in with his hand outstretched and they started talking, and soon he felt he'd known Semyon Mikhailovich all his life. Semyon Mikhailovich's sister Tanya and his mother Malanya Nikitinichna lived with us, too, and after Seryozha was born I brought my parents to Moscow and we all lived together.

In 1938, when they started arresting the cavalry commanders, most of them highly respected men and revolutionary fighters, Semyon Mikhailovich protested to Voroshilov. Voroshilov sent him to see Stalin, and Semyon Mikhailovich said to Stalin's face, "If they're jailing the people who made the Revolution they'd better jail us, too!" to which Stalin replied, "You must be crazy, Semyon!"

When Beria redeployed our troops in the Northern Caucasus during the war without telling him, he was furious and went to Stalin, who said: "Beria's from the Caucasus. He knows best what to do with our troops down there."

"But Beria's a Chekist, not a soldier. There's a difference!" Semyon Mikhailovich retorted.

Once, after the war, Budyonny took me to a banquet in St. George's Hall of the Kremlin. At the end of the meal he went off somewhere. The guests sat at tables laid out in the hall, and Stalin was passing among them with a glass in his hand. My heart was in my stomach as he moved toward me. He stopped behind my chair, and said: "Who's this, then?" When I told him he exclaimed: "So why is our Semyon Mikhailovich way over there chatting to the working class? We're all so envious of his happy family life!"

Shortly afterward, the Kremlin wives and children came for the New Year as usual at our dacha, and I did all the cooking. When the men arrived after midnight, my Semyon Mikhailovich was holding a huge bunch of flowers. "Give these to your wife," he told me Stalin had said to him. "I've kept you late and all the women are alone — they'll be angry with me."

My life with Semyon Mikhailovich was a happy one. He didn't talk much about love, but once he said: "Thank you, Maria, for prolonging my life and giving me a family. I long to come home to you after work. All my life, I've dreamed of having children."

Semyon Mikhailovich had bought us a dacha of our own at Bakovka, so we didn't use government dachas. "I'm older than you," he said, "if something happened to me you and the children could be chucked out of a government dacha within twenty-four hours."

Semyon Mikhailovich was a good man; he loved his people and tried to help everyone who came to him. When we were on holiday in the Caucasus we used to walk to the hills every day, and crowds would gather around us with flowers, everyone wanting to get close to him. I tried to keep out of the way. When our doctor saw what was happening he advised us to take our walks earlier, but people still kept crowding around us.

During the war the children and I were evacuated from Moscow with Semyon Mikhailovich's mother and sister. His mother longed for the war to end. "I hope I live to see the day," she would say. "If I die before, I won't know how it ended!"

Maria Vasilievna showed me a letter Budyonny wrote to her on September 19, 1941, during the bloody battles in the early days of war. The letter was written in pencil in a large, clear hand on a sheet of paper torn from a notebook, with not a single grammatical error.

Darling little Mother,
I have received your letter and am remembering that day in September 1937 when we joined our lives together. I feel as though we have known each other since we were children. I love you infinitely and my heart will love you until it finally stops beating. You are the most beloved and precious creature to me, for you have given me our own darling little babies. I am sure that all will end well, and that we will be together again. Give my greetings to Mother and the rest of our family. Kiss Seryozha and Ninochka for me. I wish you health and happiness. I kiss you, my darling.

Your Semyon.

I asked her about Olga Mikhailova. Maria Vasilievna explained that she had always been afraid to question her husband about the circumstances of her cousin's arrest. Olga had returned to Moscow in 1956, sick and terribly aged. She was paranoid and convinced that everyone hated her and suspected her of trying to poison Budyonny. Olga described to Maria how she had been repeatedly raped in the camps by gangs of men. Semyon Mikhailovich was convinced that all this was the product of her sick mind and arranged for her to be hospitalized. He helped her find an apartment and urged her to come and visit them. But she almost never did, and Maria Vasilievna assumed it was because she did not want to make her uncomfortable. Nothing Maria Vasilievna said to the contrary would dissuade Olga.

Insisting that Budyonny had had nothing to do with his second wife's arrest, Maria Vasilievna produced a letter from a large file of documents that he wrote to the chief military prosecutor on July 23, 1955, eighteen years after Olga had been sent to prison:

> In the early months of 1937 (I forget the exact date) J. V. Stalin informed me that Nikolia Yezhov [Beria's predecessor at the NKVD] had told him that my wife, Olga Stefanovna Mikhailova-Budyonnaya, was behaving in an improper manner and compromising me. He warned me that this could not be tolerated. Comrade Stalin said that according to Yezhov's information foreigners were drawing Olga into their net, or could well do so. He therefore recommended that I discuss the matter further with Yezhov.
>
> Shortly after this I had a meeting with Yezhov, who informed me that my wife, along with the wives of Party worker Andrei Bubnov and Marshal Alexander Egorov, was visiting the Italian, Japanese, and Polish embassies, and had once stayed at the dacha of the Japanese embassy until three o'clock in the morning. Yezhov also informed me that she was having an intimate relationship with a singer at the Bolshoi Theater named Alexeyev.
>
> She herself had told me before my conversation with Yezhov that she had gone with her women friends to the Italian embassy to sing for the ambasssador's wife, and said that she had foreseen no unpleasant results. When I asked Yezhov what specifically could be described as politically compromising in her behavior, he replied that there was nothing so far, but they would continue to keep watch on her and that I should mention nothing to her.
>
> In June 1937 I paid a second visit to Yezhov at his request. This time he said that my wife had been seen at the Italian embassy carrying a program of the racing and show-jumping events at the Hippodrome. "What of it?" I asked. "These programs are sold everywhere — they don't mean a thing!"
>
> "I think we should arrest her and interrogate her and make her tell us about her relations with Bubnova and Egorova. Then if she's innocent we can release her."
>
> I told Yezhov I saw absolutely no grounds for arresting my wife, since I had been given no evidence of her having committed any political crime. As for her intimate relations with Alexeyev (about which I had been informed by Yezhov and the Ministry of Internal

Affairs), this was an entirely personal and domestic matter, which might well end in divorce.

In August 1937 when I was out of Moscow on a ten-day visit to the Gorokhovetsk camps, Olga Stefanovna was arrested. I had played no part in her arrest; on the contrary, I had opposed it, since nothing Yezhov told me led me to believe there were any grounds for it. I knew Ministry of Internal Affairs official Dagin personally after working with him in Rostov, but I did not invite him to my house and never talked to him about my wife.

Later, after my wife's arrest and that of a number of cavalry commanders, including Alexandrov, Tarasenko, and Davydovich, I came to the conclusion that Yezhov had organized the whole thing with the purpose of provoking intrigues and rumors that might eventually lead our Party and government to arrest me.

I feel obliged here to include a brief character reference of Olga Stefanovna. She comes from a poor family. Her father was a railway worker, then a transport official. I married her in 1925. After our marriage she entered the Moscow Conservatory, from which she graduated in 1930. She studied diligently and was socially active. She never expressed the slightest hint of criticism about Soviet power. Her needs were modest, and she showed no signs of greedy materialism.

In conclusion I must say that I do not believe she could commit any crimes against the Soviet government.

Signed, Semyon Mikhailovich Budyonny

Budyonny's letter provides startling insight into the hidden workings of the infernal Party machine. Visiting foreign embassies, now cause for little more than envious curiosity, for years was regarded as highly suspect, if not criminal behavior. The fact that Olga's "crime" consisted, among other things, of taking a racing form to a foreign embassy shows the extent of the political paranoia of that time.

Many leaders' families were destroyed in 1937, and the Budyonnys were no exception. On the other hand, had Maria Vasilievna been taken during Stalin's second round of arrests of Kremlin wives in the late 1940s, Budyonny would have fought for her like a lion, rather than let her be devoured and destroyed by the system. Mother of his children, faithful wife, this strong woman was one of the few Kremlin wives who infused some domestic warmth into the frozen hell of the 1930s and the austerity of the war years. She survives to preserve the memory of Marshal Budyonny, legendary horseman and Hero of the Soviet Union.

9

In the Inquisitor's Chair

STALIN'S PERSECUTION OF HIS MARSHALS and generals often extended to their wives as well. These wives behaved with varying degrees of courage. Can we blame any woman for fearing prison, interrogation, torture, and the firing squad?

The KGB file on Olga Stefanovna Mikhailova, Budyonny's second wife, states: "Born 1905. Native of Ekaterinburg. Daughter of a railway official. Before her arrest a soloist at the Bolshoi Theater of the USSR. Wife of Marshal of the Soviet Union Semyon Mikhailovich Budyonny."

Olga's handwritten testimony, dated March 14, 1938, states:

> I was born in 1905. My father, an orphaned peasant, left his village and worked for thirty-six years on the railways. I started my education in Kursk in 1915. I have painful memories of the tsarist regime, since my father sent me to a high school, where my common speech, shabby clothes, and peasant status provoked the other pupils' derision. The teachers forbade the children of wealthy parents and government officials to play with me, telling them in my presence that they must have nothing to do with me. "Your papa's a peasant!" they would taunt me, and to avoid the sneers my father joined the local bourgeoisie.
>
> I left school at the age of fifteen and married a man named Runov, who was station manager at Vyazma. I lived uncomplainingly but unenthusiastically through the years of havoc and war. The inevitable happened: the Germans and White generals switched sides, the tsar was finished and no one could be called a peasant anymore. That satisfied me, even though I still didn't have enough to eat.
>
> Runov was an alcoholic who drank away our wages and pawned my meager wardrobe. In 1924 I left him and traveled to Georgia for

two weeks' holiday at the health resort of Essentuki, where my friends Kulik, Tyutkin, and Georgadze introduced me to Semyon Mikhailovich Budyonny. Since Marshal Budyonny was a widower he proposed that we have an affair. I agreed, and moved in with him.

Soon after this, Frunze died and Voroshilov was made war commissar. Cavalry soldiers raised their glasses to First Cavalry Commander Budyonny. Budyonny and Voroshilov were both honored, then finally Voroshilov alone, as founder of the First Cavalry and commander of the Red Army. Stalin — leader of the world proletariat — was always toasted with great enthusiasm. During the bitter and open battles with the Trotskyite opposition, the cavalry soldiers, supported by Semyon Mikhailovich, threw their weight behind Josif Vissarionovich.

As for my personal relations with Semyon Mikhailovich, I loved him for his kindness. He loved me but he made me feel that I was a trivial creature of few merits — which is perfectly true — and that I took advantage of the material benefits of his position. He received cars and dachas from the Central Executive Committee because he had earned them, he said; my job was to take care of him and look after his health and well-being, and if I wanted fame I must earn it for myself.

The file on Olga Mikhailova reveals nothing about what happened to her between this handwritten testimony and a letter she later wrote to Yezhov, in which she bitterly attacks her husband:

> During the twelve years I lived with Budyonny I discovered him to be a harsh man who would let no one stand in the way of his ambitions. In these twelve years Semyon Mikhailovich beat me, intimidated me, tyrannized me, and threatened to murder me and denounced me to the NKVD as a spy. The investigation requires me to reveal all crimes or criminal intentions against the Soviet state. I said nothing before, since this would have meant bringing up Budyonny and I lived in fear of his revenge.
>
> During the twelve years of our marriage I collected numerous facts indicating that he was involved in criminal activities against the leaders of our country, notably Stalin and Voroshilov. I shall elaborate on these facts in my statement.

Years later, after Olga Mikhailova had been released from the camps, she told Maria Vasilievna Budyonnaya that her interrogators had beaten and tortured her, forcing her to testify against Budyonny and telling her that he was already in jail and had incriminated her.

Evidently destroyed by her experiences of prison and interrogation, the poor woman wove an elaborate fantasy in which reality and fiction are mixed together:

> During the bitter battle with Trotsky I asked Semyon Mikhailovich whom we should support, Trotsky or Stalin. Semyon Mikhailovich said this was a difficult question and it was no good rushing to extremes, that we should wait a bit and see how things developed, then decide.
>
> Semyon Mikhailovich had some shady connections on the Don River. Once, on our way back from holiday, he was greeted in Vladikavkaz by a railway worker who later came to our carriage and talked at length over a bottle of wine about how he and his detachment had encircled some Reds, and that a partisan detachment had held him by the throat in a deadly grip, and that they barely managed to drag him away from the commander's corpse.

Or, she would say:

> Semyon Mikhailovich had always kept his distance from Party leader Tukhachevsky, Yakir, Army Marshal Uborevich, and Korek, but in late 1936 or early 1937 he told me that he had been to Tukhachevsky's dacha and they had made a secret pact to support each other through thick and thin — in other words to the death. It was common knowledge that Semyon Mikhailovich and Egorov were frequent visitors to Tukhachevsky's dacha.

Olga Mikhailova's KGB files at Lubyanka also contain the testimony of a fellow prisoner named "K," who was clearly a plant.

> I shared a cell with Olga Mikhailova, a singer at the Bolshoi Theater and former wife of Marshal Budyonny. According to Mikhailova, Budyonny not only knew about an anti-Stalin, anti-Soviet conspiracy within the army, but was a leading member of it. Mikhailova said she had considered reporting him, but she did not know whom to approach, fearing that Voroshilov would not believe her and that it would get back to Budyonny. She said that when the conspiratorial cells in the army were smashed and the ringleaders rounded up, Budyonny was convinced that he too would be arrested, and that during the meeting of the Central Committee in 1937 he had been acting very strangely. She said she now realizes that on his trips to Siberia between 1923 and 1930, ostensibly to chat to his old partisan comrades, he was in fact organizing insurrectionary detachments. Mikhailova was convinced that Budyonny wanted to get rid of her before she

compromised him. Only she knew the full extent of his anti-Soviet views, and he feared that if she left him for Alexeyev he would lose his influence over her and she might damage him.

As far as I know, Mikhailova revealed none of the above facts to the investigation, since according to her she was not in her right mind at the time. Secondly, she was asked almost nothing about Budyonny. Thirdly, she was afraid to talk about him. Fourthly, she has only just begun to make sense of things. And finally, she expected a just rebuke for not reporting these matters earlier. Mikhailova is now in a state of deep depression, and it is hard to talk to her or get her to reveal anything. 14.7.1938.

There follow a number of questions concerning Olga Mikhailova's connections with foreign embassies. She admitted to occasionally visiting embassies without her husband, for instance, when Italian ambassador Attolico invited her to sing. She also reported the questions she was asked:

At a reception at the Latvian embassy, a member of Muders's entourage asked me why they hadn't shot Radek, and I replied that he was still useful to them.

At the Japanese embassy they asked me where Budyonny was, and I told them that he was said to be in the Far East preparing for war against Japan.

When foreigners asked if they could see our dacha I replied that it was being redecorated. When they asked me for our telephone number I told them the telephone was broken. When they asked me if I liked Karlsbad, I replied that the waters were good but the cures were expensive.

Evidently driven almost to the point of madness, Olga Mikhailova told the interrogators about her lover Alexeyev, and about Semyon Mikhailovich's threats to have her thrown into jail. Alarmed by these threats, she said, Alexeyev had suggested that he go to the People's Commissariat of Internal Affairs and report her for some minor misdemeanor, whereupon she would spend a couple of years in a camp, he would save up a lot of money, and when she got out they would live happily ever after.

Alexander Ivanovich Alexeyev, leading tenor at the Bolshoi Theater, elegant, intelligent, and aristocratic, was clearly in love with Olga. His testimony is exemplary in that it contains no hint of criticism of her: "Yes, we occasionally discussed the current political situation. She always behaved impeccably, and I never heard her express any negative opinions."

When asked about her relations with Budyonny, Alexeyev replied that the marriage was strained by Budyonny's jealousy. When asked if he had proposed reporting Olga to the NKVD for some minor misdemeanor, he categorically denied doing any such thing.

The investigation dragged on until August 3, 1939, when Sergeant of State Security Kurkova finally stated: "There is no criminal evidence against the accused Mikhailova to present to the court," and urged that the case be dropped and Olga released from custody. On the same day Kurkova wrote to her superior, "Olga Mikhailova is seriously ill and in need of urgent medical attention." Beria was informed, but despite the lack of any evidence against Olga Mikhailova, the charges were spelled out before a Special Session of the Soviet Court in November 1939. There were two principal accusations:

> 1. That while married to Budyonny she conducted an intimate liaison with Bolshoi Theater artist Alexeyev (decd.), who is suspected of espionage activities.*
> 2. That while taking the waters in Czechoslovakia she associated with enemies of the people, known spies, and conspirators.

The case continues:

> The wives of former deputy defense commissar Egorov and former education commissar Bubnov, both arrested on espionage charges, testify that Mikhailova was a member of their ring. Egorova and Bubnova were not questioned about Mikhailova's connection with their espionage activities. Mikhailova admits that she is guilty of making dubious contacts during her unofficial visits to foreign embassies, but she denies charges of espionage. On the basis of the above evidence, the case is to be forwarded to Special Session for consideration of same.
>
> Signed, Junior Prosecutor Kurkova. November 1939.

Kurkova was obviously attempting to keep the evidence against Olga as impartial as possible. But the mighty machinery of Soviet power had made up its mind, and on November 18, 1939, Olga, by

---

* *Alexeyev died in 1939 of throat cancer. The monument on his grave is one of the finest at the Novo-Devyiche Monastery.*

now seriously deranged from prison life, was sentenced to eight years in a corrective labor camp.

Over the next six years she was incarcerated in a number of different camps and prisons. Among the KGB files on her is a letter dated August 15, 1945, from the Ministry of Internal Affairs in the province of Vladimir:

> Mikhailova told her fellow inmates of her hostility to the Soviet state, spreading slanderous lies about the leader of the Soviet government and the country's political structure, and boasting that after her sentence expired she would continue her active struggle against Soviet power. Olga Stefanovna Mikhailova is a socially dangerous element and she must not be released. . . . It has therefore been decided to keep her in jail for an additional three years.

In April 1948 Olga was living in a camp in the Eniseisk region of Krasnoyarsk, where the following unsigned letter was written by a fellow inmate:

> I was arrested in 1938, and after my sentence expired in 1953 I was deported to the province of Krasnoyarsk. It was during the building of the Eniseisk invalid home in July 1953 that I first heard of Olga Stefanovna Mikhailova, who was working as a janitor in Middle School No. 45. I knew her only as the wife of Budyonny, and had met her at several Kremlin receptions. I tried to speak to her but found her pathologically solitary and terrified of social contact. Her memories, logic, and speech were painfully muddled, and she limited herself to brief remarks about her arrest. She said she had only been arrested because she was the marshal's wife, and they had broken the sword over her head. She also informed me that she herself had interrogated the Minister of Internal Affairs, that Semyon Mikhailovich was ninety-four years old, and seriously ill, and refused to meet anyone, and so on. Mikhailova was so ill she could certainly not have left Eniseisk even if she were released.

This letter from Mikhailova's file was next to the original of Budyonny's letter of 1955, quoted earlier. Although written eighteen years too late, Budyonny's letter had the desired effect, and the following year Olga was finally released. Were it not for the workings of the infernal Party machine, Olga Mikhailova would have married her singer, just as Budyonny had his Maria. Instead, she emerged, alone and broken, into a world that no longer had any place for her.

*   *   *

Arrested at the same time was Olga's friend Galina Antonovna Egorova, wife of Marshal Egorov, the woman at whom Stalin had thrown bread pellets on the night of his second wife's death. The two thin KGB files comprising Egorova's case contain the following information about her:

> Born 1898, province of Bryansk. Film actress. Graduate of Social Studies Faculty at Moscow University. Non-Party. Russian.
>
> Evidence that as an agent of Polish espionage she passed information about the Worker Peasant Red Army to the Polish government, and that, knowing of the existence of an anti-Soviet fascist plot within the army and of her husband's leading part in it, she failed to report this to the authorities.
>
> Orders to arrest and search.

Egorova's signed testimony of January 17, 1938, looks as if it were written by a frightened child:

> Between 1916 and 1917 I studied at the Petrograd Conservatory, and it was there that I was caught up in the February Revolution. Confused about what was happening, I went home to Bryansk. After October 1917, I worked in the Commissariat of War. There I met Egorov, and in August 1919, after we married, I moved with him to Moscow.
>
> In 1927 I met some cinematographers and acted in a couple of films. My downfall began when I was lured into the diplomatic world. My head was turned by the dazzling company, stylish clothes, refined manners, foreign languages, flirtatiousness, dancing, and fun. It was a new and seductive life, which flattered me and appealed to values established in childhood by my bourgeois education.
>
> At first I only attended official receptions with my husband, but bit by bit I was drawn into a series of unofficial engagements with foreigners, informal breakfast and dinner parties, skiing holidays, trips to the theater, and so on. My presence in diplomatic circles soon made me an object of attention, but I was of particular interest to officials at the Polish mission.
>
> "Are you a Pole?" the Polish Ambassador Lukasevich asked me. He then asked me my maiden name and <u>wrote it down in his notebook</u>.*
>
> My friendship with Ambassador Lukasevich deepened, and soon all formality was dropped and we became friends. Flowers and Polish

---

* *Each surname mentioned is invariably underlined by the interrogator in red or black pencil.*

sweets were delivered via the Department of Foreign Affairs or to my home, and this was followed by private phone calls, an invitation to attend the opening party for a Polish exhibition, and so on. My feelings for Lukasevich grew, and I fell in love with him. It thrilled me to see him, dance with him, and talk to him. I couldn't resist answering his questions, and I blurted out more and more state secrets to him.

Lukasevich was mainly interested in the activities of our government officials and army commanders. On several occasions I talked to him about hostile groups within the ranks of the Soviet army, and about the anti-Soviet views of certain individuals. I told him that Tukhachevsky, Uborevich, and Yakir all bore a grudge against Voroshilov and wanted to take his place, and that each of these men believed that he had the skill and experience to do so. I also told Lukasevich about a second group around Egorov and Budyonny, which was in opposition to Tukhachevsky. I provided biographical facts and information about the places where Budyonny and Egorov had studied, served, and fought, and Lukasevich asked me about Voroshilov's relations with them.

At the beginning of 1934, Lukasevich told me that the moment had finally come when our friendship required some unequivocal proofs, and he asked me to supply him with information about our military command, specifically our air force and armed forces, and about the command structure of the Red Army in the event of war.

I understood that I was committing a serious crime against my country, but because of my infatuation with Lukasevich, the fact that he was single, led a glamorous social life, and had capital abroad, I felt unable to refuse and agreed to do so.

I knew about the proposed command structure in the event of war, since I had heard commanders of the Worker-Peasant Red Army discussing in our apartment how Voroshilov would be made commander-in-chief and Tukhachevsky or Egorov chief-of-staff. As for information about our air force, I tried to find out about this from General Alksnis, but when I next met Lukasevich, at a banquet, I had to confess that I had been unable to meet with Alksnis. Lukasevich then asked me if it was true that Egorov had traveled to the Far East.

"Yes," I said.

"What for?" he asked.

I replied that he had gone to inspect the fortified regions in the Far East, and that I would be joining him there. Lukasevich asked me to find out about these fortifications and the construction of a new road. I promised to do so. In Khabarovsk I learned about our shore fortifications, the building of a new highway along the edge of the ocean from Tikhaya Bay, and the delivery of plane and submarine parts.

I informed Lukasevich of all this at our next meeting, during a dance on the tennis court of the Italian embassy. I had still been unable to discover any information about our armed forces and air force.

All our subsquent meetings were deliberately distant and of a strictly official nature. This was because Soviet society could no longer turn a blind eye to Bubnova, Budyonnaya, Eliava, and me, and regarded our association with foreign diplomats as highly improper. In April 1934 I was summoned to see Voroshilov, who warned me about this, and word spread through the diplomatic community that "Soviet ladies had received a reprimand." I talked to Lukasevich about it during a reception at the Italian embassy, and he said we must behave formally to avoid unpleasant consequences for both of us. From then on he transferred all his favors — the first dance, sitting next to him during dinner, and so on — to Tukhachevsky's wife. Lukasevich left Moscow for a visit to Poland, and shortly afterward he left Moscow for good. The Polish military attache, Colonel Kovalevsky, kept in contact with me, and I did not see Lukasevich again.

Nineteen thirty-seven passed uneventfully, since I was unable for various reasons to attend any receptions. Between 1932 and 1935 salons had sprung up in Moscow, reminiscent of the glittering receptions held by wealthy Russians in aristocratic Russia, or of subversive aristocratic circles such as the Decembrists. Such salons were organized at the Bubnovs, Grinkos, and our house to read a new play or film script, or to hear a quartet perform a little concert.

But there was a more sinister side to these gatherings. For some reason they were invariably attended by people who had been passed over for the top jobs, people with warped minds and personal grudges against the existing state of affairs in Russia, who would slander the positive aspects of life in our country.

As we women busied ourselves in the kitchen, we would echo the views of our husbands while we discussed the latest appointments and cursed the government. Bubnova complained that Andrei Sergeyevich was being held back, despite having been one of the top five with Lenin. Tukhachevsky, a blue-blooded aristocrat, always affable and surrounded by ladies, had formed a group within the army and was campaigning openly, making no attempt to disguise his hostility to the government. This crowd of unacknowledged geniuses aspired to the leadership, caring nothing about how their aims were accomplished. Flattery, lies, and brazen sycophancy — they stopped at nothing. It was plain for all to see. When someone finally discovered their plans and stopped them in their tracks they became angry, and their anger pervaded our gatherings. Their admiration for foreigners and their scepticism about the possibility of progress in our country meant they needed people to blame, and they found these in the leadership.

Budyonny's crowd was a little different, consisting of Civil War veterans and cavalry soldiers. Semyon Mikhailovich mirrored these men's qualities and defects, and saved them from committing any kind of impropriety. I have known Semyon Mikhailovich since 1920 as a cheerful, sharp-witted man, but ambitious, vain, and something of an actor, whose political and cultural development meant that he could no longer be content with a simple Cossack girl like Nadezhda.

His first meeting with Olga Stefanovna Mikhailova took place in Kislovodsk, where I was on holiday with my husband at a sanatorium. One day Egorov, Budyonny, and I went for a drive to Lermontov rock, where we were soon joined by Kulik and Georgadze, accompanied by two women, one of whom was Olga Stefanovna. I left soon afterward with Egorov, while Budyonny stayed behind with his new friends. That was how his affair with Olga Stefanovna started. The following morning there was a jealous scene between Olga Stefanovna and Kulik, who had brought her to the Caucasus.

The Cossack girl shot herself, and literally two days later Olga Stefanovna moved in with Semyon Mikhailovich. Beautiful, young, a soloist at the Bolshoi Theater, an accomplished French speaker — all this thrilled and delighted him. She brought so much to his life. Yet after twelve years of happy married life, Olga Stefanovna was suddenly arrested. I had never seen Semyon Mikhailovich so crushed as he was at our dacha then. The tears were pouring down his cheeks. I had never imagined Budyonny could cry. Her arrest wasn't just a blow to his pride, he suffered terribly from the loss of this woman he loved, as well as the loss of his comfortable, familiar family life.

He saw in the New Year with us at our dacha. After dinner he sat down beside me and asked me if I knew about his wife's arrest. I said I did and asked him what had happened. He told me that she and Bubnova had turned out to be spies, Bubnova for three foreign governments and Olga Stefanovna for the Poles, and that Olga Stefanovna had carried out these espionage activities for seven years, had had an affair with a Pole at the embassy, and had been paid 20,000 rubles. He also told me that she and Bubnova had said under interrogation that I was the leader of their spy ring and that I had given them their assignments. He warned me to prepare myself for any eventuality.

Galina Antonovna continued her handwritten testimony on April 26, 1938:

In the testimony that I presented to the investigation in January of this year I omitted a number of circumstances that have a direct bearing on the character of my husband, A. I. Egorov, as well on my own person. I refer to the double life led by Egorov and his close associates. Although successfully passing themselves off as defenders of the Revolution and commanders of the Red Army, they were in fact out-and-out White Guards. It suited their purposes to go along with the Red Army for the time being, but their hearts were in the enemy camp on the other side of the barricades.*

As dawn was breaking these men would gather after their night's work and have dinner together. When Stalin was at the table they would congratulate each other on their spoils [sic] and raise their glasses to Soviet power and victory over the Whites. When Stalin wasn't there, all of them, including Egorov, would express their hostility to Soviet power and to Stalin personally, and drink to the imminent defeat of the Red Army.

Early in 1920 I remember Alexander Ilyich Egorov returning home in a state of high anxiety, and when I asked him what was the matter he told me Stalin's train had been accidently put on the wrong track and there had nearly been a catastrophic accident. Then Mantsev came in and the two of them had a long and heated discussion, from which I gathered that Stalin's train had almost been derailed. <u>Mantsev said, "Damn it, what bad luck!"</u>†

When I asked Alexander Ilyich why, despite his apparent friendship with Stalin and membership of the Communist Party, he behaved in such an anti-Soviet manner, he replied that he and his friends remained officers, that is, <u>men unable to reconcile themselves to Soviet power</u>. Alexander Ilyich thought constantly about escaping abroad. In 1921, at the end of the Civil War, he wrote to me urging me to learn more foreign languages since new times were coming, links with foreign countries were being made, and we should not rule out the possibility of moving there. He also encouraged me to attend frequent

---

* *Note the aggressive style here, and the preponderance of clichés evidently prompted by the investigators, as Egorova attempted to formulate her evidence in the style required of her.*
† *Underlined in the investigator's red pencil.*

banquets with foreign ambassadors, and he knew of my relations with Lukasevich. In answer to Lukasevich's questions about Egorov's anti-Soviet views, I replied that these views were shared by Bubnov and Budyonny, and that I understood from my conversations with Budyonny, Bubnov, and Egorov that they were all supporters of Rykov.

Egorov used me to persuade Lukasevich to set up a meeting for him in Warsaw with Stakhevich, the Polish Chief of Staff, who agreed to meet Egorov in a private apartment somewhere in Warsaw. When we visited Rome in 1934, we were invited to dinner by the Italian ambassador to the USSR, Attolico, and since the conversation was in English, I interpreted for Egorov as he expressed his admiration of the Italian government — which amounted effectively to a direct condonement of Italy's fascist regime.

Apart from this testimony, Egorova's files contain absolutely no evidence of any crime. Yet the court transcript of her sentencing proceedings in Moscow, on August 27, 1938, states: "The case shall be heard *in camera* without witnesses or counsel for the prosecution or defense, and the accused is to be held in custody until the trial."* The transcript of the Supreme Court session the following day continues:

The presiding judge asked if the accused was acquainted with the charges against her. The accused replied in the affirmative. The accused was informed as to her legal rights. The accused made no plea or challenge to the court. The judge asked the secretary to read out the charges, explained to the accused the nature of the accusations against her, and asked her if she pleaded guilty or not guilty. The accused replied that she was not guilty, and that she rejected the signed evidence submitted during the first interrogation.

Nobody had forced her to give incorrect testimony, she said; she had simply been stunned by the sudden arrest of her husband and her own arrest, and had lost her head and slandered herself. She had no explanation as to why her husband had produced incriminating evidence against her.

When asked if she had anything else to add, the accused replied that since she had no way to prove her innocence she could only beg for mercy. The court retired to deliver its verdict, and at 21:55 the sentence was read out.

SENTENCE. In the name of the Union of Soviet Socialist Re-

---

* *The decision to hear cases without defense or prosecution lawyers was taken after the death of Kirov in 1934, and remained in operation until Stalin's death.*

publics G. A. Egorova is found guilty of all charges against her, and the military collegium of the Supreme Court of the USSR therefore sentences Galina Antonovna Egorova to the supreme measure — death by firing squad, with the confiscation of all personal property.

The sentence is final, and according to the USSR Central Executive Committee's ruling of 1.12.1934, is to be carried out forthwith.

One might wonder why all these powerful men were in such a hurry, and what possible danger this "spy" presented to them, especially one who gave away secrets that everyone already knew. The final documents in Egorova's meager KGB file date from 1956. A letter marked Top Secret and issued by the head of the Operations Section of the Committee of State Security of the USSR declares, "In our judgment there is no case against Galina Antonovna Egorova. We possess no information suggesting any links between her and Lukasevich or Kovalevsky."

Another document, dated March 13, 1956, states:

> The case against A. I. Egorov, former marshal of the Soviet Union and deputy defense minister of the USSR, has been dropped through lack of *corpus delicti*. Having examined the files relating to the case of his wife, it has been established that since the only proof of Egorova's guilt consisted of a note containing excerpts from her husband's testimony against her, this evidence is now invalid and the case against her is dropped by lack of *corpus delicti*.*
>
> The KGB and the Soviet of Ministers of the USSR have no information as to G. A. Egorova's membership of any international intelligence agencies.

---

* *This note, the only "evidence" against Galina Egorova, is missing.*

10

The President's Wife

Mikhail Ivanovich Kalinin (1875–1946), born to a poor peasant family in the village of Verkhnyaya Troitsa, in the Kashin district of Tversk. Leaving school at thirteen, he became a footman in St. Petersburg, attended a trade school at night, and at eighteen began working as a lathe operator at a St. Petersburg factory. In 1898 he joined the Social Democratic Party and later rose steadily through the Communist Party ranks. From 1919 until his death he was president of the Soviet Republic.

STALIN TENDED TO SPARE self-effacing Kremlin wives such as Ekaterina Voroshilova, Maria Kaganovich, Maria Budyonnaya, and Nina Khrushcheva, but seems to have borne a special antipathy for those women of the Kremlin he considered emancipated — possibly because they reminded him of Nadezhda Alliluyeva.

Strong, competent, and independent, Ekaterina Kalinina was one of those who incurred his displeasure. Her file at Lubyanka reveals very little:

> Ekaterina Ivanovna Kalinina, née Lorberg. Nationality: Estonian. Date of birth: 1882. Father: day laborer. Mother: laundress. Party membership: All-Russian Communist Party (Bolshevik). Profession: government official. Previous employment: weaver. Education: primary. Employment before arrest: Commissariat of Justice, member of the Supreme Court of the RSFSR. Place of residence before arrest: the Kremlin, Moscow.

Since these notes omit any mention of the prisoner's family status, it should be added that Ekaterina Ivanovna ("Ioganovna" in Estonian), mother of five children — three of her own, two of them adopted — was the wife of Mikhail Ivanovich Kalinin, president of the Supreme Soviet of the USSR.

The girls in Mikhail's village all turned him down when he asked them to marry him. They could not make him out. He wasn't going to be a farmer like his parents. Instead, he had gone off to St. Petersburg to become a lathe operator. People said he had got caught up in the Revolution and had been on the run from the police since the upheavals of 1905. When he brought his seventeen-year-old Estonian bride back to Verkhnyaya Troitsa the following year, nobody knew much about her either.

Ekaterina came from a large Estonian peasant family and was sent out to work in a mill at the age of eleven. Moving to St. Petersburg, she joined the 1905 strike movement and was hidden from the police by a Bolshevik woman named Tatyana Slovatinskaya, who found her a job in a textile mill and hired her as a servant when her continued revolutionary activities lost her her job. It was at Slovatinskaya's house that she met the revolutionary Mikhail Kalinin, married him, and went back to Verkhnyaya Troitsa with him.

Seven years younger than Kalinin, Ekaterina was a tall, strong, graceful woman, with a snub nose and plump red cheeks. Neat and hardworking, she cleaned and scrubbed his cottage until it shone, reorganized everything her own way, was out working in the kitchen garden at dawn, and could scythe as well as any man. The weaver and the lathe worker were well matched, and she proved a good wife, mother, and comrade to him.

Shortly after the birth of their first baby, given the aristocratic name Valerian, they left Verkhnyaya Troitsa for St. Petersburg, returning for brief visits until 1910, when Ekaterina Ivanovna moved back to the village with her children, of whom there were now three. The villagers gossiped about Mikhail Ivanovich's revolutionary activities but she kept her own counsel and made plans to have a new house built in the village, a clear sign that the family intended to settle there.

War upset all her plans. She revealed that her husband was in jail in St. Petersburg awaiting deportation to Eastern Siberia as a revolutionary. Throughout 1914 she regularly left the children with his mother, Maria Vasilievna, to go and visit him, and at the end of 1916 she petitioned the government to allow him to travel to Siberia independently, rather than under armed guard, so that she and the children could accompany him there.

The girls from Verkhnyaya Troitsa who had rejected Kalinin must have been kicking themselves a few months later when suddenly the rough, self-educated Kalinin found himself not as they had predicted in some remote Siberian hut but at the pinnacle of Soviet power. After the death of Yakov Sverdlov in 1919 there appeared no better candidate to head the new Soviet state than this genuine worker of peasant origin, a true Russian. He had clean hands too, and this was a significant advantage at a time when rumor had it that Sverdlov had been murdered for his part in the tsar's execution.

In the Kremlin the Kalinins shared an apartment with the Trotskys, who also had three children, and Ekaterina Ivanovna made friends with Nadezhda Krupskaya. The object of fierce scrutiny, Kalinina disarmed all critics with her simplicity, her innate tact, her passionate desire to be useful, and her diligence in every task she undertook. Torn from the confines of her female world into the wide open spaces of political life, she enrolled in nursing courses and helped organize schools and kindergartens. As she set about tackling her own lingering illiteracy she developed a taste for this new life of cultural interests, stimulating company, and discussions about sexual equality and personal freedom.

In the summer of 1919, as the tide of civil war finally seemed to be turning in the Bolsheviks' favor and Kalinin had been appointed president of the new Soviet state, Ekaterina Ivanovna left the children first with her mother, Ekaterina Adamovna, then with Kalinin's mother in Verkhnyaya Troitsa, and set off with her husband to tour the country on the *October Revolution* agitation and propaganda train.

The *October Revolution* was a mobile medium of mass information, the equivalent of our radio, press, and television, designed to introduce people throughout large areas of Russia to the principles of the new life, tell them who their friends and enemies were, and show them the path to literacy. The new president's presence on board was considered essential. Also on board were Commissars Kamenev and Lunacharsky, plus numerous journalists, workers, foreign communists, and writers, all working in shifts to distribute pamphlets, give talks, show films, make local inspections, and force open the breadbins in areas hit by famine.

Her hair cropped short after an attack of typhus, Ekaterina Ivanovna was the *October Revolution*'s chief administrator. Quick-witted and efficient, she helped to establish kindergartens and gave talks in hospitals about the care of the wounded. Her energy was prodigious. Many decisions had to be made as they went along, and all who knew her remarked on her incorruptibility and her outstanding organizational ability.

In the summer of 1921, she returned with her children to Verkhnyaya Troitsa, where she was promptly elected to the district executive committee. In these lean years even people in the Kremlin went hungry, and she stayed on in the village with her large family until the end of that year, helping her mother-in-law by working in the kitchen garden. Gradually things improved, and in 1922 she returned to Moscow, where she completed her nursing courses, studied homeopathy, adopted two Civil War orphans, and was appointed deputy director of the Liberated Labor weaving mill.

Her granddaughter, Ekaterina Valerianovna, told me, "Everything revolved around Granny — she was the center of the family. She was a stickler for neatness, I suppose it's an Estonian trait. Neatness was an obsession with her."

As Kremlin life normalized, Ekaterina Ivanovna's desire for public service and her dramatic rise from weaver to factory manager took a toll on her time and energy. People increasingly criticized her for giving too little time to her children. But there was no stopping her now: having tasted life outside the home, nothing could induce her to return to it. The solution was to hire a housekeeper. When the beautiful, educated, aristocratic Alexandra Vasilievna Gorchakova moved in to take charge of the house and children, freeing Ekaterina Ivanovna to work undistracted, it seemed as though this former peasant, now one of the most powerful women in the Kremlin, could want for nothing more.

Yet in 1924, Ekaterina Ivanovna left her husband and children in Alexandra Gorchakova's capable hands and ran off with a woman friend named Valentina Ostroumova, a stenographer on Kalinin's staff, to the remote Altai region. The two women flung themselves into trade union work and organized a series of "Down with Illiteracy!" groups. Valentina Ostroumova wrote to Kalinin in Moscow, "The regional committee has decided to promote Katya, and the president praises her work to the skies. She'll soon be catching up to you! People's attitude to us is positive, and most of them (the masses anyway) don't know about her connection with you, so there's none of that unnaturalness she experienced in the factory."

This remark is the key to understanding why Ekaterina Ivanovna left her family and rushed off to the ends of the earth. She later explained her predicament in a letter to her husband from Altai:

> I wasn't a real person in Moscow. I was a false figure in that society that I belonged to only through you. It was a dishonest situation. A couple of people were sincere with me, but with the rest it was all lies and pretense and it disgusted me. Because I belonged to the top rank I couldn't speak and think as I wanted, like ordinary officials. I was told this to my face by fellow Communists in the top and middle ranks. What happens to the ideals we worked for if we divide up the Party into ranks, and even into classes? You can't make wheat bread from rye — if they want to sort people into groups they can leave me out. I don't need cars and privileges, and I don't need false respect — all that stops people from seeing me as I really am, just a plain ordinary weaver.

Ekaterina Ivanovna was forty-two, a woman crying out against the destruction of her ideals. All around her, inside and outside the Kremlin, the stereotypes of the new power were taking shape, and while it paraded the slogans of the new vocabulary, it was based on the timeless truth that the man with the stick is boss.

As her children grew up, Ekaterina Ivanovna's socially active nature and the revolutionary dreams of her youth had been stifled by Kremlin life. A step away from her lived unhappy Nadezhda Alliluyeva, almost twenty years her junior but equally conscientious and progressive, complex yet simple. The two women had much in common, but even though they lived near one another the difference in their ages and the scrutiny of Kremlin life meant that they could never be close.

Unable to be politically active, Ekaterina Ivanovna fled to the Urals hoping to find herself and to affirm her value as an individual. But the invisible chains of the power structure dragged her back. In the summer of 1924 Alexandra Gorchakova silenced Kremlin gossip by bringing the children to see their mother in Altai, where they spent the summer together enjoying the natural beauties of the Urals, bathing in its clear streams and picking mushrooms and berries. Then, possibly against her better judgment, Ekaterina Ivanovna returned to

Moscow and to her hated position as semi–First Lady of State. There she fell ill, went to the Pasteur Institute in Paris for treatment (occupants of the Kremlin all made use of capitalist hospitals in those days), and after her return helped to establish several large state farms.

Ekaterina Ivanovna's escape first to Verkhnyaya Troitsa in 1921 and three years later to the Urals demonstrated how unhappy she was with the ambiguousness of her official status. It is also possible that personal motives were at work here, and that her relationship with Mikhail Ivanovich was such that they had agreed to lead separate lives. Perhaps all that kept them together was the children. They may have followed the familiar pattern of couples who are unable to live together, but who miss each other when apart. Another problem may have been Kalinin's attraction for the beautiful woman who moved into their home and ran it, replacing his semiliterate, uppity Estonian wife who took over a factory and vied for power. It is also possible that, encouraged by the discussion of the woman question and free love, Ekaterina Ivanovna was emboldened to confront her husband and demand the right to live by the same standards. Cracks started to appear in the domestic stability of more than one Kremlin family at this time, and several leaders had acquired new lovers on the other side of the wall.

Whatever the causes of Ekaterina Ivanovna's restlessness, the Altai region seems to have drawn her like a magnet, and in 1931 she set off there again. By now she was forty-nine, the same age Krupskaya was when she had entered the Kremlin as its new queen. This was the highpoint of Ekaterina Ivanovna's life, too. She worked on the construction of the Chemalsk hydroelectric station and a new rest home for the executive committee. She kept pigs, grew vegetables, and rejoiced again in the opportunity to make use of her organizational skills. She was so enthusiastic about her new life that she had no qualms about using Kalinin and others to promote the development of the Altai, and wrote numerous letters begging for help. During these early years of collectivization the president's wife believed, or tried to believe, in what the Party said, and worked tirelessly to help this new world come into being and prosper. Her letters to her husband are filled with a love of life, and give the impression that the Urals had everything that could possibly make a woman happy.

When a new spa opened in the Altai, the leaders started arriving there from Moscow. Kalinin himself visited in 1934, shortly after he had celebrated the fifteenth anniversary of his presidency — without her, predictably. Her presence in Moscow would have been easy enough to arrange, but the event evidently meant little to her. He arrived home to find a letter from her apologizing for forgetting to congratulate him.

Ekaterina Ivanovna returned exhausted to Moscow at the end of 1934. In her absence the Kremlin had witnessed a number of crucially important events, including the death of Nadezhda Alliluyeva, the murder of Kirov, and Stalin's Party purges. Details illuminating the secrets of this high-powered torture chamber were plentiful.

In 1937, during the arrests and shootings of the "enemies of the people" and their wives, Ekaterina Ivanovna started working at the Supreme Court of the RSFSR. March 1938 saw the trials of Trotsky, Bukharin, and the "Right-Trotskyite bloc," and in August Beria replaced Yezhov as head of the Ministry of Internal Affairs, the NKVD. In September the Kalinins were on separate holidays, she in the Caucasus and he in Sochi, writing a pamphlet entitled "The Glorious Path of the Komsomol." On her way back to Moscow she visited him in Sochi. She left for Moscow, and shortly after departure he wrote to his daughters: "Mother has just visited and put some dynamite into our stagnant life."

A few days after Ekaterina Ivanovna's return home her old friend Valentina Ostroumova came to visit and the two women had a heart-to-heart talk about politics. Ostroumova was arrested on October 17.

Bukharin's wife, Anna Larina, who shared a cell with Ostroumova in 1938, recalls in her memoirs the dramatic developments in the investigation of her case:

> Valentina Petrovna's hatred for Stalin was such that she was prepared to repeat everything she had said to Kalinina about him: "A tyrant and a sadist, destroying the Leninist leadership and millions of innocent people." Concerned about the position of Kalinin's wife, she initially denied that the conversation had taken place. But Beria had precise and detailed knowledge of the content of their conversation, and was able to tell Ostroumova that Kalinin's wife had confessed everything. Believing Beria, Ostroumova confirmed what had been said between them. The investigator then arranged a face-to-face meeting between the two women, at which Ekaterina Ivanovna denied everything and Valentina Petrovna realized that she had been tricked.

At least that was how Ostroumova described the incident. Soon afterward she was led from the cell and was never seen again.

When Ekaterina Ivanovna was arrested they found her letters to her husband hidden behind a picture. How did anyone know where they were hidden? Was her conversation with Ostroumova bugged? Was there an informer in the Kalinins' apartment? Were the two women simply tricked into making their confession?

The minutes of Kalinina's first interrogation, on December 9, 1938, begin with the examiner demanding information on the two women's "Trotskyite counterrevolutionary activities":

KALININA: I did not carry out any Trotskyite counterrevolutionary activities. The only thing I could be accused of is having associated with people convicted as Trotskyites. I know Ostroumova as a Party member, and have never heard her make any anti-Soviet remarks.

QUESTION: Ostroumova states that she involved you in her counterrevolutionary activities, is that true?

KALININA: She's lying. I have never been involved with her in any counterrevolutionary activities, I know nothing of her counterrevolutionary activities.

Kalinina is told she is to have a meeting with Ostroumova. Ostroumova is led in.

QUESTION TO OSTROUMOVA: What do you know about the counterrevolutionary activities of Ekaterina Ivanovna Kalinina?

OSTROUMOVA: As I already indicated in my previous interrogation, I have conducted subversive espionage work against the Soviet state for several years. Apart from information of a purely intelligence nature I collected defamatory rumors about the leaders of the Party and the Soviet Government. One of the sources of these rumors was Ekaterina Ivanovna Kalinina and her associates.

Kalinina's apartment was a kind of salon where people hostile to the Party line would meet to criticize the Party's collectivization policies. Amongst those who used to attend was Abel Enukidze. Kalinina cannot fail to remember our bitter attacks on the Party and our bitter hatred of Stalin, whom we regarded as the chief culprit of its new course.

QUESTION TO KALININA: Do you confirm Ostroumova's evidence?

KALININA: It's lies, all lies!

OSTROUMOVA: Kalinina was very friendly with a Trotskyite named D. This woman was a friend of the Trotsky family and had had an intimate relationship with Trotsky before he was deported from the USSR.

QUESTION TO KALININA: Do you confirm your links with the Trot-skyites?

KALININA: I confirm only that D. was a personal friend of mine. I deny that this friendship was of an anti-Soviet nature.

The typed transcript of this meeting was signed by both Kalinina and Ostroumova and forms the body of the KGB's file on Kalinina's case. The file also contains minutes of the interrogation of "D.," who confessed to "allowing her apartment to be used twice in 1927 for the purpose of illegal counterrevolutionary meetings at which Trotsky spoke." D. was further forced to confess that she had attended one of these meetings, although she had not actually said anything.

D. even confessed to a ten-year-old affair. "I started visiting the Trotskys' apartment in the Kremlin as a friend of the family, and between 1922 and 1923, when Trotsky's wife was abroad for medical treatment, I formed an intimate liaison with Trotsky."

What this has to do with Kalinina's case is a mystery. It merely indicates how insubstantial the evidence against her was in the first place.

One can only guess what happened to Ekaterina Ivanovna between her first and second interrogation, for the tone of her replies changes abruptly after her encounter with Ostroumova. We now come to the most difficult part of her story, in which she reveals her part in the arrest of her brother:

INTERROGATOR: You are accused of conducting counterrevolutionary propaganda against the USSR. Do you admit your guilt?

KALININA: No, I do not. I have never conducted counterrevolutionary propaganda, I have always struggled against enemies of the Party and the Soviet Union and exposed them.

INTERROGATOR: Whom have you exposed?

KALININA: I exposed my own brother, Vladimir Ivanovich Lorberg. In 1924 I learned that he had been an *agent provocateur* of the tsarist secret police, and I demanded that he go to the OGPU and give himself up. He did so, and was arrested and shot.

INTERROGATOR: How did you learn that your brother had been a tsarist agent?

KALININA: I was told by my other brother, Konstantin Ivanovich Lorberg.

INTERROGATOR: What exactly did he tell you?

KALININA: He told me that the Narva Social Democrat organization in the town of Kalinin [sic] had exposed Vladimir Lorberg as a secret agent who had betrayed a number of comrades to the tsarist police.

INTERROGATOR: What did you do when you received this information?

KALININA: I immediately summoned Vladimir Lorberg and asked him if it was true. He admitted that he had had connections with the tsarist secret police and had betrayed members of the Estonian Social Democratic organization to them. I then demanded that Lorberg go to the OGPU and confess.

INTERROGATOR: Why did you not inform the Party yourself?

KALININA: I wanted my brother to tell them in person, and I warned him that if he did not I would do so myself. I personally helped him to make contact with the OGPU, and telephoned Bokio asking him to receive my brother.

If Alliluyeva was almost expelled from the Party for unpunctuality and Stalin threatened to set the Control Commission on Krupskaya for disobedience, one can imagine how threatened Kalinina must have felt by the shadow of her erring brother. It is difficult to know whether she was slandering herself to save her life, or recalling how in 1924, the critical year of her life, her blunt straightforward nature was outraged by her brother's past, and determined that he atone for his crime. It may well also be why she ran off to Altai that year.

The interrogators also accused Kalinina of meeting a White émigré woman named Levinson when she was in Paris for medical treatment, and of answering Levinson's questions about life in the Soviet Union. She then starts to slander herself in earnest:

> I confess to being a member of a right-wing counterrevolutionary organization. I was drawn to this in 1928 by my hostility to the Party's collectivization policies. Between 1928 and 1930 I regarded the peasant as an extreme individualist, and with this mentality I thought it would be impossible to change him into a state farmer.
>
> In the statement I made after my meeting with Ostroumova I admitted to being a member of a counterrevolutionary organization. I deny charges of espionage.

Her interrogator interrupts her: "Espionage charges will not be dropped. You are a spy!"

Finally comes the sentence: fifteen years' imprisonment in corrective labor camps, with an additional five years' political disfranchisement. Ostroumova's sentence was either more cruel, or less cruel, depending on your perspective. She was shot shortly afterward.

The only recorded memories of Kalinina in the camp are those of a writer named Razgon, who recalled her working in the camp bathhouse, shaking the lice from the prisoners' clothes while they were washing. Her granddaughter, Ekaterina Valerianovna, who was fond of her, says, "She didn't have to do it — I'm sure she didn't think how disgusting the lice were, but how pleasant it would be for people to wear clean clothes, even for a little while."

It is typical of Stalinist justice that Kalinina's files should contain no statement from her husband. Stalin clearly intended to keep the president under his thumb, showing the world that the great man was being magnanimously defended from his counterrevolutionary wife, and that in purging the Kremlin of the enemy within, the innocent were not touched.

Anna Larina-Bukharina wrote of the powerlessness of this man who occupied the Soviet throne:

> In the Tomsk camp, which contained mostly the wives of so-called traitors to their country (most of whom were shot), there was also a Moscow professor's wife who had evidently ended up with us by accident. This professor once received an award from Kalinin, and used the occasion to present his case. Kalinin replied, "My dear friend, I'm in the same position! I can't even help my own wife — there's no way I can help yours!"

Years passed, war broke out, and in 1944, as victory approached, the leaders talked of an amnesty. The ailing Soviet president was a particularly passionate advocate of the amnesty. This must have made Stalin smile: Kalinin was missing his wife.

Kalinin's helplessness casts new light on Budyonny's inability to help his second wife. Yet Kalinin did have the advantage over everyone else in Russia of being the first to know of Stalin's latest decrees. Learning of the amnesty that he was to sanction, he immediately summoned his children and dictated a letter to Stalin requesting that their mother be pardoned. On Victory Day, Ekaterina Ivanovna's sister traveled to the camp where she was incarcerated and gave her the

Ekaterina Ivanovna Kalinina

Five days later, after her arrest

The Kalinins outside the Kremlin

petition to sign. Ekaterina Ivanovna refused, protesting that she was guilty of nothing, but her sister shouted at her, the petition was sent, and finally the Presidium of the Supreme Soviet of the USSR, headed by Ekaterina Ivanovna's husband, decreed: "Ekaterina Ivanovna Kalinina to be released forthwith . . . and all rights restored. Signed, Secretary of the Presidium of the Supreme Soviet of the USSR, A. Gorkin."

This must have been the only Presidium decree not to bear Kalinin's signature. It was dated December 14, 1946. If family memories are accurate and the decree was not backdated, this means that it took eighteen months for the proud Estonian's letter to travel from the camp to Stalin's desk, and from Stalin's desk to the Presidium.

In the years that followed her release, Ekaterina Ivanovna battled tirelessly to clear her name. On August 24, 1954, she delivered a handwritten letter to State Public Prosecutor Rudenko:

> On April 22, 1939, I was found guilty of belonging to a Trotskyite organization, of having links with Trotskyites, and of advocating terror. The methods used in the interrogation forced me to give false testimony. My first interrogators, Ivanov and Khoroshkevich, whom I regard as direct agents of fascism, broke all Soviet laws with regard to investigation procedures, failing to show me any specific evidence, merely shouting at me that I was a terrorist, a spy, and a member of a counterrevolutionary organization, and that I had better admit it because they could prove it. I suggested that if the prosecution had slanderous material against me they should check it with me. They replied that there was nothing to check, that everything had been checked before my arrest, and it only remained for me to confess.
>
> When I was transferred to Lefortovo jail fifteen days later, I was sealed naked in a freezing basement and beaten, which made me break down and state falsely that I had expressed anti-Soviet views about collective farms. The transcript was drawn up by the interrogator, and then they made me sign it.
>
> On the night of December 9–10 I had a face-to-face meeting with Ostroumova. No transcript of this meeting was made and we signed nothing, but three months later we were made to sign a transcript, supposedly of this meeting. I don't know when and where that transcript was concocted, but it bore no relation to the evidence Ostroumova gave in my presence, even though it was signed by her.

I asked the interrogators to let me have a defense lawyer, since my reading and writing is poor. I'm not Russian and can't always express my thoughts.

In view of the above, I ask you, citizen Public Prosecutor, to protest against this unjust sentence and to exonerate me of a non-existent crime dreamed up to the advantage of our enemies.

The differences between the tone of Kalinina's letter and that of her interrogation minutes make it clear that the transcript was later fabricated to bolster the case against her. They also suggest that Ostroumova may not in fact have slandered herself and her friend after all.

The final document in Kalinina's file states:

It is clear that at the moment of Kalinina's arrest there was no evidence against her of any anti-Soviet activities, apart from the unspecified evidence of Ostroumova. Arrested on October 25, 1938, Kalinina was illegally held in custody until February 13, 1939, and the public prosecutor's permission was received only after she had made her confession. It is therefore established that Kalinina's arrest was an act of retribution by Beria and Kobulov, who were directly involved in the investigation of her case and are now exposed as enemies of the people.

The fact that this document is dated on the same day as Kalinina's letter shows that the new Khrushchev era was in a hurry to expiate old sins, and that the process was starting at the very top.

Ekaterina Ivanovna's granddaughter has collected numerous books, photographs, and papers relating to her beloved grandparents, and when the Kalinin Museum was dismantled she gathered all the archive material she could lay her hands on. Her grandmother apparently told her little of her prison experiences, and it had not occurred to her to investigate the files at the Lubyanka Prison.

She describes Ostroumova as a strong woman who worked hard in difficult circumstances to support two children on her own. She was puzzled that Ekaterina Ivanovna never mentioned Ostroumova or visited her two children when she got out, yet when told about Ostroumova's evidence against Ekaterina Ivanovna she exclaimed, "Poor

Valya, people said she was dreadfully tortured in jail — they had to carry her out when it was over!"

This generous and sensitive woman realizes that one cannot judge those who have endured torture. She will never speak ill of her extraordinary, contradictory grandmother, who fought so valiantly to remain true to the people and her principles and escape the life of a figurehead.

11

"The Personal Has No Social Significance"

Lazar Moiseyevich Kaganovich (1893–1991), born to a poor Jewish family near Kiev. At fourteen he worked as a bootmaker, and he joined the Party in 1911. From 1914 onward he worked in the Ukrainian underground, and in 1917 was elected to the Party's Central Committee, later becoming secretary of the Moscow Committee and overseer of the country's transportation system, heavy industry, and fuel production. During World War II he was a member of the State Defense Committee and strengthened the Party ranks in the Northern Ukraine. Like Molotov, considered to be one of Soviet Russia's most die-hard Stalinists, his gradual decline started after Stalin's death, and in 1957 he was expelled from the Presidium and the Central Committee and relieved of all Party posts.

As THE SOVIET SYSTEM scythed and leveled its human resources, fear was a daily staple and worked its way deep into the Russian character. While the masses lived surrounded by whispers and informers, those high up in the Kremlin focused their fears on Josif Vissarionovich, who kept even his closest entourage in a constant state of terror. The monolithic might of that one figure rendered the entire USSR population powerless. Since the leadership lived in daily fear, so did their wives, their children, and their grandchildren. Terror is what drove Galina Egorova, Olga Budyonnaya, and Ekaterina Kalinina to incriminate themselves. These strong women had expressed themselves freely and in so doing had broken Stalin's unwritten laws of conduct. In the post-Stalin era the cases fabricated against these women were said to have "violated the principles of socialist legality."

As individual needs became subsumed by the needs of society, couples had to think and act in complete unison; divorce was fraught with painful consequences for the party supporting the losing side. Lenin and Krupskaya thought alike; she often disagreed with him, but was extraordinarily good at finding common ground. Stalin and Alliluyeva's inability to understand each other was itself a kind of bond. But most Kremlin couples tried to emulate (offically, anyway) the sort of harmony that existed between Lazar and Maria Kaganovich.

Maria Markovna Kaganovich died in the 1960s. In the summer of 1991 I was able to meet with her husband, Lazar Moiseyevich, and their daughter, Maya. Lazar Moiseyevich's refusal to talk to journalists and historians has encouraged the most lurid gossip. His daughter angrily dismissed claims made in Stuart Kahan's *Wolf of the Kremlin,* which recently appeared in Russia, that she and Kaganovich's sister, her aunt Rosa, a doctor, had affairs with Stalin and had been known as "Stalin's unwed wives." "I was never even close to Stalin, and Lazar Kaganovich didn't have a sister named Rosa — there was no such person!"

According to the Kaganoviches' daughter-in-law, Serafima Mikhailovna Gopner, "Stalin did have a mistress and her name was Valya. She was his maid. It was a known fact. She apparently loved him."

Serafima Mikhailovna also told me about her relationship with the Kaganoviches' son, Yuri, a graduate from the prestigious Zhukov Military Academy:

> Yuri and I went out for five years before we married. He was a good man, his only problem was that he drank. He was surrounded by people who drank with him and bailed him out when he made mistakes. The Kaganoviches had adopted him, but they never made anything of it.
>
> Maria Markovna and Lazar Moiseyevich loved each other very much and were devoted to their family. Every weekend we all had to get together at their government dacha. We dreaded having to sit around the table listening to the same old stories. I can still see them all. Most of them were coarse, crude people, Stalin especially. As for Alliluyeva, she was a gentle soul, and she couldn't bear any of it.

We all lived in the Kremlin, to the right of the Spassky Tower. When Khrushchev arrived, he moved us to private mansions outside the Kremlin in the Lenin Hills. They were freezing cold — the walls were covered with ice in winter! The basement was like a bomb shelter. We were given a monthly food allowance of 1,000 rubles.

When Yuri was banished to the town of Engels, Serafima Mikhailovna did everything she could to get him back and lived modestly.

Maya Lazarevna Kaganovich has also lived for the past thirty years in the shadow of family disgrace. In the old photographs of her, youth softens the sharpness of her features and lends a gentle plumpness to her cheeks, which glow with the patina of Soviet well-being. It is an intelligent face. An architect with two children, Maya Lazarevna is a neat, small, timid woman with a soft, pleasant voice.

Mama was a good person. When I was sixteen she and Father decided to adopt a little boy from a children's home, and I helped choose him. We went around all the children's homes together, and we finally chose a beautiful dark little boy called Yuri — he looked just like us.

Mama loved children. For years she was director of a children's home. She was strict, though.

Long after her death, my mother's friends from work still got together once a year to visit her grave and talk about her. It touched me deeply. In the last years of her life she had been the wife of a man who was not merely disgraced and persecuted, but hated and despised.

Some in the Party might have regarded it as insulting for the Bolsheviks' wives to be distributing charity to the people they were supposed to serve. Yet Maya Lazarevna did, and I have heard of no other Kremlin wife who followed her example.

Lenin and Krupskaya set the Kremlin fashion for ostentatious simplicity. Stalin first tightened then loosened the reins, allowing the Kremlin families excessive privileges and then using these privileges as a weapon against them when he needed to. As Jews, Lazar and Maria Kaganovich tried to live by Stalin's laws, but it did not work. Lazar's brother Mikhail was shot as a spy and an "enemy of the people."

In her autobiography, the singer Galina Vishnevskaya describes her visits in the Kremlin shortly after Stalin's death. The occasion was Nikolai Bulganin's birthday party.

Various Kremlin officials and their wives were there. One could hear Kaganovich's shrill voice, with its heavy Jewish accent. Even here among friends, he was proclaiming slogans and newspaper headlines as toasts: "Glory to the Communist Party! Long live the Soviet Union!"

Most of the women were short, dumpy, and tended to say nothing. They were buttoned-up and tense. Each of them clearly wanted to go home as soon as possible, where they could rule the roost again. There could be no hint of elegance — not a single long evening dress or decent hairstyle. These women were so faceless that I wouldn't have recognized them if I had met one of them on the street the next morning. Their husbands generally did not appear with them in public, and wives were not often seen at official functions.

Tired of the rumors and innuendos about her mother, Maya Lazarevna handed me a copy of the family-approved biography.

Maria Markovna Kaganovich joined the Communist Party in 1909. She left school at a young age and went to work in various textile factories, joining the workers' revolutionary movement as a member of the underground Bolshevik organization in Kiev, the Dnepropetrovsk and Yuzov Party committees, and underground and trade union groups in various other towns.

During the period of the October Revolution and the Civil War, Maria Markovna carried out important Party assignments as president and deputy president of the Nizhny Novgorod and Voronezh Party committees, as deputy people's commissar of social welfare in Tashkent, and as member of the Regional Committee of the Bolshevik Party. In the years that followed, she worked for the Party in the major industrial centers of Gomel, Leningrad, Moscow, and Kharkov.

For her services to revolutionary activity, her dedicated hard work, and the fulfillment of the directives of the Party and the unions in the building of socialism, Maria Markovna was awarded the Order of Lenin and the Medal of Honor. Since 1958, Maria Markovna has received a special state pension.

At the end of her mother's life, after Lazar Moiseyevich's downfall, Maya Lazarevna drank the bitter cup of shame.

Everything was confiscated, and we were given a pension of 115 rubles 20 kopecks, later increased by 20 rubles. We were barred from the Kremlin medical clinic, and when Father was ill he had to go to an ordinary hospital. It was dreadful! I finally plucked up the courage to write to Khrushchev, Brezhnev, and Kosygin (that was after Mother died), and Father was admitted to the medical clinic again.

Maya Lazarevna obtained her father's agreement to be interviewed for this book. In his ninety-eighth year, Kaganovich still did not want to discuss anything personal about his wife. Maya quoted him to me, "The personal has no social significance." I decided to pass on the interview.

Kaganovich's refusal to discuss anything personal is telling but not unusual. In Stalin's Russia, private life was dead. The Bolsheviks failed to realize their dreams in good part because their search for the collective made them lose sight of the personal.

12

A Pearl Set in Iron

*Vyacheslav Mikhailovich Skryabin, 1890–1986 (revolutionary name —
Molotov), born to an educated family in Vyatka province. Drawn to revolutionary politics in 1905 at the age of fifteen, he spent two years in prison
and exile, where he became friends with Stalin. He then studied economics
in St. Petersburg and joined the* Pravda *editorial board. In October 1917
he became a member of Petrograd's Military Revolutionary Committee,
then chair of its Economic Council. During the Civil War he occupied
leading posts in various towns, and in 1921 Lenin appointed him secretary
of the Party's Central Committee. Appointed president of the Council of
People's Commissars, he became Stalin's right hand and in 1937 conducted
a massive and bloody purge of the Ukrainian CP. After Stalin's rapproche-
ment with Hitler in 1939 he replaced Litvinov as head of the Commissariat
for Foreign Affairs, where he remained until 1949. After Stalin's death
he was forced to issue a public self-criticism and was banished to a diplomatic
post in Mongolia following his unsuccessful campaign against Khrushchev.
Along with Kaganovich and Malenkov, he was expelled from the Party in
1961. He spent the years until his death tending his garden and writing,
and was readmitted to the Party in 1986.*

IN RUSSIAN, "ZHEMCHUZHINA" means pearl. A lovely name. Paulina
Semyonovna Zhemchuzhina, a poor Jewish girl from a Cossack village
in Zaporozhe, was nineteen when she was elected to attend the International Women's Conference held in Moscow in 1921. She had

been a Bolshevik for three years, and her red kerchief merged with the thousands of others gathered in the Kremlin that summer. However, Vyacheslav Molotov, who was helping organize the conference, spotted her immediately, and she did not return to Zaporozhe. Quick-witted and clear-headed, Paulina Zhemchuzhina quickly grasped all there was to know within the Kremlin, and soon became one of its most powerful women.

The Molotovs shared an apartment with the Stalins in what is now the new Palace of Congresses building. The two wives were roughly the same age and became friends. No one knew Nadezhda Alliluyeva better than Paulina Zhemchuzhina. It was Paulina Zhemchuzhina who led the distraught Nadezhda from the dining room in November 1932 after Stalin had publicly humiliated her. During their long walk around the Kremlin together afterward it was Zhemchuzhina again who comforted Alliluyeva in her distress. When Nadezhda's nurse discovered her body the next morning, the first to be called were Enukidze and Zhemchuzhina.

Many historians assume that Stalin nurtured a secret hatred for Paulina Zhemchuzhina and wonder why he waited until 1949 to arrest her. Stalin would have had no problem in disposing of her in the 1930s had he wished to; the NKVD was functioning smoothly, prying into people's most intimate secrets, especially those involving inhabitants of the Kremlin. Moreover, Paulina Zhemchuzhina had committed one glaring crime: her elder brother was an American capitalist who had left Russia at the turn of the century, and she sometimes wrote to him. A serious crime!

Yet Paulina Zhemchuzhina nevertheless climbed to a position of strength, first as deputy commissar of the food industry, then as commissar of the fish industry, and finally as director of the state perfume industry, Glavparfumeria. Like everyone else, she had occasional problems at work. According to Molotov, the Germans preferred Soviet perfumes to French brands, and in 1939 she was reprimanded and temporarily expelled from the Party when Glavparfumeria was infiltrated by German spies trying to steal the secrets of its success. But she was quickly reinstated and appointed director of the knitwear and fancy goods industry.

Throughout her life, Paulina Zhemchuzhina remained dedicated to the Party and its leader, and each of her appointments was personally authorized by Stalin.

Although it is generally assumed that Paulina Zhemchuzhina was best friends with Nadezhda Alliluyeva, contemporary accounts concur that Paulina Zhemchuzhina had been bitterly critical of Nadezhda Alliluyeva for killing herself. Far from mourning the loss of her friend, she had condemned her for selfishly abandoning Stalin and the children.

Paulina Zhemchuzhina's love for her husband and family fused with her devotion to Stalin and the Party. It appears possible that she loved the leader as a woman too, and that her devotion tied his hands.

Zhemchuzhina's photographs show a strong face, a slim figure, haughty gaze, curly hair, and elegant hands. She can hardly have been attractive to Stalin; she was too active and political for his taste. Molotov, on the other hand, was fully aware that women were prone to fall in love with Stalin. In Molotov's memoirs he describes his relationship with Stalin before the Revolution: "We wrote to each other from exile, and after we became friends we shared an apartment. Then he stole my girlfriend Marusya. Stalin was a good-looking man whom women found attractive, and he had a lot of success with them."

Molotov acknowledged Stalin's supremacy in all things and remained his shadow, but such treachery can rankle. As for Stalin and Paulina, they were liberated Marxists and close neighbors, and Stalin could do as he pleased. A complicating factor was that all the Kremlin wives feared that Stalin would marry an outsider eager to take her place in the Kremlin. Who could object if on occasion he sometimes slept with his wife's best friend and his best friend's wife? There was nothing crude here, and there was nothing vulgar about the complex and contradictory Zhemchuzhina.

She always seemed to end up on top. The Molotovs had the best apartment in the Kremlin, and under her watchful eye they built a luxurious dacha in which they held state and international receptions. After the Molotovs moved to another apartment next door, the Stalin household was filled with tension. Stalin preferred to spend his time at the Molotovs'. Clever Paulina Zhemchuzhina knew how to surround people with warmth and comfort; Stalin appreciated that. In his memoirs Molotov describes how the two families would spend intimate evenings around the table together, and how Paulina Zhemchuzhina, unlike Nadezhda, would always take Stalin's side.

When the place of First Lady of the Kremlin fell vacant after Nadezhda Alliluyeva's death, Paulina Zhemchuzhina quietly filled it —

The Molotovs and the Stalins

unofficially at first. Throughout almost the entire period of Stalin's life without Nadezhda Alliluyeva, Paulina Zhemchuzhina was always there for him. And since she herself had an army of guards and servants at her command, she was able to shoulder many of his domestic problems, including the education of his daughter, Svetlana. The Molotovs' daughter had been born shortly after the Stalins', and they had named her Svetlana, too. Who better than Paulina to supervise the upbringing of the first Kremlin girls?

She took this task seriously, though if Svetlana Stalin did not agree with her she did not insist. There were gymnastics and music lessons. ("It enhances a girl's image to sit down at the piano while the party is in full swing and play a polonaise," she said.) There were German and French classes, and English lessons with Doris Hart-Maxin, known to millions worldwide for her English-language broadcasts from the Soviet Union.

Doris Hart was a well-heeled English girl who had fallen in love with communism in the early 1930s and worked at the British Communist Party under Ivan Maisky of the Soviet embassy in London. There she met Alexei Maxin, the ambassador's chauffeur, who took her for drives in the embassy Rolls Royce. They fell in love, and he took her back with him to live in Moscow, where she ended up working for Radio Moscow. Doris gave English lessons to the two Svetlanas; English lessons with Doris Hart-Maxin had become a status symbol for the Kremlin aristocracy.

Doris recalls, "The two Svetlanas came together and studied together. They were sweet, modest girls. They wore wretchedly thin fur coats. When Svetlana Molotova caught me looking at hers, she said, 'Mama doesn't want people in town to know who I am — we have to be modest, the whole country's looking at us.' "

A man who studied with Svetlana Molotova at the Institute of Foreign Relations ten years later remembers her differently, however. "She was chauffeured to the Institute wearing a new outfit every day. Going up the stairs one would be assailed by the smell of French perfume, and know that Svetlana Molotova had just passed."

As the months turned to years, Paulina Semyonovna Zhemchuzhina — boundlessly energetic wife of the Kremlin leader, mature and powerful Soviet commissar, mistress of a large household — unobtrusively made the post of First Lady her own. As the years turned into decades, she could anticipate Stalin's moods and always knew when to step back, when to move up. Beria, for one, did not appreciate Paulina's power in the Kremlin, and must have kept his eye on her from the moment he arrived at the Ministry of Internal Affairs. Her subsequent problems make it clear that he had been collecting material against her from the start.

She was unbowed by her problems, known never to be fearful or cautious. The daughter of the Molotovs' chauffeur happened to be with her in the Crimea on June 22, 1941, the day the German Army invaded Russia. "Early in the morning of June 22, Vyacheslav Mikhailovich telephoned her from Moscow urging us to return at once. Paulina Semyonovna calmly packed her bags and summoned the hairdresser, and at midday, as she listened to Molotov's declaration of war over the radio, she had a manicure."

Evacuated early on to the village of Molotov's parents in Vyatka, Paulina Zhemchuzhina moved with her daughter to Kuibyshev, the main evacuation center. She returned to Moscow in 1942. For several years after the war Zhemchuzhina and her sizable entourage would visit the spa at Karlovy Vary, in Czechoslovakia. On their way there they would stay with Marshal Katukov, commander of Soviet troops in the GDR, whose Dresden home became a place of pilgrimage for Soviet higher-ups, enticed by Germany's fur and fabrics and all the Sevres and Meissen china that miraculously survived the war. In the 1930s, Katukov's wife, Ekaterina Sergeyevna, an intelligent woman, had married a Kremlin official who was arrested and shot, and she herself had spent two years in Butyrki jail before walking from Moscow to Berlin with the marshal and marrying him. She recalls the arrival of Paulina Zhemchuzhina and her daughter at her Dresden villa:

> They were both lavishly dressed and covered in furs — Svetlana was wearing a mink stole. Paulina Zhemchuzhina was a clever, powerful woman. There were about fifty people traveling with them on the same plane, but they all needed separate accommodations. It was a problem finding room for them all. I traveled with Paulina Zhemchuzhina and her entourage on to Karlovy Vary. Even though they had been my houseguests for several days, she never looked at me again and no longer recognized me.

Three years after the war ended Paulina Zhemchuzhina's troubles began. While Ekaterina Voroshilova, Maria Kaganovich, and other

Jewish wives held their Jewishness deep within them, Paulina Zhemchuzhina embraced with open arms the newly formed Soviet Jewish Antifascist Committee and the newly founded state of Israel. The Soviet government was the first to open diplomatic relations with Israel, and she threw a reception in honor of Israel's new ambassador to Moscow, Golda Meir. When prominent Jews urged the Party Central Committee to establish a Jewish autonomous region in the Crimea, Paulina supported the idea, and her regular meetings with Golda Meir spawned rumors that the two women had been friends since their school years and were drawing up a blueprint of the plan.

By the end of 1948 relations between the USSR and the new state of Israel had deteriorated disastrously, all talk of a Jewish homeland in the USSR had ceased, and leading members of the Jewish community were being arrested as "rootless cosmopolitans." This, however, didn't seem to deter Paulina Zhemchuzhina from pursuing her relationship with Meir and members of the Jewish Antifascist Committee. What game was Paulina playing? Had this loyal Stalinist forgotten her place?

The status of women in the Kremlin had evolved a lot over the past two decades. In the 1920s they had been mistresses of their fate. In the 1930s they turned into "Party aunties," imbued with Party spirit. In the 1940s they relaxed a little, and the more they let their hair down, the more danger they put themselves in. Meanwhile, Beria had been gathering his evidence; and the time had come to round up his witnesses and move into action. As the Jewish witch-hunt reached its height and Stalin no longer needed Paulina Zhemchuzhina's domestic warmth, Beria presented Stalin with his evidence. She was arrested at work and interrogated, but released soon afterward. Realizing that her arrest was imminent, she left the Molotov house and went to live with her brother and sister. "If the Party demands it, we'll divorce,"* she told her husband.

For the next eight months Paulina Zhemchuzhina did not communicate with her family for fear of incriminating them. Occasionally Svetlana's husband would visit his disgraced mother-in-law in the evening after work to give her news of the family and drive her to the gates of their government dacha on the outskirts of Moscow. While

---

* *Molotov told this to the poet Felix Chuev, who met him frequently in the last years of his life and published a book of interviews with him.*

this once proud and fearless woman was being crushed by the Party machine and uncomplainingly awaiting prison, her powerful husband did not ask Stalin that his wife be spared, nor did he challenge Beria to a duel. He suffered in silence in the name of communism and the future, in which he sincerely believed, just as he believed in his wife's guilt.

The following February, Paulina Zhemchuzhina was arrested along with her brother and sister at their home. Molotov described to Felix Chuev how she was summoned before the Central Committee and accused of "sustaining criminal relations with Jewish nationalists for several years, and conducting enemy work with them against the Soviet Union."

Molotov told Chuev:

> My knees trembled when Stalin read out to the Politburo the accusation against Paulina Semyonovna, which he had received from his Cheka agents. He and I quarreled about it, but there was nothing to be done. The Cheka had pounced and she couldn't escape. She was charged with associating with Zionist organizations and with the Israeli ambassador Golda Meir, and with wanting to turn the Crimea into an autonomous Jewish republic. She should have been more careful with her friends.
>
> When I told her the charges against her she screamed, "And you believe them?"
>
> She spent two years in jail and over three years in the camps. When Beria saw me at Politburo meetings he would always hiss in my ear: "Paulina's alive!"

In these terrible times, Stalin and Beria had all the power. The men of the Politburo were like spiders in a jar, each wrestling for power and with his own helplessness, not daring to raise questions, even about his own wife.

By moving in with her sister, Paulina Zhemchuzhina destroyed her, and she later died in prison. Paulina was held at the Lubyanka headquarters and interrogated. The film star Tatyana Okunevskaya, who was imprisoned there at the same time, recalls hearing a shrill female voice shouting through the open door of her cell: " 'Phone my husband! Tell him to send my diabetes pills! I'm an invalid! You've no right to feed me this rubbish!' I learned that this was Zhemchuzhina, Molotov's wife, and that he had abandoned her and might even be imprisoned himself."

Meanwhile, Molotov was in the Kremlin, sustained at Politburo meetings by Beria's mocking words of hope, "Paulina's alive!"

The case against Paulina Semyonovna Zhemchuzhina consists of four pale blue files, the first three containing the transcript of the interrogations of the accused and the witnesses, the fourth containing various relevant documents, including the accused's personal correspondence with various people, birthday greetings, petitions, and appeals.

There is a letter from the writer Galina Serebryakova, who wrote to her from the camps. A man named Belinkov wrote, pleading for the release of his son, Arkady, arrested for writing an "anti-Soviet novel." Other workers wrote her from various prisons. There is a note from Academician Lina Stern asking her to pass on a letter to Molotov.

Paulina Zhemchuzhina was meticulous about responding. She carried on correspondence with Serebryakova, asking about her latest novel and offering to have it typed for her. She tried to ease the fate of Arkady Belinkov, who was seriously ill. She wrote to public prosecutors and judges, asking them to investigate further.

The compromising material in the fourth file includes a photocopy (unsigned) of a letter written by Paulina to her brother Karp, the American capitalist. Here is her "criminal communication" with her brother and his family, written on May 10, 1946:

> My dears,
>
> Since someone is visiting your parts I am using this opportunity to drop you a line. We are all well. Throughout the country rebuilding work continues apace as we struggle to heal the wounds inflicted on us by the fascist aggressor, and the people are toiling selflessly to fulfill the new Five-Year Plan. Little Svetlanochka left her school with a certificate and a gold medal. She is now studying at the Institute of Foreign Relations. Her English is excellent, so if your daughters visit us she will have no problems in talking to them. I am working in the textile industry but unfortunately I haven't been well lately. Greetings and kisses to Sonya and the children.

An earlier letter, dated April 18, 1945, is from Salomon Mikhoels, director of Moscow's Jewish Theater:

> Esteemed Paulina Semyonovna,
>
> I hope you will forgive me for daring to trouble you. I am led to do so by a matter of public importance concerning our critic Abram Solomonovich Gurvich, who at a comparatively early age has suffered

a paralysis of the limbs. According to the doctors, his illness is curable. Knowing your generosity, I am asking for your kind help in arranging for him to be admitted to the Kremlin hospital. I repeat, I am loath to trouble you, and hope that you will forgive me. With deep respect and gratitude,

Mikhoels.

Mikhoels was no longer alive by the time of Paulina Zhemchuzhina's first interrogation on June 8, 1948, when one of the witnesses was a member of the Jewish Antifascist Committee named Fefer. It is questionable whether Paulina Zhemchuzhina played any significant role in schemes concerning a Jewish Crimea. It also seems likely that the Jews who testified against her did so because she was a woman. Her real crime was her Jewishness. The first part of her lengthy interrogation was intended to establish whether she had once attended a synagogue service three years earlier. For a Party member to visit a place of worship was considered incompatible with Party membership and thus a crime. Hence Zhemchuzhina's steadfast denial of the undeniable evidence that she had been there.

> FEFER: When Mikhoels was a member of the Jewish Antifascist Committee, he told me Zhemchuzhina used to attend plays at the Jewish Theater, and that he chatted with her once in the director's room during a performance. She said she was deeply interested in our affairs, the life of Jews in the Soviet Union, and the work of the Jewish Antifascist Committee. Mikhoels said: "She is a good Jewish daughter." He told me he once complained to her that there was so much hostility to Jews and that she had replied, "It's bad at the top."
>
> INTERROGATOR'S QUESTION TO FEFER: What did that mean?
>
> FEFER: I looked at Mikhoels and asked him how I should take these words, and he said he understood her to mean anti-Semitism wasn't just a local problem, but that many of the leaders supported this policy of oppressing and discriminating against the Jews.
>
> QUESTION TO ZHEMCHUZHINA: What do you say to that?
>
> ZHEMCHUZHINA: It's pure lies, invented either by Mikhoels or Fefer.
>
> QUESTION TO ZHEMCHUZHINA: Were you at the theater, and did you talk to Mikhoels?
>
> ZHEMCHUZHINA: I was at the theater, but I deny Fefer's account of my conversation with Mikhoels.
>
> QUESTION TO FEFER: Were you present at the synagogue on March 14, 1945?

FEFER: I rarely attend synagogue, but on that day I was there. On March 14 prayers were said for Jews killed in World War II. Many people attended, including the actors Peisen, Khromchenko, and Utesov, as well as several academicians, professors, and even generals. I also saw Zhemchuzhina there with her brother. I went in and sat down in the fifth or sixth row, facing the pulpit. According to synagogue tradition, the women sit upstairs, but exceptions are made for particularly important women and an exception was made for Zhemchuzhina.

QUESTION TO FEFER: Was Zhemchuzhina seen by everybody present?

FEFER: All the Jewish high-ups there recognized her — everybody knows her.

QUESTION TO ZHEMCHUZHINA: Were you at the synagogue?

ZHEMCHUZHINA: No, I was not, it was my sister.

QUESTION TO FEFER: Are you quite sure that it was Zhemchuzhina you saw at the synagogue?

FEFER: Quite sure. All the Jews in town were talking about it.

QUESTION TO ZHEMCHUZHINA: Do you still deny you were there?

ZHEMCHUZHINA: I was not at the synagogue.

Later that day Zhemchuzhina was confronted by Zusskind, administrator of the Jewish Theater and member of the Jewish Antifascist Committee.

INTERROGATOR'S QUESTION TO ZUSSKIND: Did Zhemchuzhina attend the funeral of Mikhoels?

ZUSSKIND: Yes, she did. On the evening of January 15, 1948, I stood beside the grave taking the wreaths from all the various organizations and there I saw Paulina Semyonovna. We exchanged greetings. I expressed my grief at Mikhoels's death, and Paulina Semyonovna asked me if I thought it was an accident or murder. I said that on the basis of the information I had received it appeared that Mikhoels had died in a car crash. Paulina Semyonovna rejected this — she said she thought it was murder, and things weren't as simple as people would have us believe.

QUESTION TO ZHEMCHUZHINA: Did you say that?

ZHEMCHUZHINA: No.

QUESTION TO ZUSSKIND: Were you at the synagogue on March 14, 1945?

ZUSSKIND: Yes, I was. I saw Paulina Semyonovna there — she was sitting right opposite me.

QUESTION TO ZUSSKIND: Are you sure it was Zhemchuzhina?

ZUSSKIND: Absolutely sure, I am inventing nothing. We exchanged greetings.

QUESTION TO ZHEMCHUZHINA: Your presence at the synagogue is confirmed by both Fefer and Zusskind, who know you well and greeted you there. What have you to say?

ZHEMCHUZHINA: I was not at the synagogue.

The same line of questioning was pursued on December 26, 1948, in a confrontation between Zhemchuzhina and an elder of the Moscow synagogue, who confirmed that he had seen her in the synagogue three years earlier and had arranged for her to sit downstairs. Yet again, Zhemchuzhina hotly denied that she had been there.

Paulina Zhemchuzhina's interrogation started in earnest on February 4, 1948, following her arrest:

QUESTION: Is Zhemchuzhina your real name?

ZHEMCHUZHINA: No, my real name is Semyonovna Karpovskaya — Zhemchuzhina is my underground name.

QUESTION: You worked in the underground?

ZHEMCHUZHINA: Yes.

QUESTION: Where?

ZHEMCHUZHINA: In the Ukraine, when it was occupied by Denikin's troops.

QUESTION: Who assigned you to do underground work behind the enemy lines?

ZHEMCHUZHINA: I assigned myself. The situation was desperate. In 1918 I was accepted into the Russian Communist Party by the Zaporozhe city Party organization, and shortly afterward I became leader of the Zaporozhe Party committee. In the autumn of 1919 Denikin advanced on Zaporozhe, and the whole regional Party apparatus was evacuated to Kiev. I was evacuated there too, along with a group of local committee workers. In Kiev we presented ourselves to the central committee of the Ukrainian Communist Party and were sent off in groups to work with various fighting units of the Red Army. I was appointed political worker with a regiment of the Ninth Army, which was stationed near Darnits, where I stayed for about two months. After that our regiment was forced to disperse under attack from the White troops, and I escaped back to Kiev.

QUESTION: It appears from your evidence that you were sent to the front to do political work with the troops, but that instead you escaped to Kiev. How would you regard this?

ZHEMCHUZHINA: I would now regard it as desertion from the battlefield, but I was young then and did not understand what was required of me. We had been told by the commissar of our regiment that the situation was hopeless and we should destroy all personal documents and get out to Kiev. That is what I did.

QUESTION: What did you do on arriving in Kiev?

ZHEMCHUZHINA: By then the town was in the hands of the White general, Bredov. I hid out for three days in the Mikhailov Monastery, unable to contact any of my comrades or receive instructions, until finally I escaped to Zaporozhe, which was also still under White occupation. In Zaporozhe I made contact with the Party organization and was sent to Kharkov to do underground Party work.

QUESTION: Why did you not stay in Zaporozhe?

ZHEMCHUZHINA: People in Zaporozhe knew I had been working for the Party committee, and I would have been identified. Only twenty-four hours after my return Denikin's counterintelligence troops started hunting for me, and they came to my home while I was out and searched it.

QUESTION: How did they treat your family?

ZHEMCHUZHINA: They didn't touch them.

QUESTION: How do you account for that? It's well known that people of Jewish background were generally punished by the Whites for no reason.

ZHEMCHUZHINA: I cannot explain it.

QUESTION: You cannot, because nothing of the sort happened?

ZHEMCHUZHINA: We were searched, the Whites ransacked my things, but I cannot explain why they dealt leniently with my family. In October or November 1919, I was in Kharkov. There I made contact with Dashevsky, who ran the passport section of Kharkov's underground Party organization. Dashevsky gave me a new passport in the name of Paulina Semyonovna Zhemchuzhina, and since then I have used this name.

QUESTION: How long did you work for the Central Committee of the Commmunist Party of the Ukraine?

ZHEMCHUZHINA: Not long. In 1921 the Ukrainian Party organization sent me as a delegate to the International Women's Congress in Moscow, and I stayed in the capital to work as Party organizer in the Rogozhsko-Simonov district. While attending the International Women's Congress I met Molotov, who was then secretary of the Central Committee of the Communist Party, and at the end of 1921, I became his wife.

Zhemchuzhina's next interrogation was six days later.

QUESTION: Are you prepared to talk truthfully about your crimes against the Soviet state?

ZHEMCHUZHINA: I have committed no crimes against the Soviet state. I deny the charges of having criminal contacts with Jewish nationalists.

QUESTION: You deny them because you want to hide the antigovernment nature of your contact with Mikhoels and other nationalists? Tell us how often you met Mikhoels.

ZHEMCHUZHINA: Not often. Our first meeting was in 1938 or 1939 at the Moscow Jewish Theater, where I attended a performance of *Tevye the Milkman*. Mikhoels came to my box at intermission and introduced himself as the theater's director. After this I had no further contact with him until the beginning of 1944, when a fellow director in the textile and fancy goods industry asked me to invite Mikhoels to talk to us about his trip to America. He accepted my invitation, and he gave his talk a few days later. In 1948 he visited our directors twice to invite me to a performance of *Freilekhs*. He also requested me to arrange for an actor at the Jewish Theater to enter the Kremlin Hospital for treatment, but I refused his request.

QUESTION: Tell us about the errands you performed for Mikhoels.

ZHEMCHUZHINA: In 1948 or 1947 Mikhoels asked me to pass on a letter to Molotov, who was then on a working trip abroad. I gave this letter to a secretary at the Soviet of Ministers to be forwarded to Molotov by the next post.

QUESTION: Did you know the contents of this letter?

ZHEMCHUZHINA: No, I did not read it and he did not inform me of what it said.

QUESTION: You're lying again! It is known that you not only agreed to pass on the letter but promised Mikhoels to raise the questions contained in it!

ZHEMCHUZHINA: I deny that. I saw nothing wrong in taking the letter from Mikhoels, and as for its contents, I repeat that I knew nothing about them.

INVESTIGATOR: Since you brazenly deny the known facts, the investigation is forced to expose you.

They led in prisoner Lozovsky, formerly head of the Informburo and member of the Soviet Jewish Antifascist Committee.

QUESTION TO LOZOVSKY: Did Jewish nationalists send slanderous letters to the Soviet government?

LOZOVSKY: Yes. In 1944 Mikhoels and Epstein, formerly chief secretary of the Soviet Jewish Antifascist Committee, received several letters from Jews in the Ukraine complaining of harassment from the local authorities. They asked me to protest this to the Soviet government. By then our nationalist work was well advanced, and after discussing the matter among ourselves we decided to write to Molotov presenting the facts cited in these letters, with the aim of forcing the Soviet government to grant concessions to the Jews. Since we received no answer, Mikhoels, Epstein, and I agreed to write another letter to Molotov, but fearing that this too would be ignored we decided to ensure a positive response from him by using our contacts.

QUESTION: You mean Zhemchuzhina?

LOZOVSKY: Yes, her.

Zhemchuzhina was then interrogated about her part in promoting a Jewish republic in the Crimea. For this they brought in Lozovsky's deputy, Yusefovich, another member of the Soviet Jewish Antifascist Committee.

YUSEFOVICH: Mikhoels and Fefer were the first to discuss the idea. We all agreed that the climate in the Crimea made it the most favorable place for the foundation of a Jewish republic.

QUESTION: It's not a question of the climate, but whether these plans to establish a Jewish state were done at the behest of your American bosses. Why conceal this?

YUSEFOVICH: That is true, but I only realized it afterward, when U. S. Congressman Goldberg visited the USSR. During Goldberg's first meeting with us in Moscow he expressed his satisfaction with our nationalist work and said the Crimea should be a Jewish glory, a Jewish California. He spoke of the Crimea's proximity to Palestine, and of the need to establish closer links between Soviet and Palestinian Jews. He clearly represented the interests of American Jewish organizations in establishing a Jewish state on Crimean territory, which could be used as a political base against the Soviet Union.

QUESTION: What was your connection with Zhemchuzhina's criminal ambitions?

YUSEFOVICH: With Goldberg's encouragement, Mikhoels and Fefer decided to use Zhemchuzhina to raise the issue with the Soviet government. Mikhoels said that he could rely on her support. We

> Jewish nationalists regarded Zhemchuzhina as our benefactor, someone who would lend a favorable ear to our requests and to Jewish problems in general. Mikhoels met her and explained our plans regarding the Crimea, and she promised to help us. Soon after this, in early 1944, he and Fefer drafted a letter about handing over the Crimea to the Jews.

Testimony was heard from all members of the Soviet Jewish Antifascist Committee interrogated during Zhemchuzhina's case, except for Academician Lina Solomonovna Stern. Stern was questioned interminably about the letter she sent Zhemchuzhina to pass on to Molotov, but refused to say anything more than "my relations with Paulina Semyonovna were of a warm and friendly nature."

The next stage of Paulina Zhemchuzhina's interrogation must have shattered her faith in humanity. Those who had ingratiated themselves with her when she was in power had turned into her accusers:

> You were a despot. When anyone tried to argue with you, you would shut them up. People were afraid of you because you were as cruel as Mother Morozova.* I'm not sticking up for you — it's all your fault I'm in prison now! You dragged us all down with you. Why should we defend you?

> Zhemchuzhina abused her position as Molotov's wife to trick the government into thinking everything was perfect at work. The whole staff of the Central Directorate knew the illegal, antigovernment methods she was using to procure extra funds. She often boasted that our Central Directorate was far better supplied than the ministry as a whole.

> On Saturdays she would gather a group of her friends together and invite us out to her dacha, where we would have a fine time eating and drinking. Knowing what we were up to, the collective at the factory didn't bother to do any work.

> She took all her colleagues' bonuses, and even their awards and medals.

Nor was Paulina Zhemchuzhina spared by her close relatives; terrified to death by the Lubyanka and demoralized by the investigation, they obviously hoped that a frank confession would save her:

---

* *Mother Morozova was a Moscow merchant of legendary cruelty.*

Polya, you weren't telling the truth. Remember when you returned from America in the spring of 1936, and you gave me a
letter and twenty dollars from Karp?

ZHEMCHUZHINA: I never gave you anything.

Polya, I've told them all about your friendship with Mikhoels, all
about your meetings with him, and all about your conversations
on so-called Jewish matters. I advise you to confess your crimes
honestly.

ZHEMCHUZHINA: I have nothing to confess, I'm guilty of nothing.

Remember, Polya, how you told me Mikhoels had described life
abroad, and he said they had real freedom over there, and that
we're not free here in the Soviet Union? And he complained that
the Soviet government had even closed our schools? You told me
yourself how he asked you to speak up for the Jews!

ZHEMCHUZHINA: I had no such conversation with Mikhoels.

And you said that when Mikhoels visited you he felt as though
he was visiting the Rabbi?

ZHEMCHUZHINA: I said no such thing.

Polya, you said the Jews were persecuted under the tsar and they're
still persecuted today, and that the government closed their eyes
when they heard about cases of anti-Semitism!

ZHEMCHUZHINA: I deny it.

A large part of Paulina Zhemchuzhina's interrogation was devoted
to prurient questions and statements about her sexual life, with frequent accusations of promiscuity and debauchery. She had a particularly painful confrontation with one of her colleagues, Ivan
Alexeyevich X., whose surname I have deliberately omitted. The previous slanders are little better, but at least these deal ostensibly with
"political" matters, about which a fair amount had already been written
in the press, whereas this man's words would simply disgrace his
surviving relatives.

QUESTION TO X: In your previous interrogation you revealed that the
Central Committee of the All-Russian Communist Party received
a letter in 1939 that contained certain allegations against you.
Who informed you of this letter?

X: Zhemchuzhina. She called me into her office and told me I had
been accused of making anti-Soviet remarks.

QUESTION: What measures were taken about this letter?

X: None. Zhemchuzhina just warned me to watch my step in future and not to indulge in any more anti-Soviet remarks.

QUESTION: So Zhemchuzhina took you under her wing?

X: I shall always be grateful to her for that.

QUESTION TO ZHEMCHUZHINA: When did you learn about the letter alleging X.'s anti-Soviet views?

ZHEMCHUZHINA: I know of no letter regarding X., and had no discussions with him on the subject.

X: Paulina Semyonovna, you called me into your office — it will be engraved in my memory for the rest of my life! Such things are never forgotten!

ZHEMCHUZHINA: I repeat, I received no letter regarding X.

QUESTION TO X: How did your relationship with Zhemchuzhina develop?

X: She proposed intimacy.

ZHEMCHUZHINA'S REPLY: Ivan Alexeyevich!

X: Paulina Semyonovna, don't deny it! You can't push me away!

QUESTION TO ZHEMCHUZHINA: Whom did you inform of your relationship with X.?

ZHEMCHUZHINA: I informed no one, since I had no relationship with X. I always regarded Ivan Alexeyevich as unreliable, and I told him so frankly several times, but I never thought he was a scoundrel.

X: Paulina Semyonovna, how can you call me a scoundrel? Think of my wife and children! If you'd thought about my family then you wouldn't have insulted me!

ZHEMCHUZHINA: Ivan Alexeyevich, are you inventing fantasies about me here in the hope of being pardoned and returned to your family? Is this how I should take your plea to think of your family?

X: You won't provoke me, Paulina Semyonovna. I remind you of my children and my broken family to make you confess your guilt toward me and them. Despite the fact that I had a wife and children, you forced me into an intimate relationship.

ZHEMCHUZHINA: I repeat, I had no intimate relationship with X. Indeed I often criticized him because people used to say that his naïveté and good nature often affected his judgment at work.

At the end of her lengthy interrogation, Paulina Zhemchuzhina denied her connection with the case of the Jewish nationalists, but admitted she was guilty of "defending arrested enemies of the people Serebryakova and Belinkov, and Party workers Dokuchaeva, Gubanova, Fedosova, and Grakhova. The list of enemies of the state defended by me is not limited to those cited in the minutes; there are numerous others, but the passage of time makes it hard for me to remember them all."*

The sentence was five years — hardly an exceptional one for the period — in the Kustanai camp in Siberia.

Paulina Zhemchuzhina's files contain several reports on Prisoner No. 12 from female secret agents at the camp:

> She said she used to live very well, and had a lot of lovely dresses. There was one she specially liked — a bottle-green worsted.

> We made pelmeni together, and she said she had a husband called Vladislav and a little girl called Svetlana. Every year on International Women's Day she celebrates the daughter's birthday.

> In the first year she drank a lot of vodka and wine.

> She said she once met Vladimir Ilyich Lenin at some congress, I don't remember which.

In January 1953, an operative group from the Ministry of State Security arrived at the camp with urgent instructions to transfer Paulina Zhemchuzhina to Moscow, ostensibly because "Prisoner No. 12 suffers from attacks of tachycardia as a result of experiencing extremes of joy or distress." In fact, Paulina Zhemchuzhina was being returned to the Lubyanka to be charged for her involvement in the "Doctors' Plot."† The agents were forbidden to tell Prisoner No. 12 the reason for her transfer, but she greeted the news with characteristic stoicism, saying: "I'm an adult woman, I don't need reasons. It's as the government decides." When she was searched before the journey to Moscow, she said: "You can turn everything upside down, but I swear on my daughter's life that you won't find anything criminal. For me the interests of the state come first." Nothing incriminating was found, though agents removed several notebooks filled with material from the Nineteenth Party Congress and résumés of the Marxist-Leninist classics.

Zhemchuzhina's second term at Lubyanka opened up yet another

---

* *Most of these women were probably not Jewish.*
† *On January 1, 1953, nine doctors were accused of having assassinated a number of Soviet leaders, the crime apparently being part of a "Zionist conspiracy."*

circle of hell for her. Contained in her files are excerpts from the interrogations of Doctors Vinogradov, Kogan, and Vovsi, who all confirmed that she was a Jewish nationalist. The writer Lev Sheinin was the only one who refused to slander her: "Zhemchuzhina and her daughter attended a performance of my play *The Duel* at the Lenin Komsomol Theater. She praised the play and regretted that her husband could not see it since the theater had no government box."

Although Zhemchuzhina's "criminal" letters were addressed to Molotov and were handed to him personally, her files predictably contain no testimony from the man with whom she had shared twenty-seven years of her life. Where was he all this time? It may be that he was interrogated, but that the interrogations of such important men were not recorded in criminal files. Zhemchuzhina had left their home shortly before her arrest, and for "Family Status" in her prison form she marked "Single."

Throughout February 1953, Zhemchuzhina was interrogated day after day at Lubyanka. Then suddenly, on March 2, it stopped. She had been incarcerated for five years.

The day of Stalin's funeral, March 9, 1953, was Molotov's birthday. After stepping down briskly from the tribune of the Mausoleum, Khrushchev and Malenkov asked him what he wanted for his birthday. "I want my Polya back!" he said tersely, and left with bowed head.

Rumors of Stalin's illness had percolated into the prison, and she must have been the only prisoner in the Gulag who passionately desired his recovery. On March 10 she was summoned to see Beria, who greeted her with the words: "You're a heroine!" She pushed him away, demanding: "How is Stalin?" On hearing the news of his death, she is said to have fallen senseless to the floor. Also present in Beria's office was her husband, Vyacheslav Mikhailovich Molotov.

According to most accounts she was released on March 10, but her files are dated March 23, meaning that Beria must have postdated his signature on the release document. The document carries one phrase that in its simplicity and singularity stands in witness to the age: "It is now established that the statements by Kogan and Vovsi in the case against Zhemchuzhina were extorted through brutality and beatings."

Zhemchuzhina's is the only case from the KGB files where I found an official admission to the use of torture.

* * *

When Paulina Zhemchuzhina was arrested, everyone assumed she would not survive the camps. Her daughter never heard from her. Despite suffering three heart attacks and undergoing major heart surgery in the seventeen years before her death, she looked better than ever. The trauma seemed not to have left a trace.

Svetlana Molotova's eldest daughter, Larissa Alexeyevna, a translator of English art books and specialist on the art of the pre-Raphaelites, was six when her grandmother, Paulina, returned from the camps. She recalls:

> They called me "Granny's little shadow." When she returned I went to live with them, and the Molotovs brought me up. She was devoted to me and took me everywhere, even to Party meetings. She and Grandfather were actively involved in my education. Everything that is good in me is their doing, everything bad is my own. She taught me everything. They developed my memory and comprehension. From an early age they would sit me down in the evenings and make me tell them everything I'd seen during the day — the waving trees, the smells. Then I had to repeat it in German.
>
> Mother never grew up. She had been terribly overprotected when she was young. She took our problems under Khrushchev terribly hard. All the lies probably hastened her death. She died suddenly of a heart attack.
>
> Granny was determined not to repeat the same mistakes with me. "Life is hard," she would say. "Things can change any moment. You must be prepared."
>
> She was like a giant bird, sheltering her nest with her wings. She helped everyone and people would crowd to see her, even when Grandfather was in disgrace under Khrushchev. People saw her as a real lady, kind and considerate.
>
> Starting in 1943 the Molotovs donated their medal coupons to a children's home.* (They both had a large number of medals, but didn't advertise that fact.) In 1957, after Grandfather was banished in disgrace to Mongolia, the Foreign Ministry received a telegram from the children's home asking why the money had stopped. It was then that they realized that the funds weren't from the Ministry at all but from the Molotovs' own pockets. A few years ago I was at the cemetery and saw an old woman at my grandparents' grave. She turned

---

* *People received coupons for medals then, which could be exchanged for cash.*

Young Zhemchuzhina, 1926. Nadezhda Alliluyeva, whose hand is on her knee, has been cut out: every family album was filled with such excisions

Vyacheslav and Paulina Zhemchuzhina Molotov with their daughter Svetlana

Zhemchuzhina after her release from prison, with her grandson

out to have been a nanny at the children's home. She was bowing from the waist and saying, "Thank you, Paulina Semyonovna! Thank you, Vyacheslav Mikhailovich! You were holy people. While you were alive the orphans did not die!"

Granny could endure anything. She went off to jail in a squirrel fur coat, and she came back in the same coat, now in tatters. All she would say of her experiences was, "You needed three things there: soap to keep you clean, bread to keep you fed, and onions to keep you well."

Upon her return she collapsed onto the sofa in the dining room, where she lay for six months. And from the sofa she directed the house. Her hands had started shaking, but she tried to control it by doing needlework. She often said she had always believed that Grandfather would save her, and we'd all be happy again. Their love was an exceptional thing. They never shared their pain, and their actions always matched their words. She created a splendid domestic routine for him. Neither of them ever raised their voice or swore. He would just say, "I'm sorry we quarreled, Polenka, I was wrong."

When asked why Molotov did not defend her, Paulina Zhem-chuzhina's younger granddaughter, Lyubov Alexeyevna, says: "He thought that speaking up for her would further destroy her. Those government men were all hostages!" She went on:

She was the dynamo of the family, the spirit of the house. She taught us grandchildren everything: cooking, sewing, knitting. She taught her own servant, a simple country girl, to be an excellent cook, and she waged an incessant war in the house for cleanliness and order. If she decided something, that was how it was done. She was an incomparably stronger character than Grandfather, of course — he lived by her rules. Meals were served at exactly the same time every day, with certain foods on certain days. On Wednesdays there were always milk noodles — come hell or high water there were always milk noodles. It was a family tradition for meals to be quickly served and cleared away. When Stalin ate with them he used to say, "I never have enough time for my food. Eat with me and we'll take our time."

In some ways her routine was a bit hard on Grandfather, but he put up with it because he needed her to organize his life for him.

Paulina Semyonovna and Vyacheslav Mikhailovich loved each other very deeply. They didn't coo over each other, but they were real lovers. I've never seen two people so much in love. Grandfather always came first for her, and only then we grandchildren.

She never spoke of prison and the camps. I only found out about all that after she died. She dedicated her life to the Party. In her last years she would summon up her last strength to attend meetings. Her faith in its ideals was totally genuine, without hypocrisy.

Excluded from power by Khrushchev, and suffering for her husband, Paulina despised the post-Stalin government for its treachery and fired off a series of letters demanding a range of privileges, including an increased pension and access to a dacha outside the town. "You may not respect him, but at least I was a people's commissar and member of the Central Committee," she wrote. As a result, the Molotovs were allowed a ministerial dacha in Zhukovka, and in 1967 their pension was increased to 250 rubles.

Paulina Zhemchuzhina remained passionately devoted to Stalin's memory. After he was unmasked in the late 1950s, at the time of "de-Stalinization," she told his daughter, Svetlana: "Your father was a genius. He destroyed the fifth column in our country, so when war came the Party and people were united." Puzzled by this loyalty, Svetlana recalled how she always added finely chopped onion to her borscht, saying "That's how Stalin liked it!"

She died on May 1, 1970. Her elder granddaughter, Larissa, recalled, "Just before her death she had a manicure. As she lay dying she called out to Vyacheslav Mikhailovich. Years later, when I sat by his deathbed, he mistook me for her, calling 'Polya, Polya!' "

All who met the widowed Molotov in the last years of his long life confirm his undying devotion to his wife's memory. Many years after her death Felix Chuev recalled, "On the November 7 holiday, Vyacheslav Mikhailovich would produce cognac and pour it out, crying, 'Lenin — One! Stalin — Two! Paulina Semyonovna — Three!' And smash the bottle."

Chuev reports that Molotov told him, "It was my great joy to have Paulina Semyonovna as my wife. Not only was she beautiful and clever, she was a true Bolshevik, a true Soviet. Life treated her badly because she was my wife, yet depite her sufferings she never blamed Stalin, and refused to listen to those who did, for history will discard those who blacken his name."

Paulina Zhemchuzhina's life, so characteristic of the interwoven faith and lies of the Stalin era, has passed almost unnoticed into history.

Which was she, Party machine or Jewish woman? Among all the reports and interrogations contained in her files there is a small piece of paper in her handwriting. It says, "With these four years of separation four eternities have flowed over my strange and terrible life. Only the thought of you forces me to live, and the knowledge that you may still need the remnants of my tormented heart and the whole of my immense love for you."

To whom were these words addressed? To her daughter? To her husband, who could not defend her? Or to Stalin? "Only the thought of you," "My immense love" — the passion these phrases conjure seems mysterious in its depth.

The Stalin-Zhemchuzhina-Molotov triangle seems to have nearly Shakespearean dimensions. All her life she thought and acted in harmony with Stalin. She even "understood" his persecution of the Jews. Perhaps she felt no need to forgive him for her arrest, since she considered herself guilty. Perhaps it was easier for her to accept her own small guilt than the immensity of his, since to acknowledge his would have meant destroying her ideals. Perhaps she knew everything, understood everything, hated everything, and suffered in silence. We shall never know.

Zhemchuzhina's granddaughters say that after Molotov's death, and even during the days of glasnost and perestroika, they were visited by secret service agents, who took away numerous papers with them. One wonders what these papers contain and where they are today.

13

Bluebeard's Women

Lavrenti Pavlovich Beria (1899–1953), son of Georgian peasants. In 1915 he attended Baku technical school, and in 1917 he joined the Bolsheviks. In 1921 he became head of the Georgian, then the Transcaucasus security police. In 1931 he was appointed first secretary of the Transcaucasus Party, and in 1935 he went to Moscow, where three years later he replaced Yezhov as head of the Ministry of Internal Affairs (the NKVD). He started by purging the police and went on to establish a regime based on torture, terrorism, and forced labor. In 1945 he was appointed marshal and put in charge of Soviet Russia's atomic research program. After Stalin's death, he was arrested and shot under mysterious circumstances.

THE GIRL IN THE APRICOT CLOUD

THE PRISONER is being interrogated by the prosecutor:

> QUESTION: Do you confess to the charges of criminal depravity against you?
>
> REPLY: Some of them, yes.
>
> QUESTION: And that your criminal depravity led you to associate with women attached to foreign intelligence agencies?
>
> REPLY: Maybe, I don't know.
>
> QUESTION: And that you instructed Sarkisov and Nadaria to keep lists of your mistresses? We have here nine lists containing the names of sixty-two women. Were these the lists of your mistresses?
>
> REPLY: Most of the women were my mistresses, yes.
>
> QUESTION: Were you infected with syphilis?

REPLY: I caught syphilis during the war, in 1943 I think, and had
treatment.

The prisoner is then charged with raping a fourteen-year-old
schoolgirl, who had his baby; the prisoner states that this was by
mutual consent.

Who is this prisoner? A medieval madman? A modern sex freak?
Leader of a gang of rapists? No, this was the Hero of Soviet Labor,
Lavrenti Beria, marshal of the Soviet Union, minister of Internal Af-
fairs of the USSR, Politburo member of the Central Committee of
the Russian Communist Party (Bolshevik), deputy president of the
Soviet of Ministers.

Beria's lengthy trial parades before us the mass murders committed over the course of several decades, the endless acts of lawlessness,
betrayal, and brutality. Coming right at the end, as is usual in such
cases, are the little details that complete this picture of depravity:
women.

Amid the flowers and celebratory air of post–World War II Moscow,
the air remained thick with anxiety. Mothers would warn their daughters not to talk to anyone on the streets for fear of Beria's Cheka
bandits, who were known to prowl the capital snatching girls to bring
to his mansion; one was said to have been abducted near the Theater
of the Red Army.

Khrushchev's son-in-law, Alexei Adzhubei, writes: "Beria's house
was on the corner of Sadovo-Triumfalnaya and Kachalov streets, not
far from Uprising Square. The building stood back from the street,
concealed by a high stone fence. The sentries standing guard outside
would follow everyone passing with a heavy gaze, and Muscovites
would quicken their step and keep quiet."

Adzhubei describes attending a party in 1947 to celebrate the
engagement of Beria's son, Sergo, to the beautiful Marfa Peshkova,
granddaughter of the writer Alexei Maximovich Gorky.

Marfa and the groom sat stiffly at the table, the guests seemed not to
be enjoying themselves much, and only Marfa's younger sister Darya,
a theater student, relaxed.

Shortly after this Beria moved L., his seventeen-year-old mistress,
into the house. When I see L. now it strikes me that beauty and
wickedness are quite compatible. She had a child by him. People said

the girl's mother once made a fuss and even slapped Beria in the face. He took it. The girl settled in comfortably, and the mother evidently grew used to it, too. His wife, Nina Teimurazovna, tolerated her presence — obviously having no choice.

There are many mysteries surrounding the evil name of Beria, and much has been embellished by past generations. One who greatly suffered at his hands was his wife, Nina Teimurazovna.

One evening during intermission at the Bolshoi Theater, I saw a woman of unearthly beauty slipping with a shy, distracted smile through a ring of soldiers. Her hair was golden, her features were sweet and gentle, and her dress was like an airy, apricot cloud flowing, rippling, and floating about her body. This was Nina Teimurazovna Beria. As I watched this lovely creature all the rumors about Beria floated up from my unconscious. With such a wife? Impossible! Why would a proud and beautiful woman endure such humiliation for the sake of the material privileges it brought her?

Thaddeus Wittlin's biography of Beria, *Commissar,* published in the 1970s in the United States and recently translated into Russian, contains a lurid account of Nina Teimurazovna's first meeting with Beria:

> During his stay in Abkhazia, Beria lived on his luxurious special train, in which he had traveled to Sukhumi. It was switched onto a siding some distance from the station building. The train consisted of three Pullman cars: a sleeper, a saloon car equipped with bar, and a restaurant car. The evening before Beria planned to depart for Tbilisi, he was approached near the station by a young girl of about sixteen years of age, of medium height, with black eyes and a creamy white complexion. The girl had come from her Mingrelian village neighboring Beria's to plead for her arrested brother.
>
> Beria noticed the beauty of the girl. Asking for more details about her brother, he invited her into his train — but not to the saloon or the restaurant. To his sleeping car. He told the girl to undress. When, frightened, she started to leave the car, Beria locked the door. Then he slapped her face, twisted her arms behind her back, pushed her onto the bed and pressed her down heavily with his body. The fragile girl was overpowered and raped. A few minutes after everything was over, Beria let her go free. Now he could order a guard to take the little waif to jail, or he could just kick her out onto the railroad track. But looking at her beautiful, tear-streaked face, Beria knew that in less than half an hour he would desire her again. He locked her up in

the compartment and went to the restaurant car for supper and some vodka.

Beria kept the girl all night. The next morning he told his orderly to bring breakfast for two. Later, before leaving for his duties, Lavrenti locked up his victim again. Beria was not only spellbound by the freshness and charm of the girl, he realized that she was the type who appealed completely to his senses. She was young and innocent, but looked mature. She was delicate but by no means thin. She had small breasts, big eyes that cast demure glances, and a full ripe mouth. Lavrenti saw that it would be stupid of him to throw such a creature away right now. Beria spent a few more days in Sukhumi to supervise the progress of the Five-Year Plan for the improvement of the country roads and highways and the construction of new dwellings, hospitals, and schools. Throughout this time he kept his prisoner locked in the train. Thus little Nina became his wife.

Wittlin has merely lifted this episode from Svetlana Alliluyeva's *Only One Year* and embellished it. And although Alliluyeva's accounts of her own experiences are an invaluable source of information, her version of the Kremlin legends that others have told her often appears close to disinformation.

Ekaterina Sergeyevna Katukova's description of Nina Teimurazovna, whom she met several times in the Czechoslovakian spa Karlovy Vary during the 1930s, appears closer to the truth:

She had golden hair with a coppery tinge, huge brown eyes, thick eyelashes curling upward like a doll, a delicate complexion, and a good figure marred by slightly crooked legs. She dressed beautifully. One dress of hers was incredibly lovely, it was made from twenty-five meters of chiffon. She never wore diamonds — no one wore diamonds in those days. She and I would play tennis together. She was an excellent tennis player. Sometimes she would play with her guards. Her husband didn't allow her to play with strange men. In Karlovy Vary I would run off to drink the waters, but she always had to be driven there. He didn't let her mix with other people. Her luxury villa was surrounded on all sides by guards. She wasn't allowed to do anything. She was very close to her son. . . .

She took good care of herself. In Dresden I often helped visiting ministers' wives to buy tea sets, hats, and furs, and if they hadn't finished their shopping they would leave me the money and I would post the things off to them with the receipts. In all the years, I never heard a word of thanks from Zhemchuzhina or Khrushcheva, but

Nina Teimurazovna telephoned me the minute she got back to Moscow, thanking me for the face cream and inviting me out to their dacha in Barvikh. When I arrived she was bicycling in the yard, with a soldier behind and a soldier in front. It was like a cage. . . .

In Dresden she once said to me: "I keep looking at you and admiring the way your husband loves you."

"What, doesn't your husband love you?"

"I'm terribly unhappy. Lavrenti's never home. I'm always alone."

Everyone who knew Beria's wife in those years agrees that she was a good, kind, and desperately unhappy person. People at the Timiryazev Agricultural Academy, where she worked, remember her for her kindness. Since Kremlin wives were not allowed to intervene in politics she was obviously unable to do much, but various attacks against agriculture were softened thanks to her influence, and her teacher, Academician Pryanishnikov, was spared.

In 1990, Nina Teimurazovna Beria was eighty-six years old and living in a small apartment in Kiev that she rarely left. Bilingual in Russian and Georgian, she spoke in Georgian during a long interview with journalist Teimuraz Koridze in the newspaper *Top Secret*.

I was born in a poor family. After Father died it was terribly hard for Mother. You could count the rich families in Georgia on the fingers of one hand then. They were anxious times — revolutions, riots, political parties. I grew up with my uncle, Sasha Gegechkori, who took me in to help Mother out. We lived in Kutaisi, and I went to the first women's school there. Sasha often went to prison for his revolutionary activities, and his wife, Vera, used to take me with her to visit him. I was young and it fascinated me. My future husband was in the same cell as Sasha. I didn't notice him, but he apparently remembered me.

After Soviet power was set up in Georgia, Sasha was transferred to Tbilisi and elected president of the Tbilisi revolutionary committee. I went with them.

I was already a grown girl by then, and Vera and I didn't get on. I remember I had one pair of good shoes, and she told me not to wear them every day so they'd last longer. I always walked to school by the back streets so people wouldn't notice my clothes.

In the first days of Soviet power I joined a student demonstration against the Bolsheviks. They turned the water cannon on us and I ran home soaked. When Sasha's wife found out what had happened she grabbed a strap and thrashed me, shouting: "When you live with Sasha Gegechkori — you don't join demonstrations against him!"

Nina Teimurazovna Beria

Tatyana Okunevskaya

Once on the way to school I met Lavrenti. After Soviet power came to Georgia he was always visiting Sasha, so I'd met him already. He insisted that I talk to him, saying, "We'll have to talk sooner or later, like it or not!"

I agreed, and we met in Tbilisi's Nadzaladevi Park. My sister and brother-in-law lived in that part of town, so I knew the park well. We sat on a bench. He wore a long black overcoat and student cap. He told me he'd been watching me for a long time, and that he liked me very much. Then he said he loved me, and he wanted me to marry him.

I was sixteen-and-a-half then, and he was twenty-two.* He told me the new government was sending him to Belgium to learn about petroleum extraction, but only on condition that he was married. I thought about it and agreed. It seemed better to be married and have my own family than to live in someone else's home, even if they were relatives. So without telling anyone, I married Lavrenti. The rumors immediately started flying that he'd abducted me. Nothing of the sort happened. I married him of my own free will.

Her indifference to her future husband appears truthful: she married him to have a home of her own. So either the three Pullman carriages and the rape scene at Sukhumi were dreamed up, or Nina Teimurazovna is lying to protect her husband. This seems hardly likely: Beria was a family friend of the Gegechkoris, and several people who knew them then are still alive. Besides, why should she lie about her youth in order to soften his posthumous fate, when she herself is approaching death?

In 1926 I graduated from the Agronomy Faculty at Tbilisi University and worked as a scientist at Tbilisi's agricultural institute. We never did go abroad. First Lavrenti postponed our trip, then problems cropped up and he was up to his ears in government work. We lived poorly, like everyone else then. It was considered wrong to live well, because the Revolution had been made against the rich.

In 1931 Lavrenti was made first secretary of the Central Committee of the Georgian Communist Party. He worked day and night and had almost no time for his family. It's easy to criticize him now, but there were fierce battles going on. Soviet power had to win. You

---

* *Nina Teimurazovna, like Nadezhda Alliluyeva, was under the legal age of consent.*

remember what Stalin wrote about the enemies of socialism? Those enemies really existed.

Meanwhile, the inventory of Beria's office after his arrest reveals the following items:

Ladies' stockings of foreign make — 11 pairs
Ladies' silk panties — 11 pairs
Ladies' silk vests — 7 pairs
Ladies' sports outfits
Ladies' blouses
Material samples for ladies' dresses
Ladies' silk scarves and handkerchiefs of foreign make
Countless intimate letters from women
A large quantity of items of male debauchery.

One can only guess what these might be; the lexicon of Party and Cheka apparatchiks, serving always to veil the real meaning of words in euphemisms, evidently collapsed in this search for words.

Before being executed the prisoner admitted his "criminal moral depravity," and his dark doings with women were well authenticated at the time. He was said to rape young women prisoners in his office and shoot them to stop them from talking, or select the younger ones for special attention. At the end of the 1940s the NKVD organized stenography courses for which young, pretty women were picked; these courses were described as Beria's secret harem, and there are those today who say that the things that went on there would scar you for life.

Even the daughter-in-law of the all-powerful Voroshilov was afraid of this man who had recently arrived in Moscow. In the summer of 1941, Nadezhda Voroshilova was walking down the street toward the Kremlin with the Voroshilovs' niece, Valya, when a black car slowed down and crawled along the curb behind them. An NKVD agent jumped out toward them, shouting, "Hey girl, haven't I seen you before?"

> Valya turned off toward the TAAS building, and I walked on in silence, with the colonel following behind me, still shouting. I had heard about Beria's debauchery, and how his colonels would snatch women off the street, and I quickened my step. The man kept up with me, the car crawled on behind, I ran, desperate to reach the Kremlin, where he would surely turn back. He ran, the car speeded up, people turned to

look. When finally I reached the gates of the Kremlin I looked around, and sure enough he was gone.

At home after I'd caught my breath I told Ekaterina Davidovna. I expected her to laugh, instead she looked at me with terror in her eyes, saying: "It's Beria! Say nothing! Don't tell a soul!"

Nadezhda Ivanovna explained: "Everyone was afraid of everyone and everything then, every family had a tragedy. Stalin and the NKVD managed to inculcate guilt in everyone, regardless of their position. All of us had someone in prison. In the Voroshilov family it was my parents, with Kaganovich it was his brother, Budyonny his wife. Jail was every Soviet family's stigma."

Thaddeus Wittlin's sensational depiction of Beria's adventures attempts the portrait of a hopeless criminal:

> His car usually stopped near the Soviet Army Theater, where a girls' high school was located. Soon after two o'clock the girls would leave the building for their homes. From behind a curtain half covering his car's greenish windows Beria would observe the girls like a prowling panther watching a herd of young does. . . . When he spotted a plump girl of fourteen or fifteen years old, with rosy pink cheeks and lips moist as the morning dew, Beria would point at her with a jerk of his chin and Colonel Sarkisov would leave the car and start toward the chosen girl. . . . From his car, often using field-glasses, Beria could see terror flash into the eyes of his horrified victim.

Actresses and dancers were especially defenseless against the NKVD machine. The singer Zoya Fyodorova was picked up one night by one of Beria's officers, who told her they were going to a large party. She was driven to a dacha and led into the dining room, where a table was laid for two.

> "Where are the others?" she demanded.
>
> "Don't worry, they'll come," he said, and disappeared.
>
> Zoya had just given birth to a baby daughter, and her milk was leaking, her head ached, and her nerves were at breaking point. Finally Beria came in. Zoya said, "If there are no more guests, let me go."
>
> "Aren't we going to have a little chat?" he said.
>
> "The milk's burning in my breasts, I have to feed my baby, and you talk garbage to me!" she shouted.
>
> Beria was furious and called an officer to take Zoya away. Another officer, evidently misunderstanding what had happened, handed her

a bunch of flowers at the door. Beria shouted: "May they rot on your grave!" She was arrested shortly afterward.

Zoya Fyodorova's murder in Moscow at the age of seventy-six is now generally known. Less well known is the fate of the film star Tatyana Okunevskaya.

THE DIVA

Today, there are many in Russia who remember the lively, temperamental beauty, Tatyana Okunevskaya, whose severe brow and dazzling smile ruled men's dreams as they stared at the giant billboards in every town of Russia.

Her first serious film role, as the heroine in Maupassant's *Boule de suif,* was followed by various roles in the classical and revolutionary stage repertory. But it was the film *Hot Days* that turned her into a star.

After the collapse of her first marriage, she married Boris Gorbatov, *Pravda* correspondent and Stalin Prize–winning novelist. Gorbatov was a flourishing representative of the style of socialist realism. Their house on Begovaya Street still bears a plaque with his name.

During the war Tatyana Okunevskaya was evacuated, and Gorbatov went off to the front. They were reunited toward the end of the war in Moscow, where she starred in a film about the Yugoslav partisans, *Night over Belgrade,* which was shown all over the country. During concerts at the front she would invariably end with the film's hymnlike battle song, which begins: "The flame of anger burns in our breast." The words combined with her beauty produced storms of applause wherever she went.

Yet throughout Tatyana Okunevskaya's youth, success and tragedy were never very far apart, and when I visited her in her tiny apartment on Petrovo-Razumovsky Street she told me that the life concealed behind her glamorous career was very different. Her father, an officer before the Revolution, had been jailed in the 1930s, denounced as a "disenfranchised person," and shot. Her grandmother died in prison, and her brother Lev, named in honor of Tolstoy, was also jailed. Okunevskaya herself was pursued throughout her life by the dark shadow of her relatives, whom she adored and never stopped visiting in prison.

"In 1945 the doors of heaven opened and Gorbatov and I were invited to the Kremlin to celebrate the anniversary of the Great October Revolution," writes Tatyana in her autobiography.

> The poor tsars' palace gazed at this feast of the elite, dressed in their frock coats and uniforms, including peasants now called collective farm workers, and handsome workers called Stakhanovites, cursing their Party membership for not allowing them to drink. The old intelligentsia — writers, actors, and artists — had now been superseded by a new wave of writers, loud, ugly, sycophantic, such as Konstantin Simonov and Boris Gorbatov, Stalin Prize laureates and terribly proud of that fact, not realizing that they had been awarded this prize for something that had nothing to do with art.

As if by magic, Tatyana Okunevskaya and Gorbatov began being invited to foreign receptions at embassies. Such visits in earlier years had not been approved of by the government, and had ended badly for Kremlin wives in the late 1930s, but times had changed in Moscow; embassy officials were no longer considered enemies, but allies. When the Gorbatovs visited the Yugoslav embassy, Tatyana Okunevskaya was invited not as Gorbatov's wife. Gorbatov was invited as her husband. The ambassador was young, handsome, and well-mannered, and he invited her to Yugoslavia to attend the opening of *Night over Belgrade*.

In Belgrade people threw flowers at her car, and all Yugoslavia was singing the partisan theme song. She gave a series of concerts, and her husband joined her. They traveled throughout Slovenia, Croatia, Montenegro, Macedonia, and back to Belgrade — a glamorous couple. In a concert for Marshal Tito and his staff, the audience held its breath as she sang: "To battle, Slavs, ahead lies the dawn!" Flowers fell at her feet, and the audience stood as she released a red gauze scarf from her clenched fist and sang encore after encore.

The next day, she went to meet Tito alone. She wrote,

> I was driven to the court of the king who had abandoned Communism. Through an ordinary gate walked Marshal Tito. At the concert he had been in uniform, now he was dressed in civilian clothes. In one hand he carried a pair of garden scissors, in the other a large bunch of black roses.
>
> At the marshal's feet lay a splendid sheepdog, gazing into my

eyes. He said: "Now we'll see how you feel about me — if it's bad, Rex will rip you to shreds! Right before my eyes."

A strange, unpleasant joke. Since the marshal was meeting the actress who had sung the praises of their countries' friendship, the intimidating tone is puzzling. But Tatyana Okunevskaya accepted everything with undaunted enthusiasm:

> Rex grumbled affectionately, and we both laughed.
> "But does he know how you feel about me?" I asked him.
> "Of course! Look, he can't take his eyes off you. He doesn't understand Serbian yet. He belonged to a German officer."
> We sat in Tito's delightful, informal little study and talked and talked. On his finger he wore a ring with a black diamond, which he said always brought him luck.

Tito then led Tatyana Okunevskaya in to dinner. "Two dozen members of his general staff rose from a huge square table to welcome us, shoulder to shoulder, tall, young, and handsome in their magnificent braided uniforms. I was seated in the center on an antique high-backed chair, like a princess."

Later, Tito visited Moscow, and a lavish reception was organized in his honor. In front of all present, the Yugoslav leader crossed the entire room and asked Tatyana Okunevskaya to dance. They danced all night, and he told her that his people would never forgive him if he married a foreign woman, even a Soviet one, but he begged her to come to Belgrade, promising that he would build her her own studio there and let her live and work as she liked.

The romance went no further and was followed by a brief and stormy affair with the Yugoslav ambassador. But by now Tatyana Okunevskaya's other life was catching up with her. She had allowed herself too many liberties, first turning the head of Marshal Tito, who was now regarded in the USSR as an "enemy of the people," and then sleeping with his ambassador. The spiral of her misfortunes started with a pleasant invitation to a private concert at the Kremlin, where People's Artists and the friends and mistresses of the leaders were to perform.

> I was told these concerts were held late at night to relax the leaders after their meetings. I was to be picked up by Beria himself. Boris wasn't in Moscow then — all the journalists were in Germany attending the Nuremberg Trials. I felt a strange sensation of dread.

A colonel escorted me to a car, and I got into the back beside Beria. I had seen him before at the Kremlin, and I recognized him at once. He was ugly, flabby, and unhealthy-looking, with a greyish-yellow complexion. He told me the meeting at the Kremlin hadn't yet ended, and we would have to wait at his house.

Once inside, the colonel vanished. There was a table laden with every kind of food one can imagine. I said I never ate before a concert and I certainly never drank, but he insisted Georgian fashion, virtually pouring the wine into my lap. He ate greedily, tearing at the food with his hands, chattering away and begging me to take a sip.

After a while he stood up and slipped silently through one of the doors. All sounds were muffled, even the traffic from the Garden Ring Road. By now it was three in the morning — our dinner had lasted two hours. He came back, drank more wine, got drunk and paid me banal compliments, telling me that a certain Koba, who had never seen me in person, wanted very much to do so. I wondered who Koba was.*

He slipped out again. I had heard they worked until dawn, but I was exhausted. Coming back, he announced that the meeting had ended, but that Koba was so tired the concert had to be postponed. I stood up and asked to leave. He said that now I must drink, and that if I didn't he would not let me go. I drank. Grabbing my waist, he pushed me through yet another door. Dribbling repulsively in my ear, he whispered that we would have a little rest, then I would be taken home. I remembered nothing more. When I came to, all was quiet. Nobody was there. The door opened silently and a woman appeared and led me back to the room where I had been the previous evening. A table laid for breakfast floated into my consciousness, and a clock said ten o'clock. I went out, climbed into a waiting car, and returned home. I had been raped. Something terrible, irrevocable, had happened. I felt numb.

Shortly after this, Tatyana Okunevskaya was arrested. "I was ill in bed with a high fever. Boris was rushing around preparing to leave on a journey somewhere. Finally he left, and my chauffeur came in and told me the yard was full of soldiers. Two soldiers came in, and said: 'You're under arrest!' I realized then that Boris had known everything, and had quietly been making his escape."

Tatyana Okunevskaya wrote later to the procurator general:

* *Koba was Stalin's Georgian nickname.*

When I was arrested the minister said: "You can see she needs a bit of punishment!" And: "Just think, what beauty, what intelligence and talent — everyone admires you, and I've arrested you!"

They shouted that I was a whore, that I held orgies, that I danced naked on the table and men played cards on my stomach. They wouldn't let me say anything — they just kept asking about Tito and his dog, and whether I believed in God.

The questions and testimonies contained in Tatyana Okunevskaya's two weighty files at Lubyanka insult the dignity of every woman with their prurient interrogation of the intimate details of her sexual life. These files, like those of Olga Budyonnaya, Ekaterina Kalinina, and Paulina Zhemchuzhina, contain no evidence of any pleas or interference from her husband. Boris Gorbatov lived in the same town, just a ten-minute bus ride away. He could have been summoned and interrogated, and he might well have helped to ease her fate.

Her letter to the procurator continues:

One night during the interrogation I was called out in my coat and driven off to another prison, where I was thrown into a freezing, pitch-dark cellar.

"Take your clothes off!" they said.

I thought I had misheard, but I hadn't. I stripped naked and stood barefoot on the icy floor. I held my stockings so I could put them on later, but they took them away and gave me back just my dress and shoes.

I lost track of the hours — the only thing left was the bread they brought me once a day. At four they threw down a board for me to lie on, and its iron clamps froze my legs. After my third piece of bread they took me out, just as I was, into the freezing yard. I was feeling very ill by now. I was led to interrogator Sokolov. I was not allowed to wash, the dirt clung to my face. I was also menstruating, and I was soaked in blood. They had taken away not only my cotton wool, but even my handkerchief. Sokolov looked at me and asked me how I felt. Understanding everything, I said: "Wonderful!"

The charges finally brought against Tatyana Okunevskaya were as follows: "Conducting virulent anti-Soviet discussions with her acquaintances, criticizing the policies of the Party and the Soviet government, praising the bourgeois order, worshiping the conditions of life in the capitalist countries, and systematically meeting with foreigners."

Thirteen months of solitary confinement were followed by the camps at Dzhezkazgan, where Tatyana Okunevskaya felled timber in the frozen forests. The women in her cell were mainly local leaders' wives, who assumed that she must be in for some crime. She was loved by the people with whom she worked at the camp's forests and building sites. "It was the ordinary people who saved me," she writes in her autobiography. "There where everything is designed to turn a person into an animal, where a mother snatches bread from her daughter, and the daughter pushes the mother into the ditch, a woman with the eyes of an icon approached me in my darkest hour and said: 'The women want you to have this kerchief — cover your face with it or you'll freeze.' "

It was some time after Beria's downfall that Tatyana Okunevskaya was finally released. She roamed Russia with nowhere to live and tried to adjust to her freedom. All her films had been withdrawn, her marriage had been annulled, Gorbatov had remarried, and by the time she left the camps he was dead.

In old age Okunevskaya is a slim, elegant woman who keeps young with daily gymnastics. The men who insulted and defiled her are now in the ground.

Kremlin wives were equally vulnerable to Beria's tactics. Beria went in person to the apartment of Komsomol leader Alexander Kosarev and arrested him. His wife, Maria Viktorovna, threw herself at his feet, crying: "Sasha, come back!" Beria arrested her, too, and she spent seventeen years in a camp.

Fifteen-year-old Anna Mikhailovna Larina first met Beria during a visit to Georgia with her parents when he was head of the Georgian GPU. "Sitting at his desk, Beria said to my father: 'I never knew you had such a lovely little girl!' I blushed with shame, and my father said, 'I don't see anything lovely about her!' Beria turned to his aide, saying, 'Mikha, let's drink to the health of this lovely little girl! A long and healthy life to her!' "

When Anna Mikhailovna met Beria again four years later in Batumi, he again praised her beauty; her third meeting took place in 1938 in his office at NKVD headquarters, where the newly appointed people's commissar had summoned her after the arrest of her husband, Nikolai Bukharin.

> "I must say you've become extraordinarily beautiful since I last saw you."
>
> "What a paradox, Lavrenti Pavlovich — after ten years in jail you'll be able to send me to Paris for a beauty contest!"
>
> After a short pause, he suddenly said, "Tell me, why do you love Nikolai Ivanovich?"
>
> I avoided the question, saying love was a purely personal matter and didn't have to be justified to anyone.

Beria sentenced Larina to fifteen years in a camp.

When he arrested twenty-three-year-old Glafira Blukher, wife of the jailed Marshal Blukher, he stared at her. "Beria conducted the interrogation himself, clearly out of simple sadistic curiosity. His appearance was repulsive and his demeanor was haughty. He conveyed an utter indifference to his victim — as though he was peering through a magnifying glass at a tiny insect."

After five months in solitary confinement Glafira Blukher was transferred to the Butyrki, then to the Karaganda camps.

The stories of Beria's female victims who managed to outwit him make more cheerful reading. One woman describes how in 1938 she worked at a secret factory outside Moscow. One of the typists got sick. Upon replacing that sick typist she addressed an envelope not to Stalingrad but to Stalin*gad*.*

> I never meant to call Stalin a swine, but they arrested me anyway and harassed me with endless questions about the envelope, demanding that I tell them which organization I belonged to and who I was spying for. The interrogator later said: "For heaven's sake why didn't you leave out the 'g'? That would have made it 'Stalin rad,'† and everything would be OK."
>
> I was a good-looking girl, although my looks were, I am told, a bit too perfect — cold as a statue and thin, the Venus de Milo come to life, is what people said of me. After six months in jail I was suddenly taken off in the middle of the night, driven to the railway station, bundled into a carriage, and locked in. We traveled for what seemed like an eternity. The carriage was shunted off to a siding, and some

* *In Russian this comes out as "Stalin swine."*
† *"Stalin happy."*

Cheka agents came and pushed me blindfolded into a car. I managed to peer through the blindfold and saw that we were driving out of a large building, which I recognized as Moscow station.

The car stopped and they untied the blindfold. We were in a forest, at the edge of a snow-covered clearing surrounded by a straight line of fir trees and a giant oak. Before us stood a large dacha. Two soldiers led me in and untied my hands. I sat down in a big armchair and looked around. The sofas and chairs were draped in white canvas covers, a reproduction of Perov's *Huntsmen at the Stopping Place* hung on the wall. My nerves became calmer. A door led into another room. I tried it but it was locked. Then out of this room jumped a monkey in a short dressing-gown. He had dark hairy legs, crooked knees, and pince-nez, just like in the photographs. The monkey smiled and said in a hoarse, high-pitched voice: "I've decided to interview you myself. You make mistakes in important letters. You say it's an accident? Rumors of your beauty have reached Moscow, but you're even better in the flesh!"

Sitting down beside me on the sofa the monkey began to scrutinize me, but I was no longer afraid. I knew why I had been brought here. I quickly realized that my looks did not appeal to him. Men liked women to be plump. I was skinny.

"Shall I take my dress off, or will I do as I am?" I asked him. "I haven't washed for a week."

The monkey flashed his gold teeth and frowned. He didn't like this. I threw off my rags and stood before him covered with goose-pimples. As I stood there shivering I saw myself from a distance. My collarbone stuck out, my stomach caved in, my breasts sagged. The monkey stepped back, evidently revolted. It was clear that he wanted to leave, and I heard myself say: "Sit down."

We had a long talk. I am good at drawing people out, and I seemed to awaken the human being in him. He told me how tired he was, and nobody understood him at home.

"Your crime's nothing," he said with his slightly Georgian accent. "I just wanted to see you for myself. Let's keep our meeting a secret. Be a clever girl and don't say a word about this to anyone."

He left the room. Pulling on my rags, I stretched out on the sofa and fell into a deep sleep, oblivious to whether I was dirtying the government chair covers with my prison filth.

I was awakened the next morning by a soldier who led me to the next room. There I was given something hot, good, and simple to eat, as well as an old but respectable overcoat. I was then driven to the center of Moscow and left there with a train ticket and a note, in which the monkey wished me success in the building of communism. It was unsigned.

When I got back to work a few people looked askance at me — few returned from prison in those days. But I had betrayed no one, and they all knew why I had been arrested. Beria left me alone not so much because I wasn't his type, but because in 1939 he was at the start of his career and not entirely sure of himself yet. Also I was twenty-six then, and it must have been obvious to him that I wasn't a virgin. He preferred innocent girls, who would be afraid and cry at his sadism. He didn't do anything to me, yet I felt the danger from him — the danger of a man with limitless power, who can do whatever he likes.

Beria's shadow hovered wherever attractive young women were found. Here is the story of an ordinary Moscow woman, now in her sixties, who fell into Beria's clutches in the summer of 1952 when she was an innocent twenty-one-year-old student. She and her two girl-friends had just graduated from the Institute of Foreign Languages, and were walking cheerfully down Kachalov Street.

I was wearing a coral-colored dress with little white flowers, and a string of pearls around my neck. I don't know if I was pretty, but I had gleaming white teeth and a nice smile that everyone noticed. Outside the large building where Beria lived stood a group of men, Beria among them.

I left my friends at the corner of Kachalov and Sadovaya streets, and as I stopped at the Garden Ring Road crossing to catch the trolley home, I was approached by a soldier. I later learned that this was Colonel Sarkisov, Beria's chief procurer of women.

"I want a word with you," he said. "You've been invited to see someone." I recalled seeing Beria a minute ago on the pavement.

"That Man wants to see you. He's inviting you to dinner."

"But Comrade Stalin warns us to be vigilant!" I said.

"You saw who I was with," the colonel repeated, obviously shaking with laughter inside at my words. "There's nothing to be afraid of. He's quite safe. He's been watching you. He wants to help you."

I had my diploma and the offer of a teaching job — what more could I want? I was afraid, mortally afraid. The colonel and I stood for a long time talking at the crossroads, then we crossed the road and argued for another fifteen minutes on the other side. He kept repeating, That Man (he never once mentioned his name) wanted to help me.

I replied, "But Comrade Stalin warns us to be vigilant!" This didn't stop him. "It won't harm you to come — it'll harm you more not to. Who do you live with?"

"My mother."

"Right, we know where you live."

My head was pounding, and I felt even more afraid.

"We know all about you. We'll come around in the car at nine and wait outside the main entrance. There's nothing to be afraid of. You're in no danger."

He left, and I caught the trolley home. Suddenly a secret service agent jumped up behind me on the bus, accompanied me to my stop, and escorted me home in broad daylight. After checking the number of my apartment he ran downstairs. Running to the sitting-room window, I saw him climbing into a black motorcar, which swung round and drove off at speed.

Mama was at work. I sat in the room, my head burning. Three girls had been walking down the street, and I had been picked. Why? Somehow the most primitive, honest reason never occurred to me, for I had been brought up to believe that all people were good, and the bad ones were only in books.

As nine o'clock approached I took out my new blue silk suit, the pride of my wardrobe, and ironed it. I assumed we would probably talk about work, and thinking that he might offer me a really good job, I pinned my Komsomol badge to my lapel.

At nine o'clock I saw the black car through the window and went out. The colonel was standing on the pavement, and I saw anxiety in his eyes as he looked at me, as though he was worried I might not get in the car. When I did, he relaxed and told me we were going to pass the new university building that was just about to be opened. He said he'd helped build it himself, and that it was thanks to That Man that there was a new university building in Moscow.

The car stopped by the parapet between the Moscow River and the university, and the colonel suggested we get out.

"You saw who I was standing with," he started again. "That Man very much wants to see you."

"What then?" I ask.

The colonel started crooning promises. "You'll live in a wonderful apartment, you haven't a telephone? You'll have a telephone. Where does your mother work?"

"The Planning Institute. Look, we don't need anything. We have everything we want. I want to know why you need me." And I repeated yet again Comrade Stalin's senseless warning to be vigilant. I could see I was boring him terribly.

"We've been watching you for a long time. You're just the sort of needy, modest person That Man likes to help. You'll get a good job."

"What do I have to do?"

This question agitated him; he evidently imagined I'd understood him, whereas of course I still hadn't understood a thing.

"We'll get in the car and go back to the building where we met. It's quite late — this will take some time."

These words brought me to my senses a little. Mother would be anxiously waiting for me by now.

We got into the car and it shot off to Beria's villa. Inside, the colonel pushed me through a small door and quickly locked it behind me. I was alone in a vast, thickly carpeted room with a long table, leather high-backed chairs, and dark maroon blinds over the windows.

Beria entered like a cat, and drawing up a leather chair for himself, he tugged my arm and told me to sit down. He was old, much older than the photographs, and he wore his usual pince-nez. He asked me my name and I told him, wondering why the colonel said they knew everything about me when they didn't even know my name.

"Has anyone in your family been arrested?"

"Yes."

"Who?"

"The husband of Mother's sister. We live with my aunt now."

He asked her name and frowned. "I don't recall her. And where does your mother work?"

After questioning me about the other members of my family, he looked at me for a long time. "Why did you change? The dress suited you. The suit's nice too, but a bit formal."

"But we'll be talking formally!" I gabbled.

"Yes, of course. But first let's eat." He pressed a button — the long table was covered in buttons — and a woman entered silently and was ordered to set the table.

He opened a door on the left and we passed through a room filled with pieces of sculpture into a smaller room, where a table was laid for two with wine, fruit, and lavash bread. He tucked into the food with gusto and poured me some wine. "I don't drink," I said. "Stalin warns us to be vigilant."

He looked at me dumbfounded. "Just have a sip, then."

I took a sip and wondered if it was drugged. The reasons why I had been brought here were starting to form in my mind, and I seemed to be developing defense reactions. He questioned me again about my family and the institute, again asked why I had changed, and repeated that he had been watching me for a long time. I wondered where. He got drunk. "Teaching's no job for you — you need something better! You live in a communal apartment? That's no good for a pretty girl."

Just then a young man entered with a sheet of paper and withdrew. I felt the gooseflesh creep over my body when Beria said: "Write, 'Dear Mother, don't worry, I'm with friends and will be back in the morning.'"

"No, no! I want to go home!" I cried, trying to pull away.

"That would be most inconvenient. How would you get back at this hour?"

The woman brought in tea. I drank, and my teeth chattered against the cup. I could see nothing, understand nothing, only that I must get away.

At last he said, "Time for bed." He took me to a bathroom and left. A huge woman appeared saying: "The bath's behind the screen. Wash yourself."

"I'm not dirty. I don't need to wash!"

I went out of the bathroom into a bedroom containing a huge double bed, and amidst a chaos of thoughts and feelings I noticed that it was laid with dazzling white batiste sheets. A woman came in — I wasn't sure if it was the same one as before — and handing me a large linen night shirt, said, "Undress here, lie down here."

She went out. I didn't put it on and lay hunched on the edge of the bed in my underwear. After about half an hour an invisible door opened and he entered the room wearing a long nightshirt. I shook with fear as he sat beside me on the bed. "What are you afraid of? You're so pretty!" he murmured, and started to kiss my shoulders. I shook even more, and pushed him away. "Don't be afraid, why are you trembling? Are you a virgin? Haven't you had a man before?"

"No!" I whisper.

"How old are you? Seventeen?"

"Twenty-one."

"And you've not had a man yet?"

"No!"

He started murmuring about work again and kissing my shoulders, repeating, "Is it true? Are you really a virgin?"

"Yes."

Suddenly he stood up and went silently out of the room. Time passed. It grew light. As I lay there awake, the colonel came in and told me that a car would be coming at six to take me home.

At five-thirty the woman came in, looked at me with undisguised contempt, and ordered me to dress. I dressed in an instant and was driven home. Mother hadn't slept all night. She'd received the note, but she didn't know what to make of it. I told her everything.

When she realized I was still a virgin she stopped worrying, but I couldn't. Next morning I visited a friend whose father was a science professor and a very clever man. When he heard what had happened he lowered the blinds on his windows and said: "Go away. Go home by a different route so that gang doesn't see where your friends live!"

He told me in detail about the women whose lives had been ruined by Beria, and about Kalinin and the operetta singers. His words hit me like a thunderbolt. He said that I was lucky to have escaped, and that Beria had let me go because he was either tired or sexually inadequate. He also said that matters wouldn't stop here, and that I must go away for the whole summer, as far from Moscow as possible.

I spent the summer with my older sister and her baby daughter in the Siberian town of Krasnoyarsk, and they returned with me to Moscow in the middle of August. My sister took the incident very seriously. Mother had also been away working over the summer, and the neighbors told us that a man had come looking for me several times and asking where I was. I had deliberately misinformed everyone as to my whereabouts.

Two days after our return a youth appeared at the door saying: "So you're back from Kalyazan? The colonel wants to see you."

The colonel instantly appeared, and armed with a strange new courage, I asked, "What do you want?"

"You know — the Comrade wants to see you."

"What Comrade? Why don't you say his name?"

At this my sister appeared with the baby in her arms, and shouted: "If you come here once more you'll be in trouble!"

This was ridiculous. Who were we to threaten them? Yet the colonel looked worried. Did he think we might have connections? Was he scared by our decisiveness?

Suddenly the baby started to wail, and the colonel went to pieces, shouting, "You listen to me! I'm working, see? I carry out orders! I do my duty!"

"So that's what you call duty!" my sister yelled. "Get out of here! You say you know all about us — we weren't anywhere near Kalyazan! You've been playing tricks on us!"

We pushed the colonel out of the door, and as he left he said: "We'll meet again. We won't forget you. That Man still wants to see you."

My sister went back home, and I started teaching in a school. All the time I felt I was being watched. My sister wrote to me: "Be very careful. Don't walk close to buildings, they might throw a tile at your head." A man kept following me. Once I turned round on him and said: "Forget the way to my house, all right?" He said nothing, of course. He was gray, like the rest of them. Another one immediately replaced him.

They followed me till November. Then one day, I realized there was no one anymore. I was still afraid that they might start following me again. Then Stalin died. In the summer of 1953 I finished my first year as a schoolteacher and went off to work as a Pioneer leader in a children's camp. While I was there I learned that Beria had been arrested and his trial had begun. I sighed with relief.

During Khrushchev's early days in office, history returned with a vengeance to the corridors where Lavrenti Beria had worked, and Nina Teimurazovna fell victim to the very machine devised by her husband for others — Beria's erstwhile friends and allies had defeated him in the battle for power.

In 1953, as some went to prison and others returned, Nina Teimurazovna and her son Sergo were arrested.

I was imprisoned in various jails. They didn't touch Sergo's family — his wife, Marfa, and her three children remained at home. At first we thought there had been a government revolution or counterrevolution, and an anti-Communist clique had come to power. I was held at the Butyrki and was called out every day for questioning. The interrogator demanded that I testify against my husband. They told me that people were angry about the things Lavrenti had done. I answered him categorically that I would not testify, good or bad, against Beria. After that they left me alone.

I spent over a year in the Butyrki. I was accused, quite seriously, of bringing a bucket of red earth back from a non-Black Earth region of Russia. When I was working at the Agricultural Academy doing research on different soil types, I had asked some people to bring me back a bucket of red earth by plane, and since it was a government aircraft they claimed I was using state transport for my own personal use.

I was also charged with exploiting the labor of others. In Tbilisi there was a famous tailor by the name of Sasha who came to Moscow and made me a dress, which I paid for. This was called "the labor of others." Another charge was that I had ridden from Kutaisi to Tbilisi on horses with golden bells. I certainly rode horses, but never with golden bells. People love to fantasize.

My time in jail was very hard. I spent over a year in a solitary confinement, in a cell so small one couldn't either sit or lie down.

Ironically, this type of inhuman cell had been created by her husband. Nina Teimurazovna was not called an "enemy of the people." But by putting her in jail they made her one with all the other women who suffered for their husbands' struggle for power.

There are many questions about Nina Teimurazovna that still remain unanswered. Was she Beria's victim or his ally? Did she really know nothing? Was she a naive woman surrounded by Cheka agents and kept away from the real life? She could have escaped from her marriage on several occasions. Had she left Beria, however, it would have meant prison or the firing squad. Closing her eyes and comforting herself with fairy-tales about the precious goal ahead, a goal in which people believed so readily in the first half of the twentieth century, was perhaps the only solution for her. Nina Gegechkori was a true Georgian girl, and her submissive life demonstrated to Josif Vissarionovich the accuracy of his mother's advice in urging him to take a Georgian girl as his bride.

Having spent most of her life in cages — first a gilded one, then in prison — the naturally wise and intelligent Nina Teimurazovna had much to think about at the end of her long life. Would she be able to describe what happened? What reason would she have to lie? I felt apprehensive at the idea of seeing her. Not too much afraid of the shadow of her husband, but apprehensive of seeing the woman who had once been so beautiful.

In the summer of 1991, still beautiful in old age, Nina Teimurazovna lived in the boundary between light and shade, guarding her devotion to her dead husband like the black-clothed widows of Georgia. She defended Stalin to me.

"Stalin was a stern man with a harsh character. But who can say whether those times required a different character, and that harshness wasn't needed? Stalin wanted to create a mighty state, and he succeeded. Of course there had to be victims. But no politician then could see any other path that would lead us to our precious goal without victims."

The women of the Kremlin were slaves, who knew from being

at the source that there was no such "precious" goal. These Kremlin women all had in common a talent for converting their fear of the Party machine into dedication to the working class.

Beria is said to have remarked: "Where there's a woman there must be money." He was lavish with government gifts. His pleasures were paid for by the State. Numerous memoirs have been written by Beria's mistresses, all seeming to compare their prowess in bed. Beria kept a young and pretty mistress by whom he had had a child. And with Nina Teimurazovna's consent, she often brought her baby to the house to play with Beria's grandchildren. I abstained from interviewing her because I had been warned that all I would hear was a syrupy account of Beria and the whole group.

To the end of her life, Nina Teimurazovna refused to accept the evidence of her husband's sexual crimes:

> The prosecutor said that 760 women had described themselves as Beria's mistresses. When would Lavrenti have found time to make these hordes of women his mistresses? He spent all day and night at work. No, it was something else. During the war and after, he did intelligence and counterintelligence work, and all these women were his secret agents and informers. He was their only contact. He had a phenomenal memory, and he kept all his contacts in his head. But when these women were asked about their relationship with their chief they could hardly say they were secret agents, so they said they were his mistresses.
>
> A man must never forget his own country. No other country will value his labor. Stalin, Ordzhonokidze, Chkheidze, Tsereteli, Gegechkori, Beria, and others all truly believed that they were fighting for the happiness of all the peoples on earth, for some common noble cause.

Nina Teimurazovna's rewriting of history left me pensive.

14

Nina Kukharchuk's Kitchen

Nikita Sergeyevich Khrushchev (1894–1970), born in the Ukraine, the son of a miner. As a small boy he worked as a shepherd, later training as a locksmith. Joining the Bolsheviks in 1918, he fought during the Civil War in the Ukraine, where he attracted the attention of Kaganovich. Throughout the 1930s he worked his way up the Party ranks, joining war councils on various fronts during World War II and taking part in the defense of Stalingrad. Subordinate to Stalin before his death, Khrushchev took over in 1953 as general secretary of the Party, and campaigned for liberalization and peaceful coexistence with the West. These desires were expressed in his speech to the Twentieth Party Congress in 1956. In October 1964 he was toppled by colleagues, and he spent the next six years of his life in semi-disgrace, writing his memoirs.

ONE OF THE MOST STRIKING PEOPLE of the post-Stalin thaw was Nina Petrovna Khrushcheva. Preoccupied with the political thaw and the increasing pressure for more and more varied food supplies, people in Russia scarcely noticed Khrushchev's wife as she modestly stepped through the oak doors of the Kremlin into the international arena. Not accustomed to seeing the smiling First Lady standing just behind her husband and to the Soviet system where Stalin was always surrounded by a gaping void, they welcomed Nina Petrovna with open arms. "Mother Nina!" "What a lovely woman!" "The soul of goodness!" "She speaks English brilliantly!"

Her appearance in America at her husband's side made a great impression and helped to offset Khrushchev's eccentric behavior, as he banged his shoe on the U.N. table and threatened to "bury the West." To the Western countries, Nina Petrovna represented important social changes in Russia. People saw the sweet smile of this typical Soviet housewife in her black skirt and white blouse, without make-up and with the shapeless figure of someone who lives on jam, bread, and potatoes, and they were charmed. After many long years of Soviet leadership without any visible sign of a Russian equivalent of a First Lady, Nina Petrovna's homely face and her ability to hold a simple conversation in English reassured terrified Americans. They saw that this vast empire was now ruled by an eccentric man and his fat provincial wife, clutching her handbag to her ample stomach. These two were for the first time people with whom one could do business.

After the Khrushchevs' visit to America and all the newspaper photographs of Nina Petrovna standing next to her husband, she became the object of various rumors. Some said that Khrushchev was under her thumb, and that she had made him pull strings to get their son a job at the prestigious Chalomey Nuclear Research Institute. Others said that it was only because her sister Maria was married to Mikhail Sholokhov that this writer carried such weight in the country. Yet America saw what it wanted to see, and Russia did likewise; few noticed what was before their eyes, the tight mouth and clenched lips, evidence of a humorless, inflexible, possibly malicious and definitely stubborn nature.

In the last years of Nina Petrovna's life she yielded to pressure from her daughter Rada to write her memoirs, and after her death Rada found this biographical sketch among her mother's papers.

I was born on April 14, 1900, in the village of Vasilev, in Kholm province. The inhabitants of Kholm were Ukrainian and the villagers spoke Ukrainian, but the village administrators were all Russian and Russian was taught in the schools, even though no one spoke it at home. In the first class of the village infant school the teacher would hit us on the hand with a ruler for various crimes, including that of not understanding Russian, which none of us knew.

When my mother, Ekaterina Grigorevna Kukharchuk, married at 16 she received for her dowry 1¼ acres of land, a small oak forest, and a trunk full of clothes and bedding. The villagers considered this very generous. Soon after the wedding, Father went off to serve in the army. My father — Pyotr Vasilievich Kukharchuk — was from a poorer family than Mother's and owned part of a three-acre allotment, an old cottage, a small plum orchard, and a cherry tree in the garden. They had no horses. My father was the oldest in the family. When his mother died he inherited the land and had to pay his brothers and sisters a hundred rubles each, which was a large sum in those days. I think the 1914 war interrupted these payments.

Vasilev was a poor village, and most of the villagers worked as day laborers for the landlord, who paid the women ten kopecks a day for picking beetroots, and the men twenty to thirty kopecks for scything hay. I remember cooking nettles and chopping them up with a big knife for the pig, which we would fatten up for Easter or Christmas. The knife would often slip and cut my finger, and I still have a scar on the index finger of my left hand.

Mother and I lived with her family: Granny Ksenya had a large cottage and Grandfather was away on military service, first in Bessarabia, later, in 1904, in Japan. We had no table, so we all sat at a wide bench and ate from one bowl. The mothers held the babies in their arms, but there was no room for us bigger children, so we had to reach over the grownups' shoulders for our food, and if we spilled some they would hit us on the forehead with a spoon. For some reason Uncle Anton was always laughing at me, and saying I would marry into a large family, my children would have runny noses, and I would have to reach over their heads for my food.

In 1912 Father put me in the cart, loaded it with a sack of potatoes and a side of wild boar, and drove to the town of Lublin, where his brother, Kondraty Vasilievich, was a conductor on the railways. Uncle Kondraty had arranged for me to study at the Lublin *progimnazium*. I had already done three years in the village school, and the village teacher had persuaded Father that I should be sent to school in the town.

I spent a year in Lublin, and when Uncle got a job as a watchman at the Kholm Treasury, I entered the second year of the *progimnazium* there. When the 1914 war broke out, I was on vacation back home in Vasilev. I was fourteen then, and my brother was eleven. That autumn Austrian troops broke through to our village and went wild, looting houses and raping the girls. Mama hid me behind the stove, ordered me not to come out, and told the soldiers I had typhus. That sent them running. Soon Russian soldiers drove the Austrians out, and we were ordered to evacuate the village. Mother, my brother, and I grabbed as many bags as we could carry. We had no idea where we were going, and we had no horses. I remember Mama was carrying a Primus stove, the object of her housewifely pride, but there was no paraffin, and she finally had to abandon it. For a long time we struggled on ahead of the advancing Austrians, until we finally reached the little railway station where my father was serving in a unit of Ukrainian auxiliaries.

Father informed his commander of our arrival, and we were allowed to stay. Mother worked as a cook at the commander's headquarters, while my brother and I lived with his unit, helping as best we could.

During a lull in the fighting the commander gave Father a letter for Bishop Evlogia of Kholm, telling him to take me to Kiev. The bishop had started an organization to help refugees in Kiev, and he arranged for me to enroll free of charge at the Maryinsky women's school, which had been evacuated from Kholm to Odessa. I lived as boarding student in Odessa until 1919.

Bishop Evlogia was a bastion of the Russian autocracy in Poland and a fanatical agent of the government's Russification policies there, turning the children from the villages of the Western Ukraine into support troops for this policy. Without his intervention I would never have been educated at state expense at the school, for the children of peasants were not accepted, only those of priests and certain officials. After finishing school I worked for a while in the school office, writing testimonials and copying out documents (we had no typewriter).

At the beginning of 1920 I joined the underground Bolsheviks and worked for the Party in Odessa and the surrounding villages. In June all the Communists were mobilized, and I went off with a unit of soldiers to the Polish front. Since I knew the Ukrainian language and conditions, I traveled around the villages with a Red Army soldier, talking about Soviet power. When the Central Committee of the Ukrainian Communist Party was formed, I was elected to lead its women's section in Ternopol.

In the autumn of 1920 we were driven out of Poland, and along with the Central Committee secretary and others I left for Moscow, where I was assigned to enroll in a new six-month Party course at the Sverdlov Communist University.

In the summer of 1921 I was sent to Bakhmut in the Donbas region, to teach the history of Western revolutionary movements at the regional Party school. Until the students arrived I was used by the regional Party commission to purge the ranks. This was my second Party purge — the first was at the Ternopol front.

Requisitioning had been abolished after the Tenth Party Congress in 1921, the markets had opened, and all sorts of things appeared for those who had money. I and a couple of the other teachers would go to the market for bread, and the three of us all caught typhus. One died, but the other girl and I survived. We didn't go to the hospital, we just lay there at the school. The patients were nursed by Serafima Ilyinichna Gopner, who was then conducting agitprop for the regional Party.

Nina Kukharchuk had fallen in with the Party, and as she started working for a new life, straight roads opened up before her. It is appropriate that she should have been noticed by Serafima Gopner, who had so influenced Ekaterina Voroshilova sixteen years earlier.

This young woman raised herself to the highest rank in the land, and she acknowledged that without Bishop Evlogia she would have had no education. Though she could not find a single kind word to say for this "bastion of the autocracy" and "fanatical agent of Russification," she nonetheless learned all she could.

In the autumn of 1922 she was sent to teach political economy at the district Party school in Yuzovka (now Donetsk), where she met Nikita Sergeyevich Khrushchev, a student at the Yuzovka workers' college. At the end of 1923, she was sent by the regional Party committee to work as a propagandist in the mines near Rutchenkovka, where Khrushchev's parents lived with the children from his previous marriage.*

In Rutchenkovka I lived in the guest house, just across from the club. When it rained the road was impossible to cross and people's boots sank into the mud and had to be tied on in a special way. Before I left for Rutchenkovka I had been warned about the mud, and as I had no boots I had to find a private shoemaker to make me some.

At my lectures for the club there were always a lot of women, who were interested in me as a woman and as the friend of Nikita Khrushchev. These were women he had met at the mines and elsewhere.

In those days there was a lot of unemployment, even among Communist miners. After the lectures my audience would follow me home, often complaining bitterly that both my husband and I had jobs while they had large families and no work. But gradually life settled down and unemployment disappeared from the mines.

* *Khrushchev had been married to Efrosinya Ivanovna, who died in 1918 of typhus, leaving behind their two children, Yulia and Leonid.*

In 1924 Nikita Sergeyevich and Nina Petrovna were married. They worked together at the Petrovsk mine near Yuzovka. When Lenin died in January 1924, Nikita Sergeyevich joined a delegation from Donetsk for the funeral. Two years after Lenin's death, Nina Petrovna went to Moscow to study political economy at the Krupskaya Communist Academy. In 1927 she returned to the Kiev Party school to teach political economy, lecturing to miners from the Western Ukraine.

By the autumn of 1927, Nikita Sergeyevich was head of the organization department of the Kiev district Party, and in 1929, shortly after the birth of their daughter, he left Kiev for Moscow to study at the Trade Academy. While he was finishing his studies his wife and baby moved to Moscow to join him.

We lived at the Academy hostel, on Pokrovka Street. We had two rooms, at opposite ends of the corridor. Rada and I slept in one, and in the other slept Yulia, Lenya, and Matryosha, the nanny Nikita Sergeyevich had found for us.

In Moscow the Party committee sent me to work at the Electrical Plant, where I set up a Party school. After a year I was elected to the Party committee and led the agitation and propaganda department of the factory's central committee. There were 3,000 Communists in the Party organization and the factory worked three shifts, so I had a lot of work, leaving home at eight in the morning and coming back at ten at night.

Then disaster struck and Radochka caught scarlet fever. She went to the hospital affiliated with the factory, and I would run out every evening to look through the little window and see how she was doing. I remember the nurse feeding her a bowl of buckwheat porridge with a big spoon, then going off to chat with a friend. Rada, who was just over a year old, put her feet in her bowl and started sobbing. The nurse either didn't hear her or else paid no attention to her crying. I was helpless to intervene. Shortly thereafter we took Rada back home with us.

I worked at the Electrical Plant until the middle of 1935, when Seryozha was born. I finished my first five-year assignment in two and a half years, and received a testimonial from the factory organization. It was at the factory that the third purge of my Party life took place. I made contact with most of the active members there, including the old Bolsheviks, Party organizers, writers, and prerevolutionary political prisoners who had been sent to work at the factory by their organizations and the collective farm workers sponsoring them. I consider these years the most active of my political and personal life.

Nikita Sergeyevich did not finish his studies at the Trade Academy, but was taken on by the Moscow Party as secretary of first the Baumann, then the Krasnopresnya district committees. There were terrible battles with the Right in the Party in those days.

Nikita Sergeyevich was a delegate to the Fifteenth Party Congress. In 1932 he became secretary of the Moscow city committee, and in 1934 he was a delegate at the Seventeenth Party Congress and was voted onto the Party Central Committee. In 1935 he was elected first secretary of the Moscow city committee to replace Kaganovich, who became commissar of transport. He remained here until early 1938, when he left for Kiev as secretary of the Central Committee of the Ukrainian Communist Party.

In Moscow Nikita Sergeyevich devoted much energy to building the first stage of the metro, the river embankments, and the establishment of the bread industry. The entire economy of the capital had to be rebuilt — with bathhouses and toilets on the streets, electricity for Moscow's factories and government, and low houses built to increase living space.

By then we had a four-room apartment in Government House on Kamenny Bridge, and Nikita Sergeyevich's parents were living with us. We had to buy food with ration cards in those days. My distribution center was not far from the factory, and Nikita Sergeyevich's was on what is now Komsomol Street. His father, Sergei Nikanorovich, used to go there for potatoes and other things, and since we had no transport he would carry the food home on his back; once he almost killed himself jumping off a moving tram with his load. He also had to carry Rada up to the kindergarten on the eleventh floor of our building, since the lift did not work. Rada adored her grandfather. Her granny, Kseniya Ivanovna, used to sit with her in her room or would bring her stool outside and sit on the street. People always gathered around her, and she would gossip with them for hours. Nikita Sergeyevich hated her sitting around like this, but she paid no attention to him.

One frequently observes comfortable Soviet wives worshiping at the shrine of their hard childhood, their unhappy youth, and the difficulties they experienced when struggling to bring up babies without adequate childcare. This is particularly noticeable in the memoirs of Nina Petrovna, who not only had a hard time as a child, but later too when she tried combining Party work with taking care of a large family.

The more one peers into the life of the Kremlin and the entire Soviet elite that underlies it, the clearer it becomes that, without the privileges of the state apparatus, the food and housing situation, the Party machine could not work.

Why should it so irritate Nikita Sergeyevich to see his mother chatting with strangers outside the house? What could a simple peasant woman possibly pick up in a house where nothing was ever said because all lived in fear that Stalin could eavesdrop in his office across the Moscow River through a secret cable? What Nikita Sergeyevich surely feared was the thought of his mother telling the neighbors about all the different foods available to the newly arrived provincial bosses and their families.

Nina Petrovna's memoirs — reproduced here almost in their entirety — are the only written testimony of a Soviet Kremlin wife to have seen the light of day. They contain no hint of any interpretation of what was happening in her country, no details of Kremlin life, no characteristics of any of the companions of her life. Why? Because Kremlin life is part of a complex distribution system of privilege that must always be kept secret. Although apparently written for her daughter, these memoirs read as though written for the Party. Virtually all personal details about those in the Kremlin are left out. The only exception is this description of an official reception at Molotov's dacha.

> When V. M. Molotov became commissar of foreign affairs — I don't remember exactly when — they built him a specially designed dacha with large rooms for foreign receptions. One day it was announced that the government was giving a reception there for commissars and leading officials of the Moscow Party.* The officials were invited to bring their wives, which is how I came to be there.
>
> The women were asked into the reception room, and from where I sat near the door I could hear the conversations of the Moscow guests. All the women present worked, and they talked about various things, including their children.
>
> We were called to the dining room, where the tables were laid out in a U-shape and we were seated according to an arranged plan. I sat next to Valeria Alexeyevna Golubtsova-Malenkova, and across from the wife of Stanislav Kosior, who had just been promoted to the

* Since Molotov was made minister of foreign affairs in 1939, and Khrushchev was then in the Ukraine, the events described are likely to have taken place early in 1938.

Soviet of People's Commissars. It was already known then that Nikita Sergeyevich Khrushchev was to take over Kosior's old job as secretary of the Ukrainian Central Committee, and I asked Kosior's wife what kitchenware I should take with me. She was very surprised by my question and replied that the house in which we would be living had everything, there was no need to bring anything. When I arrived in the Ukraine I discovered that everything had indeed been supplied by the government: all the furniture, including a full set of china and more pots and pans than I had ever seen in my life. The house also came with a cook. As for food, we did our shopping in the local government store, and were billed for our purchases once a month.

After the guests at Molotov's reception were seated J. V. Stalin came through the door of the buffet room, followed by his Politburo members, and sat down at the head table. They were greeted with lengthy applause, of course. Stalin said that a lot of new commissariats had recently been set up and new leaders appointed, and the Politburo thought it would be a good idea to hold an informal meeting for everyone to get to know one another better.

After that a great number of people got up, identified themselves, and announced their jobs, and described how they viewed their work. The women were also allowed to take the floor, and Valeria Golubtsova-Malenkova spoke about her scientific work. A lot of the women took umbrage at Malenkova's vying with the men. She was followed by the young wife of the commissar for higher education, Kaftanov, who said she would do all she could to support her husband in his new post. Her speech was received with universal approval.

We may forgive Nina Petrovna all her caution, her silences and half-statements for this remark — the women's reaction to Malenkova — clearly reveals the changes then taking place in Kremlin women's lives. All the women present worked, yet both they and their husbands greeted Malenkova's speech with open disapproval, while they applauded Kaftanova. The time had apparently come in the Soviet Union to put some politically undeveloped women in their place. Stalin had been burned by his hardworking, independent wife. Till now Kremlin women had been deeply involved in both the Revolution and building socialism; the word now was that it was time for them to return to home and kitchen. Their reward was limitless material privileges; they had no cause to grumble.

Nineteen thirty-seven had passed, the "enemies of the people" were gone, and now a Kremlin wife could be a wife, and only a wife. Clearly the evening described by Nina Petrovna gave unofficial sanction to a crucial redefining of Kremlin wives' position in the waning years of the 1930s. Krupskaya was in disgrace.

Nina Petrovna gives only a few hints as to how these changes affected her active and independent life in the years leading to the outbreak of war.

> In 1939 the Germans occupied Poland and were approaching my parents' village of Vasilev. Our troops were meanwhile moving west and capturing large areas of the Western Ukraine and Western Bye- lorussia, including the town of Lvov. Nikita Sergeyevich telephoned me in Kiev and told me that since Vasilev and the surrounding area was about to fall to the Germans, I could travel to Lvov if I wanted and be driven on to Vasilev to pick up my parents. My trip was organized by the secretary of the Ukrainian Communist Party, Com- rade Burmistenko. He informed me that I would be traveling with two women who were being sent by the Central Committee to work in Lvov. One of them, a young Komsomol member, was to work with Lvov's young people; the other, a Party official, would be working with women. We were handed revolvers and told to wear army uni- forms, so we wouldn't be stopped by army patrols on the way.
>
> Our journey passed without incident, but not far from Lvov we were almost run into by an approaching truck whose driver had not slept for three days and had fallen asleep at the wheel. The only one of us hurt was the Komsomol girl, who suffered some bruised ribs. A passing commander checked our documents and drove us the rest of the way to Lvov, where the girl was treated at the hospital and soon recovered. The other girl and I stayed at the quarters of the general in command. Semyon Konstantinovich Timoshenko was commander of the Kiev military district then, and Nikita Sergeyevich Khrushchev was a member of the Military Council. When they returned home and saw us with our revolvers and uniforms they roared with laughter, then Nikita Sergeyevich became furious and ordered us to put on our dresses again. "What are you thinking of?" he shouted. "You want to tell the local people about Soviet power, and you turn up waving revolvers? Who will trust you? They've been told for the last thirty years that we're bandits — you'll just confirm it!"
>
> I put my civilian clothes back on and set off for Vasilev with Bozhka, one of Nikita Sergeyevich's guards, to fetch my parents. We arrived safely at the cottage, and found Father and Mother at home.

Crowds of people ran up to look at me and hear the latest news. No one could imagine that the village was about to fall to the Germans — even the junior officers knew nothing.

All night long soldiers crowded into the cottage to warm themselves. Mother cooked for them, while Bozhko sat talking with them. Toward morning members of the newly organized local government arrived to arrest me as a spy and *provocateur,* and Bozhko and the tank drivers had difficulty persuading them of their mistake. That morning my parents, my brother, and his family loaded a cart with their possessions, and we drove to Lvov. I took my parents to the Lvov Palace of Fighters, where Nikita Sergeyevich was staying, and they walked around the rooms marveling at everything. My father turned on the water tap and shouted: "Hey, Mother, look at this — the water comes out of a pipe!" When he entered the room Nikita Sergeyevich shared with Comrade Timoshenko, he pointed at Timoshenko and demanded, "Is this our son-in-law?" But I didn't notice him looking too disappointed when I told him that his new son-in-law was in fact Nikita Sergeyevich.

Her father evidently would have preferred the more imposing of the two young men as his new son-in-law.

Over the next ten years Nina Petrovna — the personification of Party spirit — gradually and with a bit of guilt turned herself into the wife of the leader, thus setting the pattern for a new type of Kremlin wife for whom kitchen and children are all-important and the demands of Party work become secondary.

When I met Nina Petrovna's daughter Rada at her dacha recently outside Moscow, she said:

When Mama was young, she stopped working. She started to believe it was her Party duty to look after her family properly, and she imposed Party order on the family. This wasn't easy, not only for us children but for her servants too. Father's salary was 800 rubles, and she kept a tight hold on it. When there was a reception at the house or the dacha, she made sure that not too many bottles were put out in case the guests drank too much or the servants got drunk afterward. We children were never invited. We would sit separately and eat completely different food. Mother kept a strict eye on that. She never threw anything away. After her death we found piles of old dresses and jumpers that had been sewn and often repaired.

Mother was a strict disciplinarian, and very secretive. She never talked about herself. I was astonished when she accepted my advice and wrote her memoirs. I once asked her why they called me Rada (which means "glad"), and she said, "I was glad you were born." The two younger children, Seryozha and Lenochka, were often ill as children, and Lenochka caught tuberculosis and died when she was only in her twenties.

I was her second daughter. She had had another daughter named Nadya, who died. She had no time for her children. Until I was nine she spent almost no time at home with me, and I was looked after by nannies. She had strict Party principles, and I suffered from them. We always had a difficult relationship, even though we loved each other.

She was very strict about our schoolwork, especially with me. She wasn't so strict with the others; she didn't work then and looked after them herself, and she wasn't so tense then. Yulia and Leonid, the two children from Father's previous marriage, were a lot older. Leonid's daughter, also called Yulia, was like a sister to us, and my parents adopted her when her stepfather died.

Leonid lived in Kiev, where he worked at the pilots' school. During the war he flew in several massive bombing raids over Germany and was seriously wounded. He spent a long time in the hospital in Kuibyshev, where we were all evacuated as a family when Father was at the front. In the hospital, Leonid started to drink. One day when he was drunk he shot a man, was court-martialed, and as punishment was sent to the front line.

At the beginning of the war his sister Yulia married the theatrical administrator of the "Dumka" choir. She worked, but she was a very domestic woman at heart, more interested in sewing, cooking, and washing.

Father hardly ever spent any time with us. He felt Mother should be in charge of the home, leaving him free to do his government work. He loved me, the house was always happy when he was around; when we went off to the dacha he would sing, read poems, and take me skiing. It was almost impossible to ask Mother for anything; he was much easier.

Our children now ask us if we really knew nothing, and whether our parents ever said anything in front of us. The fact is that no one ever discussed politics at home. There were never any overt displays of the Stalin cult, although I remember when guests came to celebrate the Mayday holiday after the war, Father's first toast would always be to Stalin. Even then it seemed to me forced. But we were never allowed to say a word against Lenin or Stalin. I argued once with my grandmother when she told me to listen to her because she was older and wiser.

"What, wiser than Stalin?" I asked.

"Of course I am!" she retorted.

I was brought up not to ask questions. We children unconsciously knew what we could say and what we couldn't.

Mother was very hardworking and well organized. She had excellent handwriting; she was famous for it even at school. In our little factory settlement near Kuibyshev during the war she decided to take English lessons. I was shocked by this frivolity in the midst of war, but she soon collected a group of students, and an English teacher came to visit our apartment. Father, who was rarely at home, was nevertheless also surprised, but she cut him short, saying it was time to strengthen relations with our allies. The lessons soon stopped, however, because of life's difficulties.

When Beria was shot, Nina Teimurazovna and her son, Sergo, wrote to Khrushchev complaining that what was happening to them was illegal. He was touched by their letter and believed them. There was a lot they did not know, of course, but they could see he was floundering in the abyss, and that they were forced to flounder in the same abyss with him. After Beria's execution Mother felt very sorry for Nina Teimurazovna. She was glad when she and her son were allowed to live.

Rada's husband, Alexei Ivanovich Adzhubei, who later became editor of *Izvestia* and one of Khrushchev's closest associates, adds his own color to Nina Petrovna's portrait. "Life was divided into two eras: before and after the death of Stalin. After Stalin died, the entire Kremlin court seemed to dissolve.

"I had been part of this world before I met Rada, since my mother, Nina Gopalo, was one of the best dressmakers in Moscow and had made clothes for Svetlana Stalin, Molotov's wife, Nina Beria, and later Nina Petrovna."

Nina Petrovna's unremarkable matronly figure required simple lines; anything grand or elegant would have looked ridiculous on her, and Gopalo realized this. "Both Mother and Mother-in-law were tough nuts. Nina Petrovna Khrushcheva hadn't been one of her customers until her visit to America in 1959, when Mother happily created a wardrobe to show her off to best advantage."

Nina Gopalo had joined the Bolshevik underground before the

Khrushchev with his family

Khrushchev with Brezhnev and Mikoyan

revolution, fought with the Red Army, and was thoroughly trusted by the government. She had her own workshop in Moscow. Yet when Adzhubei married Rada Khrushcheva, Nina Beria told his mother: "It's bad that your Alexei has joined the Khrushchev family." Nina Gopalo was upset, but Beria's wife proved to be right, for this was the time of Stalin's campaign against the children of leading officials, and shortly after the wedding an anonymous letter reached the government claiming that Rada and Alexei were leading a life of luxury. Alexei Ivanovich goes on:

> Nina Petrovna's character was guarded, to say the least. When Rada and I decided to marry, she was the last to agree, and it was only after several years that her attitude toward me changed from distrust to warmth, and at the end of her life, after all her misfortunes, she began to respect me.
>
> Kremlin families led a highly unusual life. We lived as tsars and died as paupers. We never had anything of our own, we were supported by the state, since it was contrary to Party principles to own anything. The Khrushchevs always had four portraits hanging in their dining room: Marx, Engels, Lenin, and Stalin.

Nobody obliged them to hang these portraits in their dining room. For Nina Petrovna and Nikita Sergeyevich Khrushchev it was natural; these were their teachers, the creators of their ideas. Yet the children felt uncomfortable with them, and the grandchildren found them ridiculous and now ask if their grandparents really believed it all. The answer is: they most certainly did.

In 1956, when Nina Petrovna entered the place that had been occupied for the past two decades by the omnipotent and tyrannical Stalin, she did so as an experienced Kremlin wife, who had lived by its unwritten laws for almost two decades. In Stalin's Kremlin she was to face domestic desolation and graveyard cold. If her husband was a reformer, it must be assumed that she was similarly inclined as she surveyed the apartments bequeathed to him as Russia's new head of state. Although she probably did not have the deciding vote in the move from the Kremlin to the Lenin Hills, it was probably she who first considered the idea and lodged it in the temperamental brain of Nikita Sergeyevich, and in rejecting this blood-soaked legacy, her female instinct

Khrushchev, Mikoyan, Voroshilov with their wives and children

proved correct. The Soviet people naturally knew nothing of this, and the newspapers didn't comment either, so her decision appeared as a purely personal one. That decision allowed the Politburo to open the Kremlin to the public.

The comfort and space of the leaders' living quarters in the Lenin Hills corresponded, as in the Kremlin, to rank, and the Khrushchevs had the best villa. Standard mini-palaces in the "Stalin Empire" style, the new mansions and villas, constructed for the leaders and their families, are visible today behind their high stone walls. The wives and children remembered the inconveniences of the new life: the houses were built in a hurry, communications and plumbing were hastily installed, in winter the walls froze and pipes burst. Transportation, however, was no problem, since the wives had their own chauffeur-driven cars, but they were still inconveniently far from central Moscow. In their cramped Kremlin quarters it had been less obvious that everything, including the furniture, belonged to the state; the bare expanse of new walls made this fact glaringly apparent and reminded the inhabitants of the impermanence of their positions. A few of the cleverer ones, knowing that their downfall might come at any moment, preferred to move in with their families in the center of Moscow on Granovskaya Street. But most power-hungry people rarely think of impermanence.

When asked about Nina Petrovna's reaction to her husband's disgrace in 1964, Rada Nikitichna replies:

> For many years Mother had suffered from a bone condition called osteochondrosis, for which she used to take the waters in the Crimea. After the war she started visiting Karlovy Vary in Czechoslovakia, and in October 1964 she was there with Brezhnev's wife, Victoria Petrovna, when news of the government coup against Krushchev reached them. Mother did not immediately take in what had happened and understood it as a natural shift of power, saying to Victoria Petrovna: "Now I won't invite you to receptions, you'll invite me!"
>
> When she returned to Moscow she was very ill, and refused to leave her villa in the Lenin Hills. They kept trying to get her out, but she insisted on staying another month. She was in a state of shock.

Rada and her husband had their own apartment by then, as did Seryozha. Lenochka could find nowhere to live and stayed in her parents' new quarters on Starokonyushenny Lane.

I don't think Father ever slept in Moscow, he lived at their dacha in Petrovo-Dalnoe. They were offered another dacha a hundred kilometers from Moscow, but they chose the nearer one.

After Father's fall, predictably all my Kremlin friends disappeared. That day in October I met Galina Satyukova, wife of the editor-in-chief of *Pravda* and one of my father's closest associates. She knew nothing and was very friendly, insisting that we take a vacation together, and promising to call me to arrange it. I never heard from her again. My university friends didn't abandon me, though, nor did my artist and actor friends, who continued to telephone and come around.

In fact, Father and the intelligentsia never really understood each other — he loved them but they wrong-footed him. Mother had never made any friends among the government wives, and those who had hovered around soon disappeared. At the end of her life only her old friends from the Ukraine visited her.

After Father's death she was moved from Petrovo-Dalnoe to a dacha at Zhukovka, the so-called "widows' village." She lived alone there and never locked the door, she merely had to put a stick across so it could not be pushed open.

She received a monthly pension of 200 rubles, half of Father's 400, plus access to the Kremlin's clinic and food supplies and the use of a car. She quickly grew used to living alone and had an emergency telephone on her bedside table with her medicines. When she was ill in the hospital, the nurses deliberately humiliated her and refused to give her a bedpan, but she just smiled at them and didn't say a word.

Nina Petrovna's strength of character is confirmed by all who knew her. Three years after Khrushchev's death in 1974, his youngest son, Sergei, was summoned to the KGB and was asked to denounce Khrushchev's memoirs, which had recently been published in the West as *Khrushchev Remembers: The Last Testament*. He was handed a letter written by the KGB, declaring the memoirs to be a forgery and clearly intended to create a scandal in the West by discrediting the work. He was asked to sign it. Sergei Khrushchev found the proposal distasteful:

> I said I could make no decision on my own and would have to discuss it with my mother. When I told her, she asked me if I had read the memoirs. I hadn't even seen them. "So how can you say it's a forgery if you don't know the text?" she asked logically. "You can't make a statement about a book none of us had seen. We don't know how the West got hold of it."
>
> At our next meeting I told the KGB this. I knew the discussion

wouldn't be easy, but I had an irrefutable argument: Mother had forbidden it.

Even the KGB didn't dare approach Nina Petrovna, knowing full well her strength of character. Yet she had changed. It is curious that a correct Party functionary such as she should not regard the West's publication of Khrushchev's memoirs as an appalling security lapse requiring careful investigation. But in old age Nina Petrovna became politically "soft." Her feelings as a wife and mother outweighed her feelings of Party duty. She still loved the Party, yet she would not sacrifice her life's companion to its gaping maw, even though he was no longer alive.

The memoirs have proved genuine, as she must have known from the start. But she also knew the KGB and its tricks — hardly surprising for one who lived for so many years by its rules.

15

Victoria's Quiet Victory

Leonid Ilyich Brezhnev (1906–1982), born in Dneproderzhinsk, in the Ukraine. Joined the Party in 1931 and served as political commissar during the war. In 1950 he was made first secretary of the Moldavian Party. In early 1953 he became deputy chief of the political administration of the Defense Ministry. In 1954 he was secretary of the Kazakhstan Central Committee. And in 1960 he replaced Voroshilov as Soviet president. His close ties with the military served him well in the coup against Khrushchev, whom he replaced in 1964 as the Party's first secretary. His death came at the end of a long process of physical deterioration and senility.

THE FRAGILITY OF VICTORY was keenly felt in Moscow during August of 1991. The blood of those who had died during the attempted coup intoxicated the young and shook the old. Ideals were trampled beneath the barricades, and panic-stricken young people were looking for direction for this destructive unifying force.

One August day in 1991, I walked back into the past, to the world in which our late head of state, Leonid Ilyich Brezhnev, had lived and worked. It was less than a mile from the barricades around the White House to his home in a large building on Kutuzovsky Prospect, where his eighty-three-year-old widow, Victoria Petrovna, now lives alone, seeing no one and rarely going out.

I was accompanied by her daughter-in-law, Ludmilla Vladimirovna, wife of her son, Yuri. On the outside of the building a plaque bearing Brezhnev's name had recently been ripped down. In the hall was an intercom, a rug, an armchair, a bucket of flowers, an ordinary elevator. Brezhnev had been given this apartment many years earlier. He had had several opportunities to exchange it for another one. In the late 1970s a splendid brick apartment building was erected on Shchusev Street, in one of the most prestigious districts of Moscow. Increasing numbers of such buildings were then appearing in the center of Moscow for the newly arriving Party elite, but Brezhnev kept this one. This building had several distinguishing features not immediately noticeable to the untrained eye: the third floor was larger than the rest, as were the windows. This floor was designed especially for the Brezhnevs. It was said that Leonid Ilyich had participated in the discussions about the project and was the first to enter the new building, but that he refused to live there, preferring to go on living modestly without showing off.

Stopping before an ordinary door, we rang the bell. It was opened by Anya, a tall, elderly woman who has faithfully served the Brezhnevs for many years. As she went off with Ludmilla Vladimirovna to inform Victoria Petrovna of my arrival, I sat alone in the spacious lobby, separated from distant rooms by two Corinthian pillars. Before me was an open door into a large room with windows overlooking the noisy Kutuzovsky Prospect. There were two portraits of Leonid Ilyich executed by a court painter such as Alexander Gerasimov. One was obviously taken from a well-known photograph, the other an informal study of a youthful, handsome Brezhnev straining forward, his shirt unbuttoned and his hands in front of him. At one of the windows in this large room, evidently the former dining room, hung two metal cages on fine legs, containing some parakeets; the general secretary loved birds. The floor of the lobby was covered in linoleum. On the walls hung the heads of huge stuffed animals: a wild mountain ram with magnificent Ionic horns and two stags, their magnificent antlers brushing the ceiling. A medieval castle would seem a more appropriate setting for trophies such as these; Brezhnev was a passionate hunter, and many of the pictures and photographs have hunting themes: Leonid Ilyich with a gun slung over his shoulders, Leonid Ilyich with a gun in his hands, Leonid Ilyich with a dead boar at his feet.

In the mid-1970s people recounted how the general secretary's huntsmen would shackle these stags and rams and lead him through the forest for half an hour until he came upon the peacefully grazing animal. Yury Gagarin was said to have protested at this deception when he went hunting with Leonid Ilyich, but it evidently continued as Brezhnev became increasingly senile and unable to shoot.

Anya returned to tell me that Victoria Petrovna was dressing and that she was not feeling well today. Finally Victoria Petrovna entered slowly, leaning on Anya. She was wearing a dark green dressing gown, her face smooth, her gray hair drawn back in a bun, and her watery blue eyes veiled in blindness. She was radiant, tranquil, and open to her unseen guest. She sat down. What right did I have to harass this eighty-three-year-old woman by raising questions about her husband's womanizing, her relatives' timeserving, her children's alcoholism, her son-in-law's embezzlement?

The Brezhnev family was relatively small by Russian standards: Victoria Petrovna and Leonid Ilyich, their two children, Galina and Yuri, and three grandchildren — Yuri's boys, Leonid and Andrei, and Galina's daughter, Victoria.

But the extended family was large; both Leonid Ilyich and Victoria Petrovna had several brothers and sisters. This huge family clan was perpetually in need of help and support. Like many such clans, the Brezhnev's was divided internally, and relations within it were often complicated. The division occurred naturally between his relatives and hers. Although submissive to her husband in all other respects, Victoria Petrovna always defended her family against the larger Brezhnev clan, making sure that her relatives had the same privileges as his.

There were constant rumors about the Brezhnev family. The first I heard was in 1949, during a holiday in Dnepropetrovsk, where Leonid Ilyich was first secretary of the regional Party committee. People there whispered about a four-year-old girl who had wandered unsupervised through the half-open gates of the Brezhnev mansion. The guard dogs were off their chain and, it was said, tore her to pieces.

During perestroika the press picked up and legitimized many Brezhnev rumors when they reported the arrest of Yuri Churbanov, a deputy minister of internal affairs and Galina Brezhneva's third husband. These rumors would fill a fat volume, but sifting through them several "charges" stand out: debauchery, drunkenness, nepotism, and abuse of power.

What about Victoria Petrovna? She accepted it all. Leonid Ilyich was a village boy; she was said to be from the Jewish intelligentsia, the daughter of an economics teacher named Olshevsky. Her family took Leonid Ilyich in, educated him, and did all they could to help him rise to the top. And rise he did. He was handsome, tall, elegant, always laughing, and women swooned over him. They say he was unfaithful to her on their wedding day and had a succession of affairs thereafter; local Party leaders were renowned for their exploits in the bath house, with food, drink, and a limitless supply of girls. Victoria Petrovna knew everything, of course, but decided that the wisest course was to say nothing. She bore him two children, quietly tied her husband to her, like a goat on a long string. It may wander off, but always returns.

Everyone in Dnepropetrovsk knew of his affair with the beautiful T. R. He showered her with presents, and in the late 1940s they openly traveled to Germany together. When he left to work in Moldavia, she married his best friend, and Brezhnev was said to have been very depressed about it. In Moldavia, however, he quickly found consolation with another woman. Back in Moscow he took up with an actress from the Moscow Arts Theater. Victoria Petrovna always sat quietly and waited for his affairs to pass.

The stories about Brezhnev quickly became politicized. They were also a little sad, particularly toward the end when Leonid Ilyich, decrepit, was forced by his crumbling Party machine to push himself into view to stave off its final collapse.

Apart from hunting, Brezhnev's main interest was his vast collection of foreign cars. Where did he acquire them? Did he buy them with foreign money? Was he given them by foreign heads of state? These are questions still unanswered.

Speaking of Brezhnev and his array of automobiles, I have a personal anecdote. One evening in the early summer of 1980, my husband and I were driving along Leningrad Prospect toward the center, not far from the Sokolniki underground station. Suddenly out of nowhere a foreign car appeared behind us, swerving madly and trying to pass. "Who's that idiot in a foreign car?" yelled my husband, finally allowing the car to flash past us. Gripping the wheel of a large Mercedes, staring straight ahead at the empty highway, sat Leonid Ilyich Brezhnev. The seat beside him was empty, but behind him and shaking his fist at us in fury sat Vladimir Medvedev, whose face has graced our televisions for many a year: personal adjutant to Brezhnev, then to Gorbachev, Medvedev was an odd figure during perestroika.

People later had trouble understanding how the same system that judged Brezhnev guilty could allow his personal adjutant to hold onto his ill-gotten gains.

The Mercedes was followed by a black Volga filled with military men, all angrily shaking their fists at us as well. I was grateful that our adventure had no unpleasant consequences.

Eduard Gierek, general secretary of the Polish Communist Party, recalled Leonid Brezhnev in the early 1970s:

> I don't think he had any friends. Negotiations between the Czech, Soviet, and Polish delegations were always followed by a friendly get-together. A huge quantity of Soviet cognac was consumed at such gatherings. Brezhnev was coarse and plainly irritated by the repercussions of the Prague Spring.
>
> His office in the Kremlin was small, only 15 by 30 feet, with doors on either side. There was only a bust and portrait of Lenin. I wondered why the general secretary had such a modest office, and concluded that there were two possible reasons. First, right next door to it was Lenin's office, which had been carefully preserved. It was comfortable but modest; to have an ostentatious office would have been in poor taste beside the office of the revered founder of the state. Second, as ruler of one of the two most powerful nations on earth, it would look good to seem modest.
>
> Brezhnev had no home. In fact, none of the Kremlin leaders had what you would call a home. They were given apartments and dachas "for services rendered," but in fact these and all their other privileges depended upon their positions. Falling from grace in the USSR meant losing everything, and in the Stalin period frequently one's life, too. Under Stalin's successors, a banished politician would simply be evicted from his apartment, and his living standard would drop in accordance with his new position. We often compared our life in Poland to theirs, yet none of us would have changed places with them. Although there were some among us clinging by their teeth to power for power's sake, over in Russia it was a vital necessity for every member of government.

The most frequent Brezhnev rumors concerned his daughter. Galina Brezhneva was an all-too-typical product of what came to be known as the Era of Stagnation. This aging, heavy-drinking woman with a short fuse and limitless opportunities for self-gratification had a young husband, a younger lover, and a consuming passion for diamonds. It would be interesting to know where the vast fortune required to keep her in jewels came from. Those on the government payroll rarely had much money. Some said the diamonds were gifts from people who owed her favors, yet there were other, semi-official channels for this stream of jewels. According to the director of Yuvelirtorg, the state-run jewelry company, antique and contemporary pieces of jewelry that were confiscated from criminals rarely made it to shops to be sold, but went straight to women of a special government rank.

There are many "diamond legends" about Galina Brezhneva. One involved the museum in the Georgian town of Zugdidi, which contained two relics, a death mask of Napoleon and the diadem of the Queen Tamara. The heavily guarded diadem lies on velvet under a thick pane of glass in the center of the hall. In 1975, Galina Brezhneva visited the museum, and was so enamored of the diadem that she demanded that the noble Zugdidians give it to her as a present. The director of the museum, mad with grief, plucked up courage to inform the first secretary of the Georgian Communist Party, Eduard Shevardnadze, who grabbed the government telephone and told Comrade Brezhnev that while Georgia deeply respected Galina Leonidovna they could not give away their national heritage. "Send Galina home!" was her father's response.

Another diamond story dates from the end of 1981, during a festival of the Moscow circus. Galina Brezhneva adored the circus, and often took her husbands and lovers there. She and a friend, the wife of Internal Affairs Minister Shchelokov, were present, adorned in their best diamonds. However the diamonds of lion tamer Irina Bugrimova outshone the Brezhnev diamonds. A few days later Irina Bugrimova's entire collection was stolen, and the evidence pointed to Boris Buryatse, Galina Brezhneva's lover. Several days later Buryatse was apprehended at Sheremetyevo Airport; his luggage contained a portion of the Bugrimova diamonds.

These stories pained and affected the health of Leonid Ilyich, who suffered greatly in his later years from his relatives' misadventures. "The world respects you, but your own family causes you shame," he would grumble to his Party colleagues.

Perestroika turned rumors into half-facts. Many of these are filled with inaccuracies, and details were invented to allow the new political figures to rail at the old. But where there is smoke there is usually fire. Galina Brezhneva's friends were picked up and arrested, the apartments of high-placed officials were searched, and millions of rubles, gold, and valuables were confiscated. Galina stopped appearing in public. At Brezhnev's funeral, in November 1982, two burly guards were constantly by her side. People sat glued to their television sets as the funeral was broadcast and Yuri Andropov embraced Brezhnev's wife but turned his back on Galina.

Andropov ruled for fifteen months. Throughout this time the investigations continued. Boris Buryatse was sentenced to five years in prison, where he died under mysterious circumstances. After Andropov's death, during the brief leadership of Chernenko, the stories and rumors still surrounding Galina subsided and she again began appearing in public. At a major reception held in the Lenin Hills to commemorate International Women's Day, she appeared dressed in a plain blue suit, and wore only a single piece of jewelry pinned to her bosom: the Order of Lenin awarded to her in 1978 by Foreign Minister Gromyko, on the occasion of her fiftieth birthday.

Despite this hiatus, the KGB continued to unearth more and more crimes. Criminal charges were brought against Shchelokov, former minister of internal affairs, who one day in 1984 dressed himself in his army general's uniform and shot himself in the mouth.

Chernenko died, Gorbachev arrived, and Galina's husband, Yuri Churbanov, was finally arrested, along with Brezhnev's son, Yuri, formerly deputy minister of foreign trade. Searches of Galina's homes failed to yield results; some said Churbanov had hidden the diamonds, others that he had given them to friends. Galina Leonidovna's rooms were regularly searched in her presence. She was habitually drunk, signing statements without reading them, taking a friendly interest in the police, and proposing that they all drink together.

Amid the torrent of gossip about the Brezhnevs and their seemingly endless greed there is nothing whatsoever about Victoria Petrovna.

As I sat with her in her apartment, where the recently destroyed past is still embalmed, she talked to me about her life. She was born in Kursk, one of five children, where her father, Pyotr Nikanorovich Denisov, was a train engineer, her mother a housewife. After leaving secondary school she studied nursing at technical college, and it was at a dance at her nursing school in 1935 that she met Leonid Ilyich, then an agronomy student at Kursk technical college.

He asked my best friend to go out with him, and she refused. He asked her out again, and again she refused him, because he couldn't dance. "Coming, Vitya?" he said to me, so I went with him. Next day he asked my friend out again, and again she refused to go dancing with him. So once again I went with him. I taught him to dance, and he started seeing me home. I started looking at him seriously. He was respectable, well-educated. I wouldn't say he was handsome. He wore his hair with a side parting then and it didn't suit him. I persuaded him to change it, and he wore it that way ever since.

They married in 1938. Victoria Petrovna worked as a midwife until the birth of their two children. He qualified as a land surveyor, then studied at a metallurgy institute. There followed Party work, the war, and his steady climb up the Party ladder, culminating in 1966 in his appointment as general secretary.

He almost never saw the children, he was always at work. He loved it when the family got together, but when we were all sitting around the table on Sundays, the phone would invariably ring and he would be called out.

At first I couldn't cook, but I was anxious to learn, and it turned out I had a talent for it. Leonid Ilyich, the children, and our guests would praise my meals. Leonid Ilyich had a splendid appetite, he loved my cooking, especially my borscht. "No one cooks like Vitya," he used to say. There are several types of Ukrainian borscht, you know — cold or hot, vegetarian or meat. Patties, too; the secret of good patties is to beat the stuffing thoroughly before you fry them. I adore markets. When Leonid Ilyich was first secretary in Dnepropetrovsk during the late 1940s, I always went to the market and bought everything myself. In markets the chickens are always in cages. I never bought a dead chicken, always a live one, the best. Saturdays and Sundays were lovely. I would take my time choosing, then say, "Give me that one!" Then there were the fish. Dnepropetrovsk is on the river Dnepr. What perch and salmon there were! I'm on a special diet now, everything is boiled and tasteless. Only the memory remains.

When asked about the few occasions on which she traveled abroad with her husband, she says:

I never liked those trips much, I always avoided them whenever possible. You never saw anything, just sat in the car listening to the guide.

Once we flew to Paris for a magnificent reception, but in the distance people were demonstrating with banners that read,

International Women's Day, March 8. Victoria Brezhnev, third from left

Victoria Brezhnev, always in his shadow

"Victoria Petrovna, you are a Jew! Help your people leave for their homeland!" I felt uncomfortable. I'm not a Jew, you see, although people say I look like one, but I felt awkward saying I wasn't one, in case people thought I was denying my people.

At that point, Ludmilla Vladimirovna joined us, and Victoria Petrovna asked her about the shopping.

Galina Kravchenko, Nadezhda Voroshilova, Ludmilla Vladimirovna — the daughters-in-law in this book — all belong to a special category. Living in the Kremlin, submitting to its rules and accepting its privileges, they knew what it was like to have these privileges revoked. A warm, youthful woman, Ludmilla Vladimirovna has been untouched by the rumors, because there was obviously nothing negative to be said about her.

When I married Yuri Leonidovich and moved in with the Brezhnevs they welcomed me into their family. I got along with Leonid Ilyich and his expansive character from the start. I was to call them "Papa" and "Mama." I couldn't bring myself to do that right away, because my own parents were alive. It bothered Leonid Ilyich, who said to Victoria Petrovna: "Vitya, our daughter-in-law doesn't respect us. She won't call us Mama and Papa!" I quickly complied.

Victoria Petrovna is a good person, but difficult. The two of them got on wonderfully together. When he was young, Leonid Ilyich was very lively, handsome, and outgoing. He loved poetry and used to recite Merezhkovsky and Esenin from memory. Beside him Victoria seemed pale. She was a simple train engineer's daughter, shy and ordinary. When I grew more comfortable with them I would say to her: "Your mother must have been courted by an educated Jew while your father was driving his train!" and she would laugh.

They both had large families, and family feelings were in their blood. Maybe it was that common bond that brought them together. Vitya would never start dinner without him, and he never did anything in the house without her permission; all domestic questions hung on his phrase: "Ask Vitya, Vitya knows everything."

Victoria Petrovna looked after her own children and her nieces and nephews. When they went on vacation they would often be accompanied by the entire family clan — nieces, nephews, his brothers' wives.

Socially Victoria Petrovna was quiet and uncommunicative. It was hard to start a conversation with her. Receptions of any sort, even International Women's Day, were a torment for her. She would say,

"You go, Lusya, you speak." And I would say: "It's you they want to hear, not me!"

The servants especially loved Leonid Ilyich, and she cherished her husband's authority in the home. When we were on vacation in the south, after swimming and eating we would want to take a nap, but she would insist we stay at the table until he came, and he would invariably arrive with a bunch of flowers for her. Vitya and Lenya were like two doves together.

Generally at the table with Leonid Ilyich's family were his doctor, his nurse, and the maid. There were two cooks, Slava and Valera, who worked for the Brezhnevs for twenty years. Victoria Petrovna always watched them work, and would say: "It's good to see you've studied cooking, but that's restaurant food. For food to be special you must put a piece of your soul into it."

She was always cooking: pickling cucumbers and tomatoes, making home-smoked sausage, black pudding with buckwheat, cherry pies. She knitted clothes for Galina and Galina's daughter, and she brought up her granddaughter by herself; the child was named Victoria after her. She loved her nephews and her brothers and sisters, too, and often seemed to favor them over Leonid Ilyich. She gave no sign of suffering in the last phase of her life. But her voice trembled when she told me she had to leave her dacha. And later when she was being criticized for something she said in a breaking voice: "It had to be like this — I'm guilty for the war in Afghanistan!" The fact was she was totally uninterested in politics. Picking out a nice piece of lamb or some pigs' knuckles was another matter, or baking a cherry pie, or beating cream for her mother-in-law, Natalya Denisovna, or peeling apples for the pudding.

She seemed to have a natural talent for cooking. She bustled around the house from morning to night, making jam, bottling cucumbers and tomatoes, pickling, drying herbs, making pelmeni and cherry pies. Victoria Petrovna had several prize dishes, including gooseberry jam. She would labor for hours over it, and it always tasted marvelous. People loved talking about food in the house, even at mealtimes.

She hated going out. Leonid always invited people around to see them instead. If she told him Andryey Gromyko had invited them over for dinner, he would say, "Fine, but why should we go to them? Let them come here!"

Gromyko, Ustinov, and Andropov were always visiting. It was all so inconsistent: on the one hand there was the house and all the creature comforts that high office implied; on the other, a conscious show of modesty, with the grandsons forbidden to wear jeans for fear of what people might say. I had to dress plainly to avoid gossip, so I would buy the cheapest earrings, and brooches that wouldn't fasten properly.

They had a four-hundred-ruble food allowance. Victoria Petrovna never let anything be thrown away, even an old battery, in case it could become useful later on. She kept all her husband's old shirts and had them endlessly darned and mended. She and the two servants would work in the house for days on end without sitting down.

She wasn't an easy person. If she didn't like something she would fall silent but her whole figure would be filled with reproach. I never saw her in tears. When her husband was in power in Dnepropetrovsk, Moldavia, and finally in Moscow, she had to keep moving from dacha to dacha, and her first question always was, "Is there a cellar?" She never complained, she simply said, "All right, I'm ready." She had no women friends. But the wives of Mazurov, Kulakov, Gromyko, and Ustinov often visited, and they would dine together and play cards.

Leonid Ilyich shone so much more brightly than she did. He had an attractive personality and unlimited oportunities for love affairs. They never quarreled. She accepted their differences right from the start. She took care of the home, and he appreciated her ability to create a homey atmosphere. Imagine a huge table loaded with food, with Vitya seated at the head, Lenya to her left, all her relatives on her side and all his relatives on his side, as though facing off in a tournament.

In the morning she would sit beside him as he ate his breakfast. It calmed him to have her sitting there without eating. When he received his insulin shot for his diabetes she always had to be there. At night she would sit dozing until past midnight, waiting for him, and you never knew if she suspected anything. Her most striking features were her patience and endurance.

Victoria Petrovna's life represented the victory of the Kremlin family woman over Nadezhda Krupskaya and all the other progressive Kremlin women. Yet her family triumphs yielded sad results, and as she herself says: "The children gave me much happiness when I was young, but as they grew up they brought me much grief."

The path from Krupskaya to Brezhneva mirrors the various stages of development in Soviet society, from a mighty explosion to stagnation, from the birth of an epoch through degeneration to rebirth. As this blind woman faced the winter of 1991, her needs were few and she would survive. Yet she worried about the shopping, and when the old Kremlin store finally closes we can be sure that Raisa Gorbachev and Naina Yeltsin will not be standing in line for bread. But these questions were not for her. As Anya slowly led her out she smiled at me, and we said good-bye. She was so simple, so ordinary, that I almost felt that I understood nothing about her.

16

The Mystery of Tatyana

Yuri Vladimirovich Andropov (1914–1984), born in a small railway town in the Northern Caucasus, son of a station master. Leaving school at sixteen, he entered the Rybinsk Water Transport College but received his chief education at Moscow's Higher Party School. In 1953 he joined the diplomatic service and went to Hungary, where he played a significant role during the 1956 uprising. In 1957 he was responsible for liaison with foreign Communist parties, and in 1967 he became head of the KGB. A strong supporter of détente with the West, he succeeded Brezhnev as Party general secretary after the latter's death in 1982.

FOR TWENTY YEARS Andropov had reigned supreme at the KGB. And like his American counterpart, J. Edgar Hoover, he had the ability — and files — to terrorize those in high posts.

Yuri Andropov held power as general secretary for more than a year but was active for just three months, since shortly after he took office he fell ill. Yet for those three months people felt that a strong hand was in charge. Determined to preserve their illusions, people felt that this man from the KGB would provide the leadership that was needed.

The new general secretary's official biography in the *Great Soviet Encyclopedia* reveals almost nothing about his personal life. But it is a fact that during his brief tenure the dissident movement was quietly crushed.

He also issued a cheap new brand of vodka, popularly known as "Andropovka." The story goes that in one working family, the poor wife, tormented beyond endurance by her drunken husband, called the police, told them he had been drinking "Andropovka," and asked them to come and lock him up. In due course the police arrived and, ignoring the drunkard, arrested the woman and threw her in prison for two weeks for insulting the government.

While he is not be compared to Beria, and while it is true that dissidents were no longer shot in the courtyard of the Lubyanka, they were nonetheless sent to psychiatric hospitals or deported to the West. Though relatively little is known about Andropov, he was rumored to be well educated, a man who collected icons and loved poetry.*

If Andropov was somewhat of an enigma, his wife, Tatyana Fillipovna, was a total mystery. No word of her ever filtered through to the press, her face never appeared on our television screens, and her only public appearance was on the day of her husband's funeral, a large weeping woman dressed in black. I made an effort to meet her, but no one ever answered her telephone, and since I felt it was wrong in the context of this book to talk to someone's children and grandchildren without her consent, I finally gave up. Then, at the end of 1992, she died.

But I do have this from someone who worked closely with Andropov and knew his family:

> Tatyana Fillipovna was Yuri Vladimirovich's second wife. He had a daughter from an earlier marriage, who lived with her mother. Tatyana Fillipovna and Yuri Vladimirovich met in Karelia, where they both worked, and fell in love. Yuri Vladimirovich had a subtle, delicate nature and he knew how to love and respect people.
>
> Andropov was Soviet ambassador to Hungary in 1956, when the uprising occurred. Soviet wives were imprisoned in the embassy and their children were used as hostages. Tatyana Fillipovna behaved heroically, helping to evacuate the women and children and leaving with her children in a tank. A short while later she became seriously ill, and some say she really never recovered from the Hungarian earthquake.

* After his death, a collection of his poems was published, which reveals a true poetic view of the world.

17

Anna of Three Hundred Days

Konstantin Ustinovich Chernenko (1911–1985), born to a poor family in a remote Siberian village. He served with the border guards in Kazakhstan in the 1930s, then became Party secretary in Krasnoyarsk and remained in Siberia throughout World War II. His move to Moldavia in 1948 began his association with Brezhnev, who made him his propaganda chief. Brezhnev took him with him to Moscow to work on the Central Committee. After Andropov's death in 1984, Chernenko was the Central Committee's cautious choice of successor. Frail and asthmatic, the new general secretary held power for just a year and died in March 1985.

ONE DAY IN 1986, at the height of perestroika, an elderly man called me on the telephone and invited me to read my poems at a house management meeting of a building where Central Committee officials lived. He had been asked to contact me, he said, by Anna Dmitrievna Chernenko. A few minutes later Anna Dmitrievna herself called. I was leaving for Leningrad that evening and reluctant to change my plans, but it was difficult to refuse the widow of the former general secretary, so I accepted.

Later Anna Dmitrievna and I talked in her spacious apartment. I first thought her a tall, elegant, middle-aged woman of severe Party demeanor, but when she began speaking I became aware of her petite size, twinkling blue eyes, and shy smile, with a hint of sadness in her expression. As director of the University of Culture in the building which houses Central Committee officials, this woman, who was briefly First Lady, has been responsible for a wealth of lively cultural events in the building's small lecture hall, including visits from actors and writers, distinguished scientists, cosmonauts, and touring theater productions. Governments may change, but Anna Dmitrievna retains her position in the house on Kutuzovsky Prospect, and her deceased husband's position has given her access to a wide range of interesting speakers.

Why did she work for thirty years to promote culture? What was her role in the life of the shadowy figure of her gray, slow-moving husband? Her apartment is filled with family pictures and a variety of gifts to her husband from organizations and governments: the typically impersonal accessories of a high official's life. As Anna Dmitrievna reviewed her past, her memories brought laughter and tears. "There's nothing especially interesting about my life. First came work then family, and later it was family and work."

Despite her passion for political activity, she was always a shy, modest person, who spent her life battling with her nature. She was first politicized during the collectivization of the 1930s, when Pioneer and Komsomol organizations flourished and masses of children were drawn into the local chapters of the universal enlightenment machine. Sometimes with adults, sometimes on their own, children flocked to villages and farms to search out hidden grain for the hungry towns. A notice entitled *Lenin's Grandchildren* announced in a Rostov newspaper: "Pioneer Anya Lyubimova has brought to the town a red convoy bearing 1,046 poods [37,970 pounds] of bread!" Anya and her girlfriends were proud to see the newspaper story. They had little trouble finding grain. She recalls how as they were passing through one village, an old Cossack said, "Look what they're doing! Sending children! How can you refuse children!"

Born into a large illiterate family, Anya Lyubimova was the best Pioneer, the best Komsomol member, and the best science student in her class, a living example of Nadezhda Krupskaya's educational hopes and aspirations. She dreamed of building electric locomotives and studying at Moscow's Electromechanical Institute of Transport Engineers, but her friends persuaded her to study at the Saratov Institute of Agricultural Engineering instead, and she ended up designing sowing, winnowing, and mowing machines. At first she did not enjoy her work, but soon grew to like it, and her high degree of social consciousness led her to new responsibilities as she climbed the ladder from Komsomol organizer to secretary of the Komsomol committee.

She often drove tractors and could repair one as well as any man. The only problem she had with the men was their foul language; she found the constant cursing offensive, and would frequently appoint someone else to replace her. Perhaps that was why she took so long to marry: she found all the men around her too coarse, and they perhaps were put off by her.

During the war she worked tirelessly. In 1944, as the war was ending, she and three men were sent off to the Volga to organize the state grain procurement. One of these men was kind and gentle, and in the evenings after work they took strolls along the Volga River and watched the steamers. As she boarded the train back to Moscow, the man thrust a note through the window, telling her to read it only after the train was moving. The note said that he hoped to see her again in Moscow, and begged her to write to him. She did write, and several months later they were married. They lived together in love and friendship for forty-two years and had three children: Elena, Vera, and Vladimir, as well as his daughter from a previous marriage.

Anna Dmitrievna says:

> Konstantin Ustinovich was a good, sensitive man. When he graduated from the Higher Party School after the war he was sent to do propaganda work in Penza, where our two daughters were born. He worked very hard. The light in his study was always switched off last, and he was never home before two or three in the morning. I always waited up for him. When he came in he would wash, I would give him something to eat, and afterward we would sit chatting on the porch and wait for the sun to come up. Sometimes I would become silent, and he would say: "What are you thinking about? Think aloud. We must think together!"
>
> Sometimes he was very tense when he came home, and I could see he was miles away.
>
> He always knew what other people were thinking. He hated cunning and couldn't bear it when people tried to curry favor with him, but he quickly forgot about it if they didn't do it again.
>
> When he was at home on Sundays it was like a holiday. He was witty and cheerful, and his reactions were quick. He didn't have much general culture, of course; I always regretted that and tried to help him, but I didn't know how. It was impossible to drag him to the theater. "I don't have time," he would say. He was from a large peasant

family. His mother died in 1919 of typhus when he was eight, and his father remarried, to a very cruel woman who made the children's lives sheer hell. Their village is now flooded by an artificial lake, and all the people who lived there were evacuated to Novoselovo.

When we lived in Penza I worked until the children arrived. When we went to Kishinev I wanted to start work immediately, but Konstantin Ustinovich's sister, Valentina, a woman with a strong, domineering character, admonished me, "Don't be selfish, think about your husband and children! He has a good job! You should be looking after him instead of putting your own interests first. He has weak lungs!" So I didn't work, and I regretted it, of course.

Our third son, Konstantin, was born in Kishinev. My husband rarely saw the baby, he was at work for days on end. One morning he returned at five. I was in an agony of jealousy all night watching for him at the window, and when I saw him appear at the end of the street my nerves snapped. He came into the house, and I said to him, "I don't know why you bothered coming home — you should have stayed where you were!" And he replied: "Zhdanov has died. We've been writing the obituaries."*

Later, when Brezhnev left Moldavia and gathered all his most trusted officials in Moscow, we moved into this house on Kutuzovsky Prospect, and I became president of the University of Culture. I felt that my old-fashioned organizational abilities could be useful to people. The audience at our university were generally elderly, the children of peasants and workers, who had worked all their lives for the Party and the Komsomol fulfilling five-year plans, and culture had passed them by. They were happy to attend lectures, and said their studies helped them find their way in the new life and gave them something to talk about with their grandchildren.

The day Konstantin Ustinovich was appointed general secretary of the Party he stood at the door and said: "They've confirmed it!" "Confirmed what?" I said. "Andropov's funeral?" He explained that it had been discussed at great length, and it had been decided that he had the necessary experience and efficiency for the job. He was indeed an outstanding organizer, and he established a high level of record-keeping. He organized the Politburo's work, and under his leadership all paperwork was dealt with promptly.

The last year of his life is a terrible one to remember. Everyone could see that he was dying and did not have the strength to continue,

---

* *Andrei Zhdanov, Stalin's most prominent lieutenant from 1946 until his sudden death in 1948, possibly engineered by Stalin himself.*

but what could I do! When a person falls into the system he ceases to belong to himself and his loved ones. Often I would run beside his escort, grabbing their jacket and saying: "Where are you going? Look at him — he shouldn't be getting out of bed!" But they'd say: "We have to, Anna Dmitrievna, people are waiting for him, he's the head of state!"

As soon as he became general secretary, the red government telephone appeared beside his bed. I was so afraid. Of course I tried to protect him, and put the telephone beside me so when it rang I could pick up the receiver, ask who it was, and decide whether it was worth waking him or not. But when the phone rang in the middle of the night my heart would always pound!

When asked what privileges she still had, Anna Dmitrievna replied that for a while she had had the use of a government car, but now she had to pay a prohibitive fifteen rubles an hour to hire one. She was recently given a plot of land on which she and the children were building a dacha. Her warm and loving relationship with her children today justifies the sacrifices she made for them and Konstantin Ustinovich.

18

The Raisa Phenomenon

Mikhail Sergeyevich Gorbachev (1931–   ), born in a village near Stavropol in the Northern Caucasus, the son and grandson of prominent collective farm workers. A star pupil, he left Stavropol in 1950 to study law at Moscow University, where he joined the Party and met Raisa; it was said that he became a reformer under her influence. After graduating, he spent over twenty years in Stavropol, working for the Party, and became first secretary there in 1970. In 1978 he became one of the secretaries of the Party Central Committee, and after the death of Chernenko in 1985 he was elected general secretary, primarily on the basis of his grassroots Party experience.

AS MIKHAIL GORBACHEV revolutionized Soviet power, with his wife at his side, Russian people's reactions to Raisa were sharply divided. Many felt it was high time for Russia to have a real First Lady — smart, elegant, and clever — who traveled everywhere with her husband, someone we could be proud to show abroad. Others accused her of vulgarity, of stealing Gorbachev's publicity, of dressing like royalty at the state's expense, and of speaking out instead of staying in the background.

Proponents of the second view evidently prevailed over the defenders of civilized values, yet I think most Russians supported Raisa. Like Mikhail Sergeyevich, she was a child of her times. Born of war into a poor family, she was a star pupil who graduated with a gold medal, a woman on the move during the Khrushchev thaw, and the provincial wife of a Party worker who rose steadily up the ladder of power.

Since the Soviet press regarded the personal as having no political significance, almost nothing was written about Gorbachev's domestic life when he became general secretary in 1985. Yet throughout Russia millions were switching on their television sets to see Raisa's smiling face, trim figure, and wardrobe of well-tailored suits. The Gorbachevs appealed to illusions of fusion between the people and this new, unusually pleasant-looking leader. Mikhail Sergeyevich was elected leader for his "Party approach to people," and Raisa, too; they were both of the people.

I experienced this new spirit of glasnost in February 1987 when *Pravda* invited me to write something for International Women's Day. As a non-Party member, I was astonished to be offered total journalistic freedom. Then I recalled a recent speech by Gorbachev in which he said: "We must draw women into ever-wider echelons of power." My article, "The Living Female Soul," called for women to have social equality but as women, not ersatz men.

The article prompted over eight thousand replies, the vast majority favorable, and the following March, I was invited by Raisa Gorbachev to a Women's Day celebration in the Lenin Hills. In November 1988 I joined the Gorbachevs' press corps on their visit to Italy. There I saw crowds throwing themselves at Raisa's car, and in the evenings we talked together about perestroika's implications for women. Nothing would come of the recent reforms, we agreed, unless society as a whole took up the cause of saving the human family; women must take their proper place at every level of society, not merely to help men fight, spoil, and divide the world. We even discussed the possibility of a special parliament for women in Russia.

But Raisa did not please everyone. Men were offended by the spectacle of a man taking his wife around with him and treating her as his equal when she should be at home watching television. Women were also irritated by Raisa, feeling that anyone could look young and talk knowledgeably about art if she did not have to work and stand in lines all day. There were even dire hints that her thinness was the result of some unspecified but clearly serious disease. People loved to gossip about her, yet we felt bereft when she failed to appear at her husband's side during several of his trips around Russia. Just as she disappeared with her husband's fall from power, her autobiography, *I Hope,* appeared with her smiling picture on the cover.

Raisa Maximovna Titarenko was born of peasant stock in Siberia. Her mother had spun and ploughed from the age of eight and learned to read and write only in her twenties. Her father was born in the Ukraine, but moved to Siberia in 1929 to work on the construction of a new railroad in the Altai region of Western Siberia. For the rest of his life he worked on the railways. He never joined the Party. Their first child, Raisa, was born in 1932 and christened in the Russian Orthodox tradition.

In the 1930s her parents were denounced as "kulaks" [rich exploiting peasants], their property was confiscated, and her grandfather disappeared in the camps, leaving his wife to die of grief and starvation. From then on the family was constantly on the move, and when World War II broke out Raisa's father went off to fight at the front. She and her younger brother and sister attended a succession of schools, but their mother was determined to give her children the education she had never had, and her elder daughter became an avid reader. In 1949, seventeen-year-old Raisa spent her last year of school in the small Urals town of Sterlitamak, in Bashkiria. There she was awarded a gold medal for "excellent results and exemplary conduct" and the "right to enter institutes of higher education in the USSR without entry examination." She chose to enter the faculty of philosophy at the Lomonosov State University in Moscow.

In her autobiography, she describes the slow, cramped train journey to Moscow, and her pride and anxiety as she entered the old university buildings on Herzen Street. There was a rich ethnic mix among the students at that time, and a large number of older students whose education had been disrupted by war and who brought a special diligence to their studies in logic, philosophy, and psychology.

She recalls the optimism of student life in these years leading to the Khrushchev thaw: "I still find myself unable to explain how people achieved what they did in those unforgettable years. Where did they draw the strength? Factories, electric power stations, towns, and villages were rebuilt, and the land, devastated by war, was restored to life. Lord, what joy we took in everything, how proud we were!"

She writes of the student societies, the exciting discussions about

Hegel at Komsomol meetings, the passionate defense of student rights, the eminent lecturers and the radical, creative teaching. But she writes, too, of people who had overcome disaster at the cost of unbelievable sacrifices at the front, and were further humiliated by the last convulsions of Stalinism. And she describes her gradual disillusion with the dogmatic teaching methods that replaced world culture with Stalin's dreary, dogmatic texts.

Like most of her fellow students, Raisa lived in the forbidding four-story university hostel in the Sokolniki district, near the Yauza River. Each room housed eight to fourteen students; kitchens and toilets were communal. Lacking the money to buy enough food or warm winter clothes, she tried when possible to avoid paying her train fares. But unlike Moscow girls, who had more worldly things to occupy them, she was a hard worker, studying in the library most of the day and delivering her final-year lecture on "Sleep and Dreaming in the Teaching of I. P. Pavlov." But she was also popular, and all the boys wanted to dance with her.

It was at a student dance at the hostel that she and Mikhail Sergeyevich Gorbachev first met. It is not known if she had any previous boyfriends, but all university girls of her generation were under great pressure to marry before graduating. Various categories of men were considered highly eligible. First, diplomats and journalists who had the possibility of working abroad. (The bolder girls even considered foreign students.) Second, graduate students in any subject. (These were rather few at the time.) Third, professionals — scientists and teachers — providing they were from Moscow and from a good family. If all else failed, there were always one's fellow students, preferably someone older and reliable. Boys in one's own class were chosen only in cases of unreasoning passionate love, or prompted by the clock — final exams approaching meant graduation and leaving Moscow.

Raisa Titarenko was one of those beautiful, romantic girls who married boys in their own class out of love. Long walks around Moscow together were followed by outings to the cinema and the skating rink. In 1953 they parted for three months while he went off to the provinces to do his practical training as a lawyer, writing back to her of his disgust at the arrogance of the bosses and the passivity and conservatism of the masses. Mikhail proposed to Raisa that summer, and went back to his village near Stavropol in the Caucasus, where he worked as a combine driver harvesting wheat to pay for the wedding. The parents were informed only days before the ceremony that autumn at the Sokolniki registry office. The celebration afterward was attended by their student friends, after which the Gorbachevs traveled back to his native village. Raisa Maximovna writes, "We could have stayed on in Moscow after the wedding to do postgraduate work, but we didn't, and time proved this to be the right decision."

Proud and independent by nature, she might secretly have dreamed of marrying into a rich family, but she could not have endured being patronized for her humble origins, and Gorbachev felt the same. They were perfectly matched: hardworking, scrupulous, intelligent provincials, who had started from nothing and dreamed of achieving everything together.

In the Caucasus she taught philosophy at the Stavropol Agricultural Institute and the nearby farms, lecturing on logic, ethics, the problems of consciousness, contemporary sociological concepts and philosophical trends, and the views of Kant and Lenin. She also taught the history of religion and atheism, and in the 1960s she discovered the Bible, the Koran, and the Gospels.

As the focus of her studies and the subject of her doctoral thesis, however, she chose the family life, relationships, and material conditions of the peasantry. For several years she tramped around the villages in rubber boots, drinking tea with old women and war widows, visiting medical centers, nurseries, and old people's homes, and speaking at regional Party meetings. She gathered statistics from documents, archives, interviews, and over three thousand questionnaires, in which women were asked if they would give up work if their husband could earn enough; the vast majority of them replied that they would not. She later described the importance of peasant life in shaping her attitudes by saying, "The Russian village is where we all have our roots, the source of all our strengths and perhaps our weaknesses, too."

Shortly after the birth of the Gorbachevs' daughter, Irina, in January 1957, Raisa was again probing the depths of village life for her thesis, entitled "The Development of New Features in the Life of the Peasantry in Collective Farms." But her thesis was never completed. As she ascended the professional ladder as a teacher, Gorbachev was ascending the ladder of the Stavropol Party organization, and it quickly became apparent that he was overtaking her. Couples embarking on their professional lives together generally find that one quickly takes the lead and that the other has to choose. Generally it is the man who takes the lead; when it's the other way round the family often breaks up. The man is unable to accept her "strength," and the woman his "weakness."

Raisa evidently had no desire to compete with her husband. There was even talk that she was offered the position of dean of the Stavropol philosophy department, but turned it down. She wanted to be perceived as the "weak" woman, and she saw this as her strength.

For twenty years she lived as a provincial nomenklatura wife who had to defer to the wife of the Stavropol Party boss. This could not have been easy for someone with her independent temperament, but her own training as a teacher protected her from such humiliations. She knew how to find harmony in any situation. When she became wife of the boss, and the other wives had to defer to her, she was once again protected by her teaching work and her relationship with her pupils.

The wife of one of Gorbachev's Stavropol subordinates did not find Raisa easy to get along with. "Her didactic tone and her unspoken assumption of her own infallibility grated on people's nerves. It was impossible to criticize her narrow-minded Party correctness, as this might reflect on her husband."

Arrogance toward subordinates coexisting with the desire to please superiors is a typical trait of those who come to power, and although not an inherent part of Raisa's nature, it became identified with her. She was a kind and generous woman who cared for orphans and gave her money to children in the best traditions of her Kremlin predecessors. Yet she naively imagined that goodness should be reciprocated, whereas paradoxically the more she gave, the more she irritated people. "So what if she gives her money away? She has nothing else to do with it!" people said. Or: "She lords it over people — it's vulgar!"

After Mikhail Sergeyevich's election to the Central Committee in 1978 the Gorbachevs moved to Moscow. Despite Raisa's new professional opportunities and the improved housing and increased privileges, she was repelled by the cold, hierarchical nature of her new life, and by the wives' narrow interests.

When Gorbachev became general secretary his wife inherited the tradition that stemmed from Stalin's day: the absence of any right to a public, official existence. Hence her new presence at the Kremlin

Raisa and Mikhail Gorbachev

Raisa

Raisa

created a sensation. With no training in diplomatic protocol, she had to learn as she went along — on the protocol of seating, dressing, and dining when she accompanied Gorbachev on his meetings with Presidents Reagan and Bush, Prime Minister Thatcher, and the Queen of England. On her travels around Russia with her husband, she talked to women about jobs, pensions, schools, and children's homes. In Moscow she threw herself into a variety of public activities and helped to promote the Soviet Foundation for Culture. But her chief concern was the welfare of children. She visited children crippled and orphaned by the Armenian earthquake and the Chernobyl disaster and supported a Moscow children's hospital and an organization called Hematologists of the World for Children. Although deluged with requests concerning children, health, education, and culture, she handled all correspondence without secretarial assistance.

After the publication of her autobiography and her reappearance by her husband's side, the Gorbachevs again became the subject of comments, jokes, and rhymes. Yet Raisa once said to me: "I'm afraid we won't last four years." Did she fear that perestroika would not last? Surely she must have realized that the process would take decades. Her words indicate her personal involvement in the political process. No wonder the boorish Yeltsin's reaction to her in the early days of perestroika was so inadequate, evidently assuming that a woman should function as some sort of fifth wheel, serving men's domestic and physical needs.

Behind the conventional acts of charity, Raisa played a far greater role in Russian politics than any other Kremlin wife had before her, including Nadezhda Krupskaya. Krupskaya had served Lenin, who was the embodiment of her all-consuming ideal. Raisa's ideal was Gorbachev, and he was always right. Despite her independence, she went even further than Victoria Brezhneva in subordinating herself to her husband. As she stood behind him, aided by the television cameras and her famous charm, she transformed the political kitchen of socialism into a cozier, stylish place with a subtle hint of capitalism. Yet when told that her appearance on television enlivened the tedium of official life, and that if she were not there people would not listen to Gorbachev, she would invariably protest: "That's terrible! You *must* listen to him!" Her conduct was most remarkable during the coup in August 1991, when she behaved like a woman afraid for her family.

Her fear came through in gentle words, but it taught the victors nothing and, exhausted, she fell ill.

Mikhail Gorbachev had the choice of repairing the machine or destroying it. In trying to repair it he destroyed it, and as always throughout our history, Russia's male leaders failed to foresee the bloody retribution that would inevitably follow.

In the seventy years of the Soviet Union's history, the leaders' wives complemented their male partners to an astonishing degree, whether as allies or as opposites. The quiet spirit of rebellion lived within all of them, from Nadezhda Alliluyeva to Victoria Brezhneva, yet ultimately all were prisoners of the male power machine. Princesses in their own domestic realm, they differed from other women in Russia only in the material privileges Kremlin life temporarily offered them. Those who refused to serve the machine were doomed to meet the fate of Nadezhda Alliluyeva, Olga Budyonnaya, and Ekaterina Kalinina. Most Kremlin wives have been but the pale shadows of frighteningly powerful men. Yet these men, too, were afraid, and even Stalin lived out his years of power in a state of fear and paranoia. Had men linked their fates not with every passing fanatic doctrine but with the women who shared their lives, then perhaps together they might have built a strong, secure Russia for their children.

Select Bibliography

Two publications widely quoted are given in abbreviated form. These are *Novy zhurnal* [New Journal], represented here as *NJ,* and *Sovershenno sekretno* [Top Secret], *SS.*

Adzhubei, A. "Te desyat let" [Those ten years]. *Soviet Russia,* 1989.

Alexandrova, V. "Pervaya voennaya zima v Rossii" [Russia's first winter of war]. *NJ,* no. 4, 1943.

Alexinskaya, T. "1917 god" [The year 1917]. *NJ,* nos. 90–94, 1968.

Alliluyev, S. *Proidyonny put'* [The path traveled]. Moscow: OGIZ, 1946.

Alliluyeva, N. S., obituaries. *Pravda,* 10, 12, 16 November, 1932.

Anin, D. "Perspektivy i vnutrennie protivorechiya bolshevisma" [The prospects and internal contradictions of Bolshevism]. *NJ,* no. 36, 1954.

Annenkov, Y. *Dnevnik moikh vstrech* [Diary of my meetings]. 2 vols. Moscow: Mezhd. Literatura, 1966.

———. "Vospominaniya o Lenine" [Memories of Lenin]. *NJ,* no. 65, 1961.

Antonov-Ovseenko, A. *Stalin bez maski* [Stalin without mask]. Moscow: Vsya Moskva, 1990.

Arbatov, Z. *Ekaterinoslav 1917–1944.* Vol. 12, Berlin. Archive of the Russian Revolution.

Armand, I. *Sta'ti, rechi, pis'ma* [Articles, speeches, and letters]. Moscow: Polit. Literatura, 1975.

Arsenidze, R. "Iz vospominanii o Staline" [Recollections of Stalin]. *NJ,* no. 72, 1963.

Avtorkhanov, A. "Koba i Kamo" [Koba and Kamo]. *NJ,* no. 110, 1973.

———. "Lenin i Ts.K. v oktyabrskom perevorote" [Lenin and the Central Committee in the October Revolution]. *NJ*, no. 100, 1970.

———. "Ts.K. protiv planov Lenina o vosstanii" [The Central Committee against Lenin's plans for the uprising]. *NJ*, no. 101, 1971.

Berberova, N. *Zheleznaya zhenshchina* [Iron woman]. New York: Russica Publishers, 1982.

Berdyaev, N. *Istoki russkogo komunizma* [The sources of Russian communism]. Moscow: Nauka, 1990.

Berter, I. "E. D. Stasova." *NJ*, no. 103, 1971.

Bocharnikova, M. "Boi v zimnem dvortse" [The battles at the Winter Palace]. *NJ*, no. 68, 1962.

Bonch-Bruevich, M. *Vsya vlast' sovetam* [All power to the soviets]. Moscow: Voenizdat, 1958.

Borev, Y. *Staliniada*. Moscow: Sovetskii pisatel', 1990.

Breshkovskaya, E. "1917 god" [The year 1917]. *NJ*, no. 38, 1954.

Bunin, I. *Pod serpom i molotom* [Under the hammer and sickle]. London/Canada: Zarya, 1975.

———. *Okayannye dni* [Cursed days]. Moscow: Sovetskii pisatel', 1990.

Burt, V. "Zinochka iz 1917-ogo" [Zinochka from 1917]. *SS*, no. 8, 1990.

Buranov, Y. "Poedinok s gensekom" [Duel with the general secretary]. *SS*, no. 7, 1991.

Chernov, V. *Pered burei* [Before the storm]. New York: Chekhov Press, 1953.

Chernova, O. "Kholodnaya zima. Moskva 1919–1920" [A cold winter. Moscow 1919–1920]. *NJ*, no. 121, 1975.

Chuev, F. *Sto sorok besed s Molotovym* [One hundred forty conversations with Molotov]. Moscow: Terra, 1990.

Dan, P. "1970 god" [The year 1970]. *NJ*, no. 87, 1967.

Domontovich, A. *Zhenshchina na perelome* [Woman at the turning point]. Moscow/Petrograd, 1923.

Dodolev, E. "Taina zolotykh byustov" [The secret of the golden busts]. *SS*, no. 3, 1991.

SELECT BIBLIOGRAPHY

Drabkina, E. "Zimnii pereval". [Winter crossing]. *Novy Mir,* no. 10, 1968.

Dridzo, V. *Nadezhda Konstantinovna.* Moscow: Detskaya Literatura, 1969.

Druzhnikov, Y. "Blizhnyaya dacha" [The dacha next door]. *SS,* no. 4, 1991.

Dumova, N. *Konchilos' vashe vremya* [Your time is over]. Moscow: Polit. Literatura, 1990.

Essen, M. *Inessa Armand.* Moscow: Gosizdat, 1925.

Feuchtwanger, L. *Moskva 1937* [Moscow 1937]. Moscow: Polit. Literatura, 1990.

Garvi, P. "1970 god" [The year 1970]. *NJ,* no. 87, 1967.

Geller, M. *Mashina i vintiki* [The machine and the cogs]. London: OPI, 1985.

Gide, A. *Vozvrashchenie iz SSSR* [Return from the USSR]. Moscow: Polit. Literatura, 1990.

Gins, G. "Perevoploshchenie Peterburga" [The reincarnation of St. Petersburg]. *NJ,* no. 58, 1952.

Gorky, M. *Vladimir Il'ich Lenin.* Moscow, 1924.

Gul, R. "Ya unes Rossiyu" [I took Russia away]. *NJ,* nos. 132–138, 1978–1989.

———. *Krasnye marshaly* [The red marshals]. Moscow: Molodaya Gvardia, 1990.

Gurvich, A. "Artisticheskaya Moskva 1917–1920" [Artistic Moscow 1917–1920]. *NJ,* no. 129, 1977.

Guseinov, E. "Syn partii" [Son of the party]. *Izvestia,* 14 November, 1982.

Hippius, Z. "Dnevnik. 1938 g." [Diary for 1938]. *NJ,* no. 92, 1968.

Kerensky, A. "O revolyutsii 1917 goda" [The revolution of 1917]. *NJ,* no. 15, 1947.

———. "Dva Oktyabrya" [Two Octobers]. *NJ,* no. 17, 1947.

———. "Kak eto sluchilos?" [How did it happen?]. *NJ,* no. 34, 1953.

Kheraskov, M. "Obshchestvo blagorodnykh" [Noble company]. *NJ,* no. 14, 1946.

Khodasevich, V. *Literaturnye sta'ti i vospominaniya* [Literary articles and memoirs]. New York: Chekhov Press, 1954.

Kolesnik, A. *Mify i pravda o sem'e Stalina* [Myths and truth about Stalin's family]. Moscow: Tekhinvest, 1991.

Koltsov, P. *Diplomat Fyodor Raskolnikov* [The diplomat Fyodor Raskolnikov]. Moscow: Polit. Literatura, 1990.

Koridze, T. "Interv'u N. T. Beria" [Interview with N. T. Beria]. *SS*, no. 9, 1990.

Kozhenova, T. "Budni sovetskoi zhenshchiny" [Everyday life of the Soviet woman]. *NJ*, no. 34, 1953.

Kramov, I. *Utrennii veter* [Morning wind]. Moscow: Sovetskii Pisatel'.

———. *Literaturnye portrety* [Literary portraits]. Moscow: Sovetskii Pisatel', 1962.

Krasnopolskaya, I. "Komandarm" [Army commander]. *Moskovskaya Pravda*, 2 August, 1987.

Kravchenko, G. *Mozaika minuvshego* [Mosaic of the past]. Moscow: Iskusstvo, 1975.

Kreidlina, L. *Bol'shevik dragotsennoi proby* [A bolshevik of precious worth]. Moscow: Polit. Literatura, 1990.

Krivorotov, V., and S. Chernyshev. "Zagadka Lenina" [The mystery of Lenin]. *Literaturnaya Gazeta*, 17 April, 1991.

Krotkov, Y. "KGB v deistvii" [The KGB in action]. *NJ*, nos. 108–112, 1973.

Krupskaya, N. *Pedagogicheskie sochineniya* [Pedagogical writings]. 11 vols. Moscow: Akademia Ped. Nauk, 1957–1963.

Kunetskaya, L., and K. Mashtakova. *Krupskaya*. Moscow: Molodaya Gvardia, 1985.

Kuskova, E. "Davno minuvshee" [The distant past]. *NJ*, no. 54, 1958.

Larina-Bukharina, A. *Nezabyvaemoe* [The unforgotten]. Moscow: APN, 1989.

Lenin, V. I. *Pis'ma k rodnym. 1893–1922* [Letter to family]. Complete Collected Works, vol. 37. Moscow: GIPL, 1957.

Lukomsky, A. *Vospominaniya* [Memoirs]. 2 vols. Berlin: Otto Kircher, 1922.

Manukhin, I. "Vospominaniya o 1917–1918" [Memories of 1917 and 1918]. *NJ*, no. 54, 1958.

Medvedev, R. *Oni okruzhali Stalina* [They surrounded Stalin]. Moscow: Polit. Literatura, 1990.

———. "Konets 'sladkoi zhizni' dlya Galiny Brezhnevoi" [The end of the "sweet life" for Galina Brezhneva]. *SS*, no. 2, 1990.

———. *O Staline i Stalinizme* [Stalin and Stalinism]. Moscow: Progress, 1990.

Melgunov, S. *Krasny terror* [The red terror]. Moscow: 1990.

———. "Osada zimnego dvortsa" [The siege of the Winter Palace]. *NJ*, no. 17, 1947.

Naglovsky, A. "Lenin." *NJ*, no. 88, 1967.

———. "Vospomominaniya" [Memoirs]. *NJ*, no. 90, 1968.

Nikolaevsky, B. "Porazhenie Khrushcheva" [The defeat of Khrushchev]. *NJ*, no. 25, 1951.

Nord, L. *Marshal Tukhachevsky*. Paris: Lev, 1978.

Olesin, M. *Pervaya v mire. Biograficheskii ocherk ob A. M. Kollontai* [First in the world. A biographical essay on A. M. Kollontai]. Moscow: Polit. Literatura, 1990.

Oskotsky, V. "Glavny ideolog" [The chief ideologist]. *SS*, no. 5, 1991.

Pestkovsky, S. "Vospominaniya o rabote v Narkomnatse" [Memories of work in the Commissariat of Nationalities]. *Proletarskaya revolyutsiya*, no. 6, 1930.

Pilnyak, B. *Ubiistvo komandarma* [Death of a commander]. London: Phlegon Press, 1965.

Pleshakov, L. "I styla krov pri imeni ego" [The blood froze at his name]. *SS*, no. 3, 1990.

Popov, I. *Odin den's Leninym* [A day with Lenin]. Moscow: Sovetskii Pisatel', 1963.

Pribytkov, V. "Pomoshchnik genseka" [The general secretary's assistant]. *SS*, no. 7, 1990.

Prushinsky, K. "Noch v Kremle" [Night in the Kremlin]. *SS*, no. 7, 1990.

Pushkarev, S. "Oktyabrsky perevorot 1917 g. bez legend" [The October 1917 revolution without legends]. *NJ*, no. 89, 1967.

Reisner, L. *Izbrannye proizvedeniya* [Selected works]. Moscow/Leningrad: GIKhL, 1956.

Rolitsky, Ya. "Bol'shoi brat" [Big brother]. *SS*, no. 5, 1991.

Rotin, I. *Idem za rytsaryami revolyutsii i lyubvi* [Let us follow the knights of revolution and love]. Moscow: Molodaya Gvardia, 1978.

Rubanov, S., and S. Netinsky. *Krupskaya v Peterburge* [Krupskaya in Petersburg]. Leningrad: Lenizdat, 1975.

Satina, S. "Obrazovanie zhenshchin v dorevolyutsionnoi Rossii" [The education of women in prerevolutionary Russia]. *NJ*, no. 76, 1964.

Semyonov, Yu. "Taina Kutuzovskogo prospekta" [The secret of Kutuzovsky Prospect]. *SS*, no. 6–7, 1989.

Shelest, P. "Kak eto bylo" [How it was]. *SS*, no. 6, 1990.

Shturman, D. *V. I. Lenin*. Paris: YMCA Press, 1989.

Shub, D. "Tri biografii Lenina" [Three biographies of Lenin]. *NJ*, no. 77, 1964.

———. "Kupets revolyutsii" [The merchant of the revolution]. *NJ*, no. 87, 1967.

———. "Iz davnikh let" [From bygone years]. *NJ*, no. 99–110, 1970–1973.

Simonov, K. "Glazami cheloveka moego pokoleniya" [Through the eyes of a man of my generation]. *Znamya*, no. 6–7, 1988.

Tolstaya, A. *Probleski vo tme* [Glimmers in the dark]. Washington, 1965.

Tolstaya, O. "Dozhd i solntse" [Rain and sun]. *NJ*, no. 132, 1979.

Turov, N. "Vstrecha s Abbakumovym v tyurme NKVD" [A meeting with Abbakumov in the NKVD jail]. *NJ*, no. 98, 1970.

Tyrkova-Williams, A. *To, chego bol'she ne budet* [What will not be again]. Paris: Vozrozhdenie, 1953.

Valentinov, N. "Chernyshevsky i Lenin" [Chernyshevsky and Lenin]. *NJ*, no. 26–27, 1951.

———. "Lenin v Simbirske" [Lenin in Simbirsk]. *NJ*, no. 37, 1954.

————. "Rannie gody Lenina" [Lenin's early years]. *NJ*, no. 40–41, 1955.

————. "Vydumki o rannei revolyutsionosti Lenina" [Fabrications about Lenin's early life as a revolutionary]. *NJ*, no. 39, 1954.

————. "Vstrecha Lenina s marxismom" [Lenin's encounter with Marxism]. *NJ*, no. 53, 1957.

————. "O lyudyakh revolutsionnogo podpolya" [People of the revolutionary underground]. *NJ*, no. 63, 1963.

————. *Vstrechi s Leninym* [Meetings with Lenin]. New York: Chekhov Press, 1953.

————. *NEP i krizis partii posle smerti Lenina* [The New Economic Policy and the crisis of the Party after Lenin's death]. Hoover Institutions Press, 1971.

Vasetsky, N. *Likvidatsiya* [Liquidation]. Moscow: Moskovskii Rabochii, 1989.

Vishnevskaya, G. *Istoriya zhizni* [History of a life]. Moscow: Novosti, 1991.

Volkonogov, D. *Triumf i tragediya* [Triumph and tragedy]. 2 vols. Moscow: Novosti, 1989.

Voslensky, M. *Nomenklatura*. London: OPI, 1990.

Vulf, B. "Krupskaya chistit biblioteki" [Krupskaya purges the libraries]. *NJ*, no. 99, 1970.

Zemtsov, I. *Chernenko. Sovetskii soyuz v kontse perestroiki* [Chernenko. The Soviet Union at the end of perestroika]. London: OPI, 1989.

Zenzinov, V. *Perezhitoe* [Experiences]. New York: Chekhov Press, 1953.

Zykina, L. "V moei zhizni vse bylo krasivo" [Everything in my life was lovely]. *SS*, no. 3, 1991.

Anthologies

Chetyrnadtsatyi s'ezd RKP(b). Stenograficheskii otchet [The Fourteenth Party Congress, a stenographic record]. Moscow/Leningrad: Gosizdat, 1926.

Dodnes tyagoteet [A burden to this day]. Moscow: Sovetskii Pisatel', 1989.

Larisa Reisner v vospominaniyakh sovremennikov [Larissa Reisner remembered by her contemporaries]. Moscow: Sovetskii Pisatel', 1969.

Odinnadtsatyi s'ezd RKP(b). Stenograficheskii otchet [The Eleventh Party Congress, a stenographic record]. Moscow: Gosizdat, 1922.

Ot ottepeli do zastoya [From thaw to stagnation]. Moscow: Sovetskii Pisatel', 1990.

"Partiinaya etika." Diskussii 20-kh godov [Party "ethics." Discussions of the 1920s]. Moscow: Polit. Literatura, 1989.

Reabilitatsiya [Rehabilitation]. Moscow: Polit. Literatura, 1991.

Reabilitirovan posmertno [Posthumously rehabilitated]. Moscow: Yuridicheskaya Literatura, 1989.

Shestnadstaty s'ezd RKP(b). Stenograficheskii otchet [The Sixteenth Party Congress, a stenographic record]. Moscow: Gosizdat, 1950.

Trinadtsatyi s'ezd RKP(b). Stenograficheskii otchet [The Thirteenth Party Congress, a stenographic record]. Moscow: Gosizdat, 1924.

Vozhd', diktator, khozyain [Leader, dictator, master]. Moscow: Patriot, 1990.

Vozvrashchennnye imena [Returned names]. Moscow: APN, 1989.

Books in English

(English translations of Russian books are cited wherever possible)

Alliluyeva, S. *Letters to a Friend*. Translated by Priscilla Johnson. London: Hutchinson, 1967.

———. *Only One Year*. Translated by Paul Chavchavadze. New York: Harper and Row, 1969.

Clark, W. *The Man Behind the Mask*. London: Faber and Faber, 1988.

Conquest, R. *The Great Terror*. New York: Oxford University Press, 1990.

Engels, F. *The Origin of the Family, Private Property and the State*. New York: Penguin, 1986.

Fisher, L. *The Life of Lenin*. London: OPI, 1964.

Gorbachev, R. *I Hope*. Translated by David Floyd. New York: HarperCollins, 1991.

SELECT BIBLIOGRAPHY

Krupskaya, N. *Reminiscences of Lenin.* New York: International Pubs. Co., 1970.

Mandelstam, N. *Hope against Hope.* Translated by Max Hayward. New York: Atheneum/Macmillan, 1970.

———. *Hope Abandoned.* Translated by Max Hayward. New York: Atheneum, 1974.

Rayne, R. *The Rise and Fall of Stalin.* London: W. H. Allen, 1965.

Trotsky, L. *History of the Russian Revolution.* New York: Anchor Foundation, 1980.

———. *My Life.* New York: Pathfinder Press, 1970.

———. *Stalin: An Appraisal of the Man and His Influences.* New York: Scarbrough House, 1970.

Tucker, R. *Stalin as Revolutionary, 1879–1929: A Study in History and Personality.* New York: Norton, 1974.

Wittlin, T. *Commissar: The Life and Death of Lavrenty Pavlovich Beria.* New York: Macmillan, 1972.

Index

Adzhubei, Alexei Ivanovich, 162,
  198–200
Afghanistan, 42, 44
agit-train (October Revolution), 118–19
Akhmatova, Anna, 22, 39, 44, 45
Aldanov, Mark, 15
Alexander II, Tsar, assassination of, 3, 4
Alexander III, Tsar, 8
Alexeyev, Alexander Ivanovich, 96,
  101–2, 106–7
Alksnis, General, 110
Alliluyev, Sergei Yakovlevich, 57–58, 61,
  76
Alliluyeva, Anna, 61, 76
Alliluyeva, Nadezhda, 57–77, 120
  childhood, 57–60
  death, 70–77, 122
  early employment with Lenin, 63–65
  life with Stalin, 60–70
  paternity of, 73, 76–77
  and Paulina Zhemchuzhina, 137–38
Alliluyeva, Olga Evgenyevna, 63, 76
Alliluyeva, Svetlana, 73–74, 140
  Letter to a Friend, 65
  Only One Year, 61–63, 164
amnesty, for "enemies of the people,"
  126–29
Andreyev, Leonid, 39
Andreyev, Vadim, 39
Andropov, Yuri Vladimirovich, 211, 215,
  218–19
Andropova, Tatyana Fillipovna, 219
Annenkov, Yuri, 28
anti-Semitism, 90, 141–54
Antonovskaya, Anna, 54
Anya (Brezhnev family servant), 206

Arbatov, Z. Yu., memoirs, 85–86
Archive of the Russian Revolution,
  85–86
Arkhangelsk, 83
Armand, Alexander, 11–13
Armand, Alexander (son), 13
Armand, Andrei (son), 13
Armand, Boris, 13
Armand, Fyodor (son), 13
Armand, Inessa, 11–17, 18–19, 23–24,
  33, 35
Armand, Inessa (daughter), 13
Armand, Varvara (daughter), 13
Armand, Vladimir, 13–14
Askenazy family, 13–14
Attolico (Italian ambassador), 106, 114
Aurora, 33, 38

Babi Yar massacre, 90
Babushkin, Ivan Vasilievich, 7
Baratov campaign, 93
Bazhanov, Yuri, 66, 67
Bedny, Demyan, 72
Belinkov, Arkady, 144, 153
Beria, Lavrenti Pavlovich, 99, 122, 129,
  141, 142–44, 155, 161–85, 198
  debauchery of, 162–63, 168–70
  female victims of, 175–83
  mistress of, 184–85
  and Nina Teimurazovna, 163–64, 167
  and Tatyana Okunevskaya, 172–75
Beria, Nina Teimurazovna, 163–68,
  183–85, 198–200
Beria, Sergo, 162, 183, 198
Blok, Alexander, 22, 39, 43, 44
Blukher, Glafira, 176

INDEX

Bolsheviks, 32, 33
  ideas about marriage and family life,
    34–37, 63
  post-Revolution behavior, 65
  takeover of Kremlin, 18–21
  women's rights and, 33–37
Bolshoi Theater, 78–79
books, banning of, 22–23
Bredov (White general), 148
Brest-Litovsk peace treaty, 68
Brezhnev, Andrei, 207
Brezhnev, Leonid (Yuri's son), 207
Brezhnev, Leonid Ilyich, 205, 220
  background and rise of, 207–8,
    211–12
  hobbies, 206–9
  later years and rumors, 208–10
  Ludmilla's memories of, 211–16
Brezhnev, Victoria Petrovna, 202
  and Leonid Brezhnev, 208
  life story, 211–16
  present life, 205–8
  simplicity of, 216–17
Brezhnev, Yuri, 205–6, 207, 211
Brezhneva, Galina, 207
  legends about diamonds of, 209–11
Brezhneva, Ludmilla Vladimirovna,
    205–6
  memories of Brezhnev family,
    214–16
Brezhneva, Victoria (Galina's daughter),
    207
Bubnov, Andrei Sergeyevich, 114
  wife of, 101, 107, 111
Budyonnaya, Malanya Nikitinichna, 99
Budyonnaya, Maria Vasilievna, 96–102,
    116
  and Nadezhda Alliluyeva's death, 74
Budyonnaya, Nadezhda Ivanovna,
    93–94
Budyonnaya, Ninochka, 98
Budyonnaya, Olga Stefanovna
    Mikhailova, 94–97, 100–108, 111,
    112, 131–32, 174
Budyonnaya, Tanya, 99
Budyonny, Misha, 98

Budyonny, Semyon Mikhailovich,
    84–86, 92–102, 110, 112, 114
  helplessness in face of arrests, 126
  and Maria Vasilievna, 96–102
  and Nadezhda Ivanovna, 93
  and Olga Stefanovna, 94–96, 101–2,
    104–7
  pre-Bolshevik period, 92–93
Budyonny, Seryozha, 98
Bugrimova, Irina, 210
Bukharin, Nikolai Ivanovich, 25, 64, 67,
    75–76, 176
  trial of, 122
Bukharina, Anna Larina, 122, 126
  Nadezhda Alliluyeva's death and,
    75–76
  The Unforgotten, 75–76
Bulgakov, Mikhail Afanasyevich, 22
Bulganin, Nikolai Aleksandrovich,
    133–34
Burmistenko (Ukrainian Communist
    Party secretary), 195
Buryatse, Boris, 210, 211
Butyrki (prison camp), 53, 176

capitalism, 31
Cheka, 45, 66, 99, 162
Chernenko, Anna Dmitrievna, 220–24
Chernenko, Elena, 222
Chernenko, Konstantin (son), 223
Chernenko, Konstantin Ustinovich, 211,
    220, 222–24
Chernenko, Valentina, 223
Chernenko, Vera, 222
Chernenko, Vladimir, 222
Chervyakov (Executive Committee
    member), 61
Chuev, Felix, 159
Churbanov, Yuri, 207, 211
Civil War, 23, 24, 38, 40–42, 81, 84, 93,
    118, 186
collectivization, 31, 121
communism, 36
Crimea, 79–80
  as Russian Jewish state, 142, 143, 145,
    150–51

INDEX

"D." (prisoner), testimony of, 124

Davydova, Vera, 79

Denikin, Anton, 147–48

Denisov, Pyotr Nikanorovich, 211

détente, 218

divorce, in Stalinist era, 132

"Doctors' Plot," 154

Dokuchaeva ("enemy of the people"), 153

Donskoy, Mark, 52

Dostoevsky, Fyodor, 22

Drabkina, Elizaveta, 23

Duma, 18

Dybenko, Pavel, 34–35

Dzerzhinsky, Felix, 81

Dzhezkazgan (prison camp), 175

Dzhugashvili, Artyom, 63

Dzhugashvili, Josif Vissarionovich. See Stalin

Dzhugashvili, Nadezhda. See Alliluyeva, Nadezhda

Dzhugashvili, Svetlana. See Alliluyeva, Svetlana

Dzhugashvili, Vasily, 63, 64

Dzhugashvili, Yakov (Stalin's son), 56, 63, 64, 73

Egorov, Alexander Ilyich, 105, 110, 113–14

Egorova, Galina Antonovna, 101, 107, 109–15, 131–32

Eisenstein, Sergei, 50

Eliava ("enemy of the people"), 111

"enemies of the people," 153
  amnesty for, 126–29

Enukidze, Abel, 54, 58, 70, 79, 83, 123, 137

Epstein (chief secretary, Jewish Antifascist Committee), 149

Era of Stagnation, 209

Esenin, Sergei, 22

Evlogia, Bishop of Kholm, 189, 190

family life
  Bolshevik attitude toward, 34–37, 63
  in the Kremlin, 193, 200–202

and perestroika and glasnost, 226

Fedosova ("enemy of the people"), 153

Fefer (Jewish Antifascist Committee member), 145–46, 150–51

Figner, Vera, 3

First Cavalry, 84–85, 93, 104

free love, 33–34, 63, 121

French Socialist Party, 14

Frunze, Mikhail, 86

Fyodorova, Zoya, 169–70

Gagarin, Yury, 207

Gegechkori, Sasha, 165

Georgadze (friend of Olga Budyonnaya), 104, 112

Gerasimov, Alexander, 83, 206

Gierek, Eduard, 209

glasnost, and women, 226

Glebova (Kamenev's paramour), 50, 52

Goldberg (U.S. congressman), 150

Golubtsova-Malenkova, Valeria Alexeyevna, 193–94

Gopalo, Nina, 198–200

Gopner, Serafima, 83, 84, 132–33, 190

Gorbachev, Irina, 229

Gorbachev, Mikhail Sergeyevich, 211, 225–26
  professional life of, 229–30
  and Raisa Maximovna, 228–29

Gorbachev, Raisa Maximovna Titarenko, 217
  I Hope, 227
  Kremlin life, 230–32
  life story, 225–29
  popular opinions about, 225–27
  professional life of, 229–30
  role in Russian politics, 232

Gorbatov, Boris, 170, 171, 175
  and Tatyana Okunevskaya, 173–74

Gorbman, Golda. See Voroshilova, Ekaterina Davidovna

Gorchakova, Alexandra Vasilievna, 119–21

Gorky, Alexei Maximovich, 162

Gorky, Maxim, 22, 28

Grakhova ("enemy of the people"), 153

Grinko family, 111
Gromyko, Andrei, 211, 215, 216
"Group of 92," 73
Gubanova ("enemy of the people"), 153
Gumilyov, Nikolai, 22, 39–40, 44
Gurvich, Abram Solomonovich, 144–45

Hamburg uprising, 45
Hart-Maxin, Doris, 140
Hitler, 78, 136

Ilyinichna, Anna, 50
Ilyinichna, Maria, 80
Informburo, 149
Ioffe, Adolf, 68
Israel, 142
Ivanov (interrogator), 128

Jewish Antifascist Committee, 142, 145,
    149–51
Jews
    Russian Jewish State for. See Crimea
    in Stalinist Russia, 90, 141–54
    women married to Russians, 81,
        83–84

"K." (prisoner), testimony of, 105–6
Kaftanov, wife of, 194
Kaganovich, Lazar Moiseyevich,
    131–35, 136, 186, 192
Kaganovich, Maria Markovna, 80, 116,
    132–35, 141
Kaganovich, Maya Lazarevna, 132,
    133–35
Kaganovich, Mikhail, 133
Kaganovich, Rosa, 132
Kaganovich, Yuri, 132–33
Kalinin, Mikhail Ivanovich, 116,
    117–18, 122
    and Alexandra Gorchakova, 121
    and Ekaterina Ivanovna, 117, 126–28
Kalinin, Valerian, 117
Kalinina, Ekaterina Ivanovna, 116–30,
    131–32
    abandonment of family, 119–20,
        121–22

arrest of, 116, 122–26, 129, 174
arrest of brother, 124–25
battle to clear name, 128–29
family life and marriage, 121
Kremlin years, 118–19
and Mikhail Ivanovich Kalinin, 117,
    126–28
pardon of, 126–28
Kalinina, Ekaterina Valerianovna, 119,
    126
Kalinina, Maria Vasilievna, 117
Kalinin Museum, 129
Kamenev, Lev Borisovich, 25, 30, 34, 47,
    49–52, 54, 67, 68, 81, 118
Kamenev, Lyutik (Alexander Lvovich),
    48, 49–53, 55
Kamenev, Yuri Lvovich, 50, 52–53, 54
Kameneva, Olga Davidovna, 48, 49–53,
    54, 56, 79
Kaplan, Fanya, 23
Karaganda (prison camp), 176
Karlovy Vary, 141, 164, 202
Karp (brother of Paulina
    Zhemchuzhina), 144
Karpovskaya, Paulina. See Zhemchuzhina,
    Paulina Semyonovna
Katukov, Marshal, 141
Katukova, Ekaterina Sergeyevna, 141,
    164–65
Kazan, battle for, 40
KGB
    Andropov's reign in, 218
    confiscation of Voroshilov documents,
        91
    and Ekaterina Kalinina, 116, 123–26,
        128–29, 174
    files on unnamed women, 174
    and Galina Egorova, 109–15
    and Kremlin marshals and wives,
        103–15
    and Nadezhda Alliluyeva's death, 72
    and Nikita Khrushchev, 204
    and Olga Stefanovna Budyonnaya,
        103–8, 174
    and Paulina Zhemchuzhina, 144–54,
        174

INDEX

and Tatyana Okunevskaya, 174
use of torture in, 155
and Valentina Petrovna Ostroumova,
122–24
See also NKVD
Khodasevich, Vladislav, 22, 47–48
Khoroshkevich (interrogator), 128
Khrushchev, Leonid, 190, 191, 197
Khrushchev, Nikita Sergeyevich, 69, 70,
73, 133, 136, 159, 183, 186–87,
192
amnesty under, 129
coup against, 205
death of, 203
*Khrushchev Remembers: The Last
Testament,* 203–4
life after disgrace, 202–3
and Nina Petrovna, 190–91
thaw during rule of, 227
Khrushchev, Sergei Nikanorovich, 192,
203
Khrushchev, Seryozha, 191, 197, 202
Khrushcheva, Efrosinya Ivanovna, 190
Khrushcheva, Kseniya Ivanovna, 192
Khrushcheva, Lenochka, 197, 202
Khrushcheva, Nadya, 197
Khrushcheva, Nina Petrovna, 116,
186–204
Lenin Hills life, 200–202
life story of, 187–96
reaction to disgrace of Nikita
Khrushchev, 202–4
recollections of Rada and Alexei
Ivanovich, 196–200
Khrushcheva, Rada, 187, 191, 192,
196–98, 202
marriage to Adzhubei, 200
Khrushcheva, Yulia, 190, 191, 197
Khrushcheva, Yulia (daughter), 197
Kirov, Sergei, 47, 81
murder of, 52n., 122
Klasson (friend of Nadezhda Krupskaya),
6
Koba. *See* Stalin
Kobulov (Ekaterina Kalinina case), 129
Kogan (doctor), 155

Kollontai, Alexandra Mikhailovna, 24,
33–35, 53–54
Komsomol groups, 221–22
Korek (Party member), 105
Koridze, Teimuraz, 165
Korutsky, General (NKVD), 54
Kosarev, Alexander, 175
Kosareva, Maria Viktorovna, 175
Kosior, Stanislav, wife of, 193–94
Kovalevsky (Polish colonel), 111
Kozhevnikov (Lenin's doctor), 27
Krasin, Herman, 7
Kravchenko, Galina Sergeyevna, 30,
48–55, 69, 214
Nadezhda Alliluyeva's death and, 74
Kravchenko, Vitaly Alexandrovich
(Vitalik), 52, 53–54, 55
Kremlin, 18–21, 34
Bolshevik life in, 65–67
family life in, 193, 200–202
paranoia in, 89
philandering in, 138
power struggle in, 24–28
Stalinist and post-Stalinist atmosphere
in, 198
Stalin's purging of, 78–80
wives and women in, 37, 103–15,
120–21, 175–76, 233
women's rights in, 142, 194–96, 214
Kronstadt Bolsheviks, 40, 44
Krupskaya, Elizaveta Vasilievna, 2–4, 6,
8–9, 10'
and Inessa Armand, 14–16
Krupskaya, Konstantin Ignatievich, 2
Krupskaya, Nadezhda Konstantinovna,
1–35, 80, 118, 216
childhood of, 2–4
death of, 32
and Inessa Armand, 14–16, 19
and Lenin, 7–11, 24–28, 69
life after death of Lenin, 28–32
obituary for Nadezhda Alliluyeva,
71–72
revolutionary zeal of, 4–8, 10, 18, 23
schooling of, 2–3, 4, 6
Shushenskoe years, 9–11

INDEX

and Stalin, 25–32, 59, 61–63
teaching career, 18, 20–21
thyroid illness, 11, 15
women's movement and, 34–35
Krupsky, Konstantin Ignatievich, 3
Kuibyshev, Valerian Vladimirovich, 78, 141
Kukharchuk, Ekaterina Grigorevna, 187–89
Kukharchuk, Kondraty Vasilievich, 188
Kukharchuk, Nina Petrovna. See
    Khrushcheva, Nina Petrovna
Kukharchuk, Pyotr Vasilievich, 188–89
Kulakov, Feodor, 216
kulaks, 227
Kulik (friend of Olga Budyonnaya), 104, 112
Kuritsyna, Nina, 21–22
Kurkov (sergeant of state security), 107
Kurnatovsky, Viktor Konstantinovich, 10, 14–15, 58
Kuzmin, Mikhail, 43

Larina, Anna Mikhailovna, 175–76
Lebedev, Alexei, 69
Lebedeva, Ekaterina, 69–70
Lenin, 1, 5, 6, 7–8, 58, 59
    Development of Capitalism in Russia, 13
    illness and death of, 24–28
    and Inessa Armand, 14–17, 19, 23–24
    and Larissa Reisner, 40
    and Nadezhda Alliluyeva, 63–65
    and Nadezhda Krupskaya, 7–11, 24–28, 69
    reputation of, in Russia, 11
    return to Russia after exile, 17
    Revolution work with Nadezhda Krupskaya, 18–23
    shot by Kaplan, 23
    and Stalin, 25–32, 59
    "Testament" about Stalin, 25–27, 65
    and Trotsky, 29
Leningrad. See Petrograd
Lenin Hills, Khrushchev's move to, 200–202

Lenin Museum, 90
Lepeshinsky (revolutionary), 9
Levinson (Paris acquaintance of Ekaterina Ivanovna Kalinina), 125
Libedinsky, Yuri, 39
literacy programs, 20–21, 33
Litvinov, Maxim, 136
Lorberg, Ekaterina Adamovna, 118
Lorberg, Ekaterina Ivanovna. See
    Kalinina, Ekaterina Ivanovna
Lorberg, Konstantin Ivanovich, 125
Lorberg, Vladimir Ivanovich, 124–25
Lozofsky (Jewish Antifascist Committee member), 149–50
Lubyanka Prison, 129
    file on Ekaterina Ivanovna Kalinina, 116
Lukasevich (Polish ambassador), 109–11, 114
Lunacharsky, Anatoly, 35, 40, 81, 118
Lyadov-Mandelstam, 35, 36

Maisky, Ivan, 140
Malenkov, Georgy, 136
Mandelstam, Nadezhda, 39, 43, 44
Mandelstam, Osip, 43, 45
Mantsev (plotter against Stalin), 113
marriage
    Bolshevik attitude toward, 33–35, 63
    in Stalinist era, 132
Marx, Karl, Das Kapital, 5, 6
Marxism, 6, 18, 21
Marxist Union of Struggle for the Emancipation of the Working Class, 1
Matryosha (Khrushchev family nanny), 191
Maxin, Alexei, 140
Mazurov, Kiril, 216
Medvedev, Vadim Andreyevich, 208–9
Meir, Golda, 142, 143
Mensheviks, 31
Mikhoels, Salomon, 90, 144–46, 149–52
Mikoyan, Ashkhen, 98–99
Ministry of Internal Affairs. See NKVD

INDEX

Molotov, Vyacheslav, 81, 136–44
  and Nadezhda Alliluyeva's death, 74
  and Paulina Zhemchuzhina, 143–44,
    155, 158–59
  reception at dacha of, 193–94
Molotova, Larissa Alexeyevna, and
  Paulina Zhemchuzhina, 156–58
Molotova, Lyubov Alexeyevna, 158
Molotova, Svetlana, 140, 141
Molotovs, dispensations to, in post-Stalin
  era, 158–59
Moscow, 19
  during World War II, 78–79
Mukholatka, 52

Nicholas II, Tsar, execution of, 22
Nikulin, Lev, 43
NKVD, 122, 137, 161, 168, 169. *See also*
  KGB
Novocherkassk, Battle of, 93
Novo-Devyiche cemetery, 68

October Revolution (agit-train), 118–19
Okunevskaya, Tatyana, 143, 170–75
Okunevsky, Lev, 170
Olshevsky (Victoria Brezhneva's father),
  208
Optimistic Tragedy, An (Vishnevsky), 38
Ordzhonikidze, Sergo, 23
Ostroumova, Valentina Petrovna, 119,
  122–24, 126, 129–30

Panina, Countess, 38
Pasternak, Boris, 22
  Doctor Zhivago, 46
People's Will Party, 8, 11
perestroika, 207, 210, 226, 232
Perovskaya, Sofia, 3
Peshkova, Darya, 162
Peshkova, Marfa, 162
Pestkovsky, Semyon, 60
Petrograd, 17–19, 56, 59–60
Petrograd Battalion of Women, 33
Pilnyak, Boris, 86
Pioneers, 221
Platonov, Andrei, 22

poetry, Russian love of, 43
Politburo, 19, 45, 90, 143, 194, 223
Popov, Ivan, 16–17, 24
Populists, 2
Poskrebyshev (Stalin's secretary), 53, 80
Poverty (newspaper), 86
Prague Spring, 209
Pudovkin, Vsevolod, 48
purges, 56, 61, 78–80, 122, 161. *See also*
  Reign of Terror
Pushkino, 11, 18
Pyatakov, Yuri, 80

Radchenko, Anna Ivanovna, 58–60
Radek-Sobelsohn, Karl, 31, 45–46, 106
Radio Moscow, 140
Raskolnikov, Fyodor, 40, 42, 44–45, 46,
  48
Razgon (prisoner), 126
Red Army, 40–42, 92, 93, 104
Red Guards, 61
Red Marshals, The (Gul), 82
Reign of Terror, 52n., 56, 131–32, 169.
  See also KGB; NKVD; purges
Reisner, Larissa Mikhailovna, 38–46,
  47–48
  Afghanistan, 44
  Coal, Iron and Living People, 45
Revolution and Culture (magazine), 66,
  68
"Right-Trotskyite bloc," trial of, 122
Romm, Abram, 54
Rosenfeld, Lev Borisovich. *See* Kamenev,
  Lev Borisovich
Rostov, Battle of, 93
Rothstein, Andrew, 39
Rozhdestvensky, Vsevolod, 39, 43–44
Rudenko (public prosecutor), 128
Rudin (literary journal), 39
Runov (Olga Budyonnaya's first
  husband), 103
Russian Revolution, 17–23, 33
Rykov, Alexei, 114

Sarkisov (Beria's aide), 169, 178
Satyukova, Galina, 203

INDEX

Schneider, Volodya, 48
Sedova, Natalya (Trotsky's wife), 49, 64
Serebryakova, Galina, 144, 153
Shalamov, Varlaam, 45–46
Shchelokov (minister of internal affairs),
    211
Sheinin, Lev, 155
Shevardnadze, Eduard, 210
Sholokhov, Mikhail, 187
Sholokhova, Maria, 187
Shpiller, Natalya, 79
Shushenskoe, 9–11
Simonov, Konstantin, 171
Skryabin, Vyacheslav Mikhailovich. See
    Molotov, Vyacheslav
Slava (Brezhnev's cook), 215
Slovatinskaya, Tatyana, 117
Smolny Institute, 38
Social Democrats (Marxist), 11
Socialist Revolutionary Party, 31
Soviet of People's Commissars, 1
Spiridonova, Maria, 79
Stakhevich (Polish chief of staff), 114
Stalin, 11, 30–32, 35, 47, 56–77, 99,
    104, 135, 194
  death of, 155
  domestic habits of, 65–67, 76
  drinking habits of, 65, 66, 76
  first trials of, 68–69
  and Hitler, 136
  and Lenin, 25–32, 59
  mistress of (Valya), 132
  and Nadezhda Alliluyeva, 60–70
  and Nadezhda Alliluyeva's death,
    70–77
  and Nadezhda Krupskaya, 25–32, 59,
    61–63
  and Olga Budyonnaya, 101–2
  paranoia of, 66–67
  and Paulina Zhemchuzhina, 137–42,
    159–60
  philandering of, 79, 138
  poetry by, 43
  protocol about, 197–98
  and Trotsky, 30, 65, 68, 105
  and Voroshilovs, 89–90

World War II, 56, 78–79
Stalinism, 32
Stalin-Trotsky conflict, 30, 65, 68,
    105
Stasova, Elena, 31
Stephane, Inessa Theodorovna. See
    Armand, Inessa
Stephane, Renée, 11–13
Stern, Lina Solomonovna, 144, 151
Svanidze, Ekaterina, 56–57, 66
Sverdlov, Yakov, 23, 118

Tamara, Queen, diadem of, 210
Terentevna (Lyutik's nanny), 50
Tiflis (Georgia), 58
Timoshenko, Semyon Konstantinovich,
    195–96
Tito, 171–72
Tolstoy, Leo, 5, 13
Tolstoya, Tatyana, 5
Tomsk (prison camp), 126
Top Secret (newspaper), interview with
    Nina Beria, 165–68
torture, use in KGB, 155
T.R. (Brezhnev's paramour), 208
"Trial of the Industrial Academy," 68
Trial of the Sixteen, 47
trials, 68–69. See also KGB; NKVD
Trotsky, Leon, 25, 31, 46, 49, 56–57,
    64, 67, 68, 124
  Lenin's death and, 29–30
  opinions about Nadezhda Alliluyeva's
    death, 74–75
  and Stalin, 30, 65, 68, 105
  trial of, 122
Trotsky, Seryozha, 49, 52
Trotsky family, 118
Trotskyites, 47, 123–24
"tsaritsas," 20
Tsaritsyn, 61, 65, 67, 81, 84
Tsvetaeva, Marina, 22
Tukhachevsky, Mikhail, 105, 110, 111
Twentieth Party Congress, Khrushchev's
    speech to, 186
Tyrkova, Ariadna, 3–4, 5, 6
Tyutkin (Olga Budyonnaya's friend), 104

INDEX

Uborevich (army marshal), 105, 110
Ulyanov, Alexander, 8
Ulyanov, Vladimir Ilyich. *See* Lenin
Ulyanova, Maria Alexandrovna, 8
Ustinov, Dmitri Fedorovich, 215–16
Utin, Nikolai Isaakovich, 3

Valera (Brezhnev's cook), 215
Valya (mistress of Stalin), 132
Vinogradov (doctor), 155
Vishnevskaya, Galina, 133–34
Volga campaign, 40–42, 48
Voloshin, Maximilian, 22
Voroshilov, Klim (son), 82, 87
Voroshilov, Kliment Efremovich, 81–91,
    104, 110, 111
Voroshilov, Kolya, 86
Voroshilov, Petya, 81–82, 84–85, 86
    marriage to Nadezhda Ivanovna, 87
Voroshilov, Volodya, 87
Voroshilova, Ekaterina Davidovna, 57,
    80, 81–91, 116, 141, 190
    death of, 90–91
    memoirs of, 91
    Stalin's relationship with, 89–90
    stern and guarded nature of, 86–90
    youth, exile in Arkhangelsk, 83–84
Voroshilova, Nadezhda Davidovna,
    168–69, 214
Voroshilova, Nadezhda Ivanovna, 83, 87,
    88
Voroshilova, Truda, 86
Voroshilova, Valya, 168
Vovsi (doctor), 155

What Is To Be Done? (Chernyshevsky), 13
White Army, 93, 147–48
White Czech Legions, 40–42
White Guard, 33, 40–42, 113
White Party, 61
Winter Palace, 38, 40
Wittlin, Thaddeus, 169

The Commissar, 163–64
Wolf of the Kremlin (Kahan), 132
women
    Jewish, 81, 83–84
    in Kremlin politics, 184, 233
    Kremlin wives, persecution of, 103–15
    place in Soviet society, 216–17
    as revolutionaries, 3–4
women's rights, 18, 20–21, 121
    and the Bolsheviks, 33–37
    under glasnost and perestroika, 226
    in the Kremlin, 142, 194–96, 214
    and the Russian Revolution, 78
Worker-Peasant Red Army, 110, 111
Worker Woman's Life (Bolshevik
    magazine), 18
World War I, 16, 93
World War II, 78, 131, 186, 227
    Stalin and, 56, 78–79

X., Ivan Alexeyevich, 152–53

Yakir (Party official), 105, 110
Yeltsin, Naina, 217
Yezhov, Nikolai, 101–2, 122, 161
Yusefovich (Lozofsky's deputy), 150–51

Zasulich, Vera, 3
Zhdanov, Andrei, 223
Zhemchuzhina, Paulina Semyonovna, 37,
    70, 80, 136–60
    anti-Jewish actions against, 142–54
    arrest of, 144–55, 174
    and "Doctors' Plot," 154
    and Nadezhda Alliluyeva, 137–38
    post-prison life, 155–58
    and Stalin, 137–42, 159–60
Zhizneva, Olga, 54
Zinoviev, Grigory, 34, 47, 67, 68
Zugdidi Museum, 210
Zusskind (Jewish Theater administrator),
    146–47